PRAISE FOR *THE TRAGEDY OF FATHERHOOD*

"This fresh and original study turns our notions of paternal power and its dominance upside down to argue through texts from literature, psychoanalysis, philosophy, and political theory that history has been written mainly by the son, who is both heir and victim. Freud, Greek tragedy (Laius, Oedipus), and philosophy (Aristotle) are joined to the Hebrew Bible (Abraham), among others, in order to offer another set of readings, especially of German authors (Hofmannsthal, Lessing, Kleist), that will challenge the reader to think our familiar tropes anew."
Froma I. Zeitlin, Emerita, Ewing Professor of Greek Language & Literature and Professor of Comparative Literature, Princeton University, USA

"This important study is of immense value to any reader interested in the history of family formation, the relationship between antiquity and modernity, the precursors of psychoanalysis in Greek tragedy, and representations of fatherhood in Western culture."
Anette Schwarz, Associate Professor of German Studies, Cornell University, USA

NEW DIRECTIONS IN GERMAN STUDIES
Vol. 9

Series Editor:
Imke Meyer

Editorial Board:
Katherine Arens, Roswitha Burwick, Richard Eldridge,
Erika Fischer-Lichte, Catriona MacLeod, Stephan
Schindler, Heidi Schlipphacke, Ulrich Schönherr, James
A. Schultz, Silke-Maria Weineck, David Wellbery, Sabine
Wilke, John Zilcosky.

Volumes in the series:

Improvisation as Art: Conceptual Challenges, Historical Perspectives
by Edgar Landgraf

The German Pícaro and Modernity: Between Underdog and Shape-Shifter
by Bernhard Malkmus

Citation and Precedent: Conjunctions and Disjunctions of German Law and Literature
by Thomas O. Beebee

Beyond Discontent: 'Sublimation' from Goethe to Lacan
by Eckart Goebel

From Kafka to Sebald: Modernism and Narrative Form
edited by Sabine Wilke

Image in Outline: Reading Lou Andreas-Salomé
by Gisela Brinker-Gabler

Out of Place: German Realism, Displacement, and Modernity
by John B. Lyon

Thomas Mann in English: A Study in Literary Translation
by David Horton

The Laughter of the Thracian Woman: A Protohistory of Theory
by Hans Blumenberg, translated by Spencer Hawkins (forthcoming)

Vienna's Dreams of Europe: Culture and Identity beyond the Nation-State
by Katherine Arens (forthcoming)

The Tragedy of Fatherhood

King Laius and the Politics of Paternity in the West

Silke-Maria Weineck

BLOOMSBURY
NEW YORK • LONDON • NEW DELHI • SYDNEY

Bloomsbury Academic
An imprint of Bloomsbury Publishing Plc

175 Fifth Avenue	50 Bedford Square
New York	London
NY 10010	WC1B 3DP
USA	UK

www.bloomsbury.com

First published 2014

© Silke-Maria Weineck, 2014

All rights reserved. No part of this publication may be reproduced or transmitted in any form or by any means, electronic or mechanical, including photocopying, recording, or any information storage or retrieval system, without prior permission in writing from the publishers.

Whilst every effort has been made to locate copyright holders the publishers would be grateful to hear from any person(s) not here acknowledged.

No responsibility for loss caused to any individual or organization acting on or refraining from action as a result of the material in this publication can be accepted by Bloomsbury Academic or the author.

Bob Dylan, "Highway 61 Revisited," cited with kind permission of the Bob Dylan Music Company. Leonard Cohen, "Story of Isaac," cited with permission of Sony/ATV Music Publishing. Versions of Chapters One, Two, and Nine have previously appeared, respectively, in *Dreams of Interpretation/ The Interpretation of Dreams*, ed. Catherine Liu, John Mowitt, and Thomas Pepper, University of Minnesota Press, 2007; *Cultural Critique* 74 (2010), special issue on "Classical Reception and the Political," 131-146; *Eighteenth Century Studies* 37-1 (2003), 69-89. I thank the editors.

Library of Congress Cataloging-in-Publication Data
A catalog record for this book is available from the Library of Congress.

ISBN:	HB:	978-1-6289-2818-1
	PB:	978-1-6289-2789-4
	ePub:	978-1-6289-2078-9
	ePDF:	978-1-6289-2895-2

Typeset by Fakenham Prepress Solutions, Fakenham, Norfolk, NR21 8NN
Printed and bound in the United States of America

For Stella, Leon, and "The Unknown System"

Contents

Acknowledgments		ix
Introduction: The Silence of the Father		1
Section I Freud's Fatherhood I		
1	Revenants	15
Section II The Tragic Father		
2	The Laius Complex	33
3	Oedipus Patêr	45
4	"I Must Do What I've Been Told": Abraham and the Conditions of Unconditional Paternity	58
Section III The Political Father		
5	Aristotle and the Body of the Father	77
6	Paternity and the Perfect City	88
7	Hobbes and the End of the Paternal Triad	107
Section IV The Rise of the Son		
8	Lessing: Paternal Abdication	127
9	Kleist and the Resurrections of the Father	144
Section V Freud's Fatherhood II		
10	The *Gschnas*, or the Path to the Fatherless Society	165
Conclusion: Dead Children		184
Bibliography		195
Index		205

Acknowledgments

I am in such deep debt.

To my institution, the University of Michigan, for giving me time, a salary, and the sheer magic of a place that is devoted, above all, to the production and dissemination of knowledge. And to the Alexander von Humboldt Foundation, which allowed me to leave that place behind for a year, only to return to my brilliant, eloquent colleagues in the Departments of German Studies and Comparative Literature. To Haaris Naqvi, my fabulous editor, for his unwavering support.

To the many men who have talked to me about their children, helping me understand, or misunderstand, what it means to be a father, among them Eric Baker, Henry Bean, Hartmut Böhme, Jonathan Freedman, John Kushigian, Marc Lipschutz, Bill Miller, Georg Rosenwald, Arthur Suits, Robert Ziff, anonymous guy on the bus. These conversations – sometimes about doubts, sometimes about fears, but always, always about love – have been one of the great joys of this project.

My relationship to the concept of family is deeply ambivalent, but my feelings about friendship are simple: I would not know how to think or write or indeed live without my friends. I wish I could thank all you wonderfully smart, kind, generous, disputatious people individually, and I can only hope you know how important you have been: Seemee Ali, Farrukh Azfar, Kerstin Barndt, Birgit Dahlke, Andreas Gailus, Eckart Goebel, John Hamilton, Daniel Herwitz, Kay Hymowitz, Peter Janz, Vassilis Lambropoulos, Marjorie Levinson, Thomas Pepper, Yopie Prins, Anton Shammas, Scott Spector, Heidi Schlipphacke, Annette Schwarz, Vivason Soni, Claus-Jürgen Thornton, Rochelle Tobias, Johannes von Moltke.

Some of you have been there for decades now: Susanne Goedde, Daniel McLean, Michael McShane, Imke Meyer, Helmut Puff, Patricia Reuter Lorenz, Gwendolyn Wells, Elizabeth Wingrove. Did I say I was ambivalent about the family? Nah, you *are* my family. I love you.

To my children, Stella and Leon, who lent such urgency to the project, and to their father, Paul Sunstein. They really lucked out there.

To my father (†), with reservations. He was whom I needed to understand. And to my mother, without reservations. And to my brother (†), with whom I wish I could talk just one more time.

To Stefan Szymanski who came to this late, kept me in roses, and forced me to finish by threatening to make me go jogging or watch cricket if I didn't.

To Jochen Schulte-Sasse (†). I am so sad that he will not see this book. I would not have written it if it were not for him.

Thank you.

Introduction: The Silence of the Father

The male voice of the last century has been the voice of the son, speaking to and about the father in tones of anger and regret, rebellion and longing, contempt, condemnation, guilt, fear, and, at times, love. Franz Kafka's voice is not the loudest of these, but perhaps the most insistent one, the one best remembered. Here is a famous passage from his "Letter to the Father":

> Sometimes I imagine (*stelle ich mir vor*) the map of the earth unfolded, and you diagonally stretched across it. And then I feel as if, to save my life, I could only consider those regions that you either do not cover or that are not within your reach. And according to the image (*Vorstellung*) I have of your magnitude, these are not many and not very comforting regions, and marriage especially is not among them.[1]

Kafka tells us twice that this is a father of the imagination, not Hermann Kafka, Prague shopkeeper. One of the most striking aspects of the letter is, after all, how unimpressive Hermann looks here, how ill suited to assume the role of global giant. If it weren't for Franz, Hermann would not even *be* on the map, much less cover it all across. Max Brod did well, then, in titling the text "Letter to *the* Father" rather than "Letter to *my* Father."[2] It is not Hermann whose body spans the earth, nor any individual father, but the father *entsprechend der Vorstellung*, in accordance with and literally speaking out of the imagination.

---

1 "Manchmal stelle ich mir die Erdkarte ausgespannt und Dich quer über sie hinausgestreckt vor. Und es ist mir dann, als kämen für mein Leben nur die Gegenden in Betracht, die Du entweder nicht bedeckst oder die nicht in Deiner Reichweite liegen. Und das sind entsprechend der Vorstellung, die ich von Deiner Größe habe, nicht viele und nicht sehr trostreiche Gegenden und besonders die Ehe ist nicht darunter." Franz Kafka, "Brief an den Vater," in *Hochzeitsvorbereitungen auf dem Lande und andere Prosa aus dem Nachlaß* in *Gesammelte Werke*, 8 vols., ed. Max Brod (Frankfurt am Main: Fischer, 1983), 1:158.
2 Kafka himself did not title the letter; writing in 1919 to his sister Ottla, he calls it "Brief an den Vater," and in writing to Milena in 1920, he refers to it as "der Vater-Brief." Cf. *Briefe an Ottla und die Familie*, ed. Hartmut Binder and Klaus Wagenbach (Frankfurt am Main: Fischer, 1975) 74–6; *Briefe an Milena*, ed. Jürgen Born and Michael Müller (Frankfurt am Main: Fischer, 1991), 85, 165, 196.

2   The Tragedy of Fatherhood

Psychoanalysis will give us a word for this: the father has become an inner object, and it is probably not a coincidence that the theory of inner objects arises from a theory of mourning and melancholia.³

Hermann Kafka, it is said, never read the letter, and certainly did not write back. It is unlikely that he was meant to. When Kafka wrote it, in 1917—incidentally the same year "Mourning and Melancholia" was published—, the father had already fallen into silence, that very silence that allows the son to imagine him as large enough to nearly cover the earth. The modern father can only remain "the" father as long as he is silent during the construction of his image, the filial *Vorstellung* out of which the paternal voice echoes in all its distortions. Silence is the source of his power, but also his great weakness. And indeed, we hear Hermann only in Franz's paraphrase, in sentences his son claims to remember or imagines him to speak. Ironically enough, none of them sound as if they could belong to that monstrous body, that near boundless reach, a figure whose voice ought to sound as if it issued from a wrathful deity, perhaps like the voice of God at the end of the book of Job.

When Kafka writes, God is dead, Hermann lives on, and Franz constructs his merciless prose, prose to which there can be no response precisely because it throws open a gap between the father and his image so wide that no answer could travel across it. Franz's own writing contains all the answers he needs: "You could respond," he begins the long penultimate paragraph that contains Hermann's imagined reaction, and comments, with disarming logic: "My answer to this is, first, that this whole interjection (*Einwurf*), which in part could be turned against you as well, is, after all, not from you, but from me."⁴

Indeed. Writing is one of those few and allegedly disconsolate regions that exceed the father's grasp, and while Hermann certainly appears present enough in this letter, he is, despite all his physical bulk, far too slight, even pathetic a figure to carry the weight of the global father. So Franz will have to answer himself. As Deleuze and Guattari point out, concerning this letter: "Kafka knows very well that nothing in it is true." It contains, they write, "a reproach that is so strong that it becomes unattributable to any particular persons"

---

3   The term "inner object," central to object-relations theory, is not part of Freud's essay on "Mourning and Melancholia," but it is there that Freud first fully articulates the consequences of the notion that our emotional life consists of our relations not to people but to our internal representations of them—they are psychic, not material objects. The essay is of foundational importance to the theory of object relations as Melanie Klein and Donald Winnicott will articulate it.
4   "Darauf antworte ich, daß zunächst dieser ganze Einwurf, der sich zum Teil auch gegen Dich kehren läßt, nicht von Dir stammt, sondern eben von mir." "Brief an den Vater," 162.

(in fact, the word *Schuld*, guilt, by itself or in numerous derivations, appears no fewer than 50 times in the text) and they refer, quite compellingly, to the passage cited above as an "Oedipalization of the universe."[5] There is more than a difference in perspective between being Hermann and seeing Hermann, between the position of the father and the father's image as it looms in the mind of the son. Hermann has effectively been removed from the scene, and only the fantasy of Hermann remains.

The oedipalization of the universe is not Kafka's invention. While Deleuze and Guattari are right and the letter may be oedipalization's parody at least as much as its manifestation, their own *Anti-Oedipus* bears ample testimony to the dire cultural, political, and emotional consequences of that sweeping oedipalization. But even that active and brilliant critique of "the imperialism of Oedipus," of "Oedipus as dogma,"[6] can be said to be written from the position of the sons—in its very resistance to the oedipal logic, it cannot do without the gesture of filial revolt. This is Freud's cunning: the very act of intellectual rebellion against Oedipus emerges as oedipal in structure, including the one that rejects or resists the symbolic positions of the nuclear family: as we will see in Chapter 3, it was Oedipus himself who claimed that he had no family, that he was the son of fortune, brother to the moons.

Kafka, however, realized more clearly than anybody else that modern writing is the domain of the son—the son who writes about nothing as passionately as about his father or his fathers, the son who, in an odd entanglement of authorial paternity and filial subjectivity, indeed begets the father in writing.[7] The father falls silent in the wake of Freud because Freud is the one who sealed Oedipus's fate as both the quintessential subject and the quintessential son, whereas the father becomes, alternatively or simultaneously, the symbol of all power and its parody (see Chapters 1 and 10). But Freud did not invent the logic of filiarchal culture. In 1835, Heinrich Heine writes that "in literature, ... the fathers are slain by the sons as soon as they grow old and feeble," not as a new phenomenon but by "custom and tradition."[8] And indeed,

---

5   Gilles Deleuze and Félix Guattari, *Kafka: Towards a Minor Literature*, trans. Dana Polan, intro. Réda Bensmaïa (Minneapolis: University of Minnesota Press, 1986), 9–10.
6   Gilles Deleuze and Félix Guattari, *Anti-Oedipus: Capitalism and Schizophrenia*, trans. Robert Hurley, Mark Seem, and Helen R. Lane (Minneapolis: University of Minnesota Press. 1983), 51.
7   For a superb account of literary paternity, see Stanley Corngold, "Nietzsche, Kafka, and Literary Paternity," in *Lambent Traces: Franz Kafka* (Princeton, NJ: Princeton University Press, 2004), 94–110.
8   "Nein, und er [A. W. Schlegel, in his treatment of Bürger] handelte nach Brauch und Herkommen. Denn in der Literatur wie in den Wäldern der

in modernity, cultural capital increasingly accrues to the innovators and the rebels, who, the more their rebellion succeeds, risk becoming fathers in turn, and next in line to be slain (Freud's own fate is a case in point). Needless to say, such a logic actually *needs* to uphold an image of (literary) history as a family romance, and it especially needs the figure of the father, which it construes, according to its multiple needs, in three molds: as the benign ancestor whose name is evoked as a guardian spirit of the young, as the tyrant who needs to be violently overthrown, and as the obsolete one, Heine's feeble old man who is ritually consecrated to the superannuated past against which the present defines itself.

Psychoanalysis has reflected at length on the first two functions, notably in Lacan's logic of the "no(m)-du-père," which presents the father as the one who both gives his name along with a place in the social order and says no. I suspect, however, that the third father, the feeble one who holds no power, the one who knows that he is destined to be superseded not in violent rebellion but in casual dismissal, is the one with whom contemporary fathers are most likely to identify—we find one of his finest embodiments in *Peter Pan*'s Mr. Darling, the man who banishes the dog Nana from the house since he "had sometimes a feeling that she did not admire him."[9] The owls of psychoanalysis, in other words, flew at dusk: by the beginning of the twentieth century, the semiotic system that made the father both powerful and terrible still operated everywhere, but its foundation had been crumbling for centuries. Thus, the father may still function as the *figure* of the law, but his traditional double function—to protect and prohibit—had long been absorbed by a state that ceased to resemble the family and had become a disembodied system. Hegel remains the premier theorist of this process, but it is Hobbes who articulates it first (see Chapter 7).

It is no accident that Paul Federn, who coined the influential term of the "fatherless society" in 1919,[10] was a left-leaning psychoanalyst who wrote his essay by the same title in response to the fall of the Hapsburg monarchy. The loss of the charismatic political father figure—lamented or welcomed, as the case may be—reinforces and is reinforced by the concomitant weakening of the divine father, the long and meandering process Nietzsche called the death of God. "The royal remains," as Eric Santner calls them, mingle with the (also remaining) divine remains to form both a

---

nordamerikanischen Wilden werden die Väter von den Söhnen totgeschlagen, sobald sie alt und schwach geworden." Heinrich Heine, *Die Romantische Schule. Zur Geschichte der Religion und Philosophie in Deutschland*, ed. Hans Kaufmann, vol. 9 of *Sämtliche Werke* (Munich: Kindler, 1964), 59.

9 J. M. Barrie. *Peter Pan in Kensington Gardens: Peter and Wendy* (Oxford: Oxford University Press, 2008), 84.

10 Paul Federn, *Zur Psychologie der Revolution. Die Vaterlose Gesellschaft* (Leipzig and Vienna: Anzengruber Verlag, 1919).

halo and a cloud of ashes around the father, who, in the absence or fading of god and king, has lost the support of the sytem I call "the paternal triad."

This triad, a complex system of explicit or submerged analogies in which paternal, royal, and divine authority mutually reinforce each other, has organized theories of power for a very long time, but—and this has gotten far less attention—it may have been contested for just as long, though with varying intensity and success. There is no clearly dateable beginning to that process, though there are, I maintain, texts, both literary and theoretical, that mark watersheds in symbolic paternity's long history, movements of critique and crisis that strike me as particularly significant. In this study, I will consider such movements in fifth- and and fourth-century BCE Athens, over the course of a very long eighteenth century (beginning with Thomas Hobbes, who is the first seminal modern political theorist to dispute the natural right of fathers), and at the turn of the nineteenth century, with psychoanalysis and its aftermath.

Needless to say, neither the democratization nor the secularization of power—perhaps because both remain unfinished projects—abolished fatherhood as a central institution of social and of psychic life, but in losing much of its metaphysical and political grounding, fatherhood was progressively cut off from that very long history that created, defined, and legitimized its position. By Freud's time, its metaphors were still firmly in place, and paternal authority within the family remained largely uncontested, but in many regards, the father who lays down the law to his children had become a caricature. The patricides of expressionism were killing a ghost they had to conjure first, and evocations of this sort continue to this day, particularly in Germany, and often with remarkable tedium (there is something quite curious about writers and scholars who, in the middle of their lives, speak of the father as if he were always someone and somewhere else, as if they, if only in their function as, say, university professors, had not occupied his position for years or decades). Certainly, the incommensurability of individual fathers, symbolic fathers, patriarchal structures, or paternal metaphors is habitually stressed in these discourses, but they all live off the affectively invested word "father," and they all return to the man who begets or the man who raises children, that is, to the father within the family. Jean-Joseph Goux, to give an example, will readily admit that the "'paternal' hegemony . . . determines *a certain mode of historicity* as 'paternal' domination (far beyond a specific parental figure),"[11] but

---

11 Jean-Joseph Goux, *Symbolic Economies after Marx and Freud*, trans. Jennifer Curtiss Gage (Ithaca, NY: Cornell University Press, 1990), 217. The volume comprises selections from *Freud, Marx: Economie et symbolique* (Paris: Editions du Seuil, 1973) and *Les iconoclastes* (Paris: Editions du Seuil, 1978).

there is a curious tension here between the scare quotes surrounding "paternal," as if fatherhood were a term under erasure, and the parenthetical qualification that declares specific fathers to be the beyond of paternal structures.

None of these preliminary remarks ought to be misconstrued as a dismissal of the many studies devoted to the hegemonic structures governing reproduction and their metaphoric and symbolic equivalents in the political realm. Goux's complex dialectical account of history's relation to the maternal is very suggestive, Andrew Parker's reflections on the mobility and multiplicity of maternity are useful,[12] and the Lacanian reconstruction of symbolic paternity against bodily fatherhood, to which both are indebted, has been exceptionally productive. This book, however, focuses on the father-child dyad rather than on the family, and while theories of motherhood are, of course, deeply important to theories of fatherhood, only some of the chapters that follow engage questions of maternity or the gender binary in conceptions of parenthood. This is not because they don't matter—they matter tremendously—, but because they have been so well explored in the past. *The Tragedy of Fatherhood* is not just indebted to but rather enabled by the pathbreaking work of scholars like Brown, Elshtain, Hartsock, Hunt, Moller Okin, Naffine, O'Brien, Pateman, or Stevens, who have analyzed the ideology, metaphors, and reproductive strategies and practices of various patriarchal or semi- or quasi-patriarchal cultures.[13] Mothers, however, are not this book's central concern, and neither is the family, in either its premodern or modern varieties, and while my decision to relegate questions of gender to the background of this study has been a cause for some displeasure among a number of my most cherished interlocutors, I maintain that anything I could have said has been said, and said much better, by those before me.

---

12 Andrew Parker, *The Theorist's Mother* (Durham, NC: Duke University Press, 2012).

13 Wendy Brown, *Manhood and Politics: A Feminist Reading in Political Theory* (Totowa, NJ: Rowman and Littlefield, 1988); Jean Bethke Elshtain, *Public Man, Private Woman: Women in Social and Political Thought* (Princeton, NJ: Princeton University Press, 1981); Nancy Hartsock, *Money, Sex and Power* (New York: Longman, 1983); Lynn A. Hunt, *The Family Romance of the French Revolution* (Berkeley: University of California Press, 1992); Ngaire Naffine, *Law and the Sexes* (Sydney: Allen and Unwin, 1990); Mary O'Brien, *The Politics of Reproduction* (London: Routledge, 1981); Susan Moller Okin, *Justice, Gender and the Family* (New York: Basic Books, 1989) and *Women in Western Political Thought* (Princeton, NJ: Princeton University Press, 1979); Carole Pateman, *The Sexual Contract* (Cambridge: Polity Press, 1988); and Jacqueline Stevens, *Reproducing the State* (Princeton, NJ: Princeton University Press, 1999).

Introduction: The Silence of the Father

What, then, are the goals of this book? One of its aspirations is to hear the fathers speak, in however mediated a way. While psychoanalytically shaded reflections on paternity elide the "specific father" on principle, studies of the tropes and politics of reproduction—with exceptions such as Lynn Hunt's very sensitive *Family Romance of the French Revolution*—rarely engage the position of the father from within. He is either dead, absent, or the enemy—in short, he remains Oedipus's father as Freud wanted us to see him, the Laius of my subtitle.

The absence of the father's voice as anything but a distorted echo in the writings of sons—or those who pose as perennial sons for complicated reasons of their own—has led to a pervasive failure to articulate the place of the father as a subject position. While many writers have addressed the death or the weakening of the father in historical, political, psychological, cultural, or scientific terms, they often tend to neglect the consequences for the father who lives on. For a long time, the son's voice was the only audible one in the Freudian appropriation of the oedipal, and while feminist studies have done much to develop Jocasta's position and perspective as well, by and large, Laius has remained offstage to this day. As we will see in Chapter 2, the few who make Laius speak—Hofmannsthal, Pasolini, or psychoanalytic critics like John Munder Ross or Marie Balmary—show us a monster, a child murderer, a sensual fascist, a pedophile rapist, a bitter old man who visits his sins upon his son. And yet, Laius was once a tragic hero—how did he turn into a murder victim who had it coming?

In order to address this question, this book will explore a number of heterogeneous texts and discourses that show fatherhood in crisis: literature and philosophy, biology, political theory, law, and psychoanalysis all play a role—none of them negligible, none of them decisive. In the end, I believe that literature and myth have the most to teach us, for a number of reasons, foremost among them the very traits that they share with that "legal fiction" of fatherhood, as Joyce called it.

Like paternity itself, literature and myth mediate between the abstract and the sensual, aesthesis and intellection. They can (and do) argue, but they are under no obligation to mount arguments, and under no obligation to commit to the ones they do make—in other words, literature and myth need not choose between the competing but mutually exclusive logics that have supported fatherhood for so long. Literature is of its time, but again, it is not beholden to its time, but functions freely, like the institution of fatherhood itself, as a repository of that which is incommensurable and nonsynchronous. It moves between the public and the private, however construed, and mediates between them, a mediation that, pace Adorno or Marcuse, more often than not takes the shape of failure or sacrifice.

Just as importantly, literature has long seen itself in competition with fatherhood, as a parallel and superior mode of generation, a paternity more pure, uncontaminated by mothers and their rivaling claims, and, for the most part, less threatened by its offspring—though Plato was the first to point out that the poem may belong to the poet even less than the child belongs to its father, a thought that will, with very different investments and consequences, come back to haunt writing at the turn of the twentieth century and beyond. Over millennia, images of creation and procreation converge and diverge, support and repel each other, drawing on the very models of nature and culture that fatherhood, mutatis mutandis, both depends on and subverts.

Of more particular interest to me is literature's affinity to metaphor. While we have long understood that all discourse relies on and is structured by tropes, over time, literature has been unique in consistently affirming and celebrating this dependence *as a form of knowledge*. Literary texts, then, are, I believe, in a privileged position to reflect the relationship between concepts of fatherhood and concepts of political power, particularly that of sovereignty, a relationship that depends on the dangerous logic of metaphor which oscillates between the claim that two terms are interchangeable and the claim that they are not.

Carl Schmitt famously claimed that "all significant concepts of the modern theory of the state are secularized theological concepts."[14] In a nutshell, this book suggests that the central "theological" concept in the political realm is, in fact, a procreative one: theories of power—divine or secular, and at the junction of the two—have been enmeshed with theories of fatherhood, which functions as the model and master trope of both legitimate and benign power.[15] The most significant political concept is not a secularized theologeme, as the proponents of the secularization thesis have told us, but a theologized, legalized, retrospectively posited, and fantasmatically transformed relation that hovers ambivalently between soma, bios, and nomos. This leaves sometimes-subtle traces: thus, when Carl Schmitt avers that "all significant concepts of the modern theory of the state are secularized theological concepts," he uses the term "prägnante Begriffe." The most straightforward translation of *prägnant* is "concise," but Schmitt is surely too much of a Latinist not to hear the echo of *prægnans*, pregnant. Significance itself reveals itself as a process of impregnation.

But how does a concept become pregnant—fecund, heavy, rich with possibilities? A term's fertility can be measured by its metaphorical

---

14 Carl Schmitt, *Political Theology: Four Chapters on the Concept of Sovereignty*, trans. and intro. George Schwab (Chicago: University of Chicago Press, 2005), 36.
15 See Silke-Maria Weineck, "'Invisible Person' Carl Schmitt and the Master Trope of Power," *Germanic Review* 84, no. 3 (Summer 2009): 199–221.

potential, its capacity to accrue, over time, all the implications that have been transferred to and from it. As we know from classical rhetoric, a metaphor has three parts: *primum comparandum*, the first term to be compared, *secundum comparatum*, the second term that the first one is compared to, and *tertium comparationis*, the third term of the comparison, the element common to both that makes the comparison possible. And the metaphoric operation that has linked God to kings has consistently depended, for its success, on a third term. The link between theology and politics, the hyphen in the theologico-political as it were, is the trope of paternity, and its overdetermined figure continues to haunt the intersection of the two discourses. This is not to say that familial fatherhood holds the key to political or theopolitical organization. Supplementing the idea of the theopolitical dyad with that of the paternal triad brackets the question of origin. Neither royal nor divine nor spermal fatherhood can lay a clear claim to being the "literal" meaning of paternity, and different theoretical structures will designate any one of them as "first," even though the familial notation is, I believe, the one that mediates the others most frequently, most insistently, and most effectively.

If metaphor is crucial to the cross-legitimation of the fatherhoods of the paternal triad, its structure also mirrors the relationship of father and son, since metaphor and metonymy are forms of speech that simultaneously posit identity and difference, continuity and rupture—replacing one word with another on the basis of a hidden quality that unites them performs sameness on the basis of a difference both erased and preserved. Such is the structure of the perennial idea that the son, as an extension of his father, guarantees the latter's immortality: the son can only live on *as* his father because he is *not* him. And while all affirmative theories of power that take recourse to paternity as their master trope envision the succession as a harmonious process, both history and literature tell us differently—over and over again.

The Tragedy of Fatherhood engages with poetry and prose, but I believe that the genre that has the deepest investment in the theory and the phenomena of fatherhoods both symbolic and somatic, the one that tells us the most of its variable fates, is, indeed, tragedy. Aristotle said that violence threatening or befalling *philoi* is more frightening and hence better suited to the emotional response appropriate to tragedy, but kinship is only one form of *philia*, and conflicts between friends largely remained the domain of the epic (friendship is, in fact, the dominant human relationship in the Homeric texts, as Daniel McLean pointed out to me). By contrast, the vast majority of tragedies revolve around kinship, and while the relations at stake are not limited to the father-child dyad that is the focus of this book, all patriarchal kinship systems depend on the paternal past—*Antigone* or *Seven against Thebes* may be "about" fraternity, but Oedipus is always present in absence, like Laius was before him.

Tragedy is particularly suited to the representation of fatherhood, however, not (just) because it evokes strong and complex emotions. First, tragedy as a genre—at least in the definition to which I am partial—is devoted to the eruption of a conflict whose conditions precede its proper plot, the kind of conflict Aristotle called "necessary." If fatherhood, as I argue, is at core the always-tenuous incorporation of potentially conflicting if temporarily reconciled claims to legitimacy, then its form is itself tragic.

Second, and relatedly, tragedy's clear affinity to the analysis of political power and its dissolution can find in the institution of fatherhood both power's master trope and the crucial element of power's demise, that is, the internal self-contradiction entailed by overdetermination. Fatherhood has proven to be such a powerful model for political rule because it a) has long been coded "natural" and b) promises to bring body, law, and social affect into alignment as long as fatherhood is simultaneously defined as biological (via sperm or the discourse of shared blood), legal (predominantly, here, as the husband of the mother and highest authority of the *oikos*), and ethical (as the head of the household whose members are entrusted to the father's care). While fatherhood's multiplicity accounts for its great resilience over time, it also marks the paternal position as mobile and always potentially unstable the moment its constitutive elements no longer align—Oedipus cannot fathom that the oracle is not talking about Polybus, and so it begins.

Third, parenthood is the only position of power that writes power's end into its structure without inverting its logic: slavery does not envision slaves turning into masters, andrarchy does not envision women becoming men, feudalism does not envision peasants becoming aristocrats, but sons are meant to become fathers. Conversely, democratic and republican structures envision rulers and ruled exchanging places, theories of revolution envision the seizure of power, but while the son is meant to become a father, the father is not meant to become a son. In other words, the temporality of the succession of power unique to fatherhood interferes with the transposition of paternity as a model for other forms of rule, and vice versa.

The Tragedy of Fatherhood will show how all of this plays out at various textual, historical, or theoretical moments I believe to be signaling crises of fatherhood, or moments where its tragic structure reveals itself. It is not, I want to stress, a history of fatherhood. Rather, I want to think of paternity as one of those "absolute metaphors" Hans Blumenberg introduces in *Paradigms for a Metaphorology*. They are "absolute" because they cannot be dissolved into the conceptual systems that Descartes had still been able to imagine as pure. Such absolute metaphors, Blumenberg argues, constitute a reserve of images "from which the universe of concepts continually renews itself, without thereby converting and exhausting" it.[16] While they prove resistant to terminological demands, they are not removed from history. On the contrary, they "have history in a more radical sense than concepts, for the historical transformation of a metaphor brings to light the metakinetics of historical horizons of meanings." Their study, metaphorology, "seeks to burrow down to the substructure of thought, the underground, the nutrient solution of systematic crystallizations; but it also aims to show the 'courage' with which the mind preempts itself in its images" (5).

In the belief that every time fatherhood enters into crisis we glimpse the possibility of thinking and feeling differently about power and its loss, this book is dedicated to those acts of courage.

---

16 Hans Blumenberg, *Paradigms for a Metaphorology*, trans. Robert Ian Savage (Ithaca, NY: Cornell University Press, 2010), 13.

Section I

Freud's Fatherhood I

One Revenants

> *Die Liebe zu den Kindern ist immer eine unglückliche.*
> Arthur Schnitzler, *Aphorismen und Betrachtungen*

Only the most committed Freudians would maintain that Freud's model of the nuclear family is anything but a brilliant fiction, if an extremely illuminating and potently productive one, and nobody at all would claim that the family of the twenty-first century is the same family Freud found—or invented—at the turn of the nineteenth century. And nonetheless, any reflection on the fate of fatherhood must start with Freud, whose terms continue to dominate the debate, be it in the writings of his heirs or his foes. For better or for worse, Freud's fatherhood remains the theoretical touchstone for all thought regarding paternity. No matter how often, how passionately, or how plausibly the oedipal model has been contested, the fact is that we still do contest it, and with an urgency no competing articulation of the family has engendered. In the long history of the paternal triad, Freud, the great secularist, succeeded in fundamentally changing the terms: after Freud, it is no longer the royal, the divine, or the familial father who matters the most, but the psychic father, the father as inner object.

Here is the first sentence of the most fateful subchapter of *The Interpretation of Dreams,* "Dreams of the Death of Dear Persons" (V.D.β): "Another series of dreams that may be called typical are those with the content that a dear relative, parents or siblings, children etc. has died."[1] We all know where this is going, but it is worth lingering a bit: this is a very strange sentence, particularly from a stylist as meticulous as Freud. German does not mix singulars and plurals like this, and the odd grammatical structure—a singular verb following multiple subjects—heralds a peculiarity about those typical dreams of parents, siblings, and children. It is really only one dear relative whose dreamed demise will matter to psychoanalysis—the father, whose death, according to

---

1 "Eine andere Reihe von Träumen, die typisch genannt werden dürfen, sind die mit dem Inhalt, daß ein teurer Verwandter, Eltern oder Geschwister, Kinder usw. gestorben ist." Sigmund Freud, *Die Traumdeutung,* in *Studienausgabe,* ed. Alexander Mitscherlich, Angela Richards, and James Strachey, vol. 2 (Frankfurt am Main: S. Fischer, 1972), 253. All quotations are from this edition; all translations are my own.

Freud's widely accepted autobiographical narrative, gave rise to his self-analysis and hence to psychoanalysis as we know it.

In his later writings, Freud will repeatedly stress that psychoanalysis stands and falls with the Oedipus complex, an assertion echoed in the literature over and over again. Not that long ago, Slavoj Žižek wrote, "When we speak about myths in psychoanalysis, we are effectively speaking about ONE myth, the Oedipus myth—all other Freudian myths (the myth of the primordial father, Freud's version of the Moses myth) are variations of it, although *necessary* ones."[2] A little later, he claims that "the Oedipal 'myth'—and, perhaps, mythic 'naivety' itself—serves to obfuscate some prohibited *knowledge*, ultimately the knowledge about the father's obscenity" (11–12).

If, in the wake of psychoanalysis, masculinity and even becoming-human itself emerge as oedipal, then we all came to be defined and marked by the name of the quintessential son whose mask even the most patriarchal of twentieth-century grand theorists could don without raising too many questions. In *The Interpretation of Dreams* Freud, father of six, habitually presents himself as the son reflecting on his father's death. To be sure, he will still have things to say about dreams concerning the death of siblings and of parents of both sexes, but there is one of those typical dreams he will barely explore—the father's dream of his son's death,[3] what we may call King Laius's dream. And when he finally arrives there, in the Dream of the Burning Child, all the rules he has laid out will be broken. This will be the one dream that escapes the interpretative machine that had turned even the most horrendous visions into wishes. All of them—but not that one.

The Interpretation of Dreams, the discipline that grew from it, and all the theories indebted to it are built on this elision, the erasure of fatherhood. Seeing the prominence of the very word "father" in psychoanalysis, this may sound like a counterintuitive claim, and of course, I am neither suggesting that psychoanalysis does not reflect on fatherhood as an institution nor that it does not reflect on fathers—it obviously has done both, to a great extent and to tremendous effect. But it denies to fatherhood all interiority: we see the father through the son's eyes only, as if paternity were a fantasmatic extension of filiality but not a distinct realm of masculine experience that gives rise to a subject position of its

---

2 Slavoj Žižek, *Did Somebody Say Totalitarianism? Four Interventions in the (Mis)Use of a Notion* (London: Verso, 2002), 9.
3 It should be mentioned from the start that the following remarks concern the father-son dyad almost exclusively. This is not because daughters or mothers do not matter, but because father-daughter relationships are a different story, and the elucidation of the role of the mother in the configurations sketched here would necessitate a separate discussion.

own. This is the great irony: it is precisely the intense analytic preoccupation with the (name of the) father that blocks him from view. Like Laius, he is always already offstage, significant only after his death, to which he must consent in order to gain the power ascribed to the function he is called upon to embody.[4] The disappearance of the father is mirrored in the wildly and strangely successful myth Freud offers in *Totem and Taboo*, where the brothers' murder of the father and his subsequent ambivalent enthronement as totemic and later divine authority is posited as the beginning of civilization. As Eric Santner paraphrases it: "The institution of the symbolic (and so, *dead*) father serves to immunize the group from attempts to usurp the place of the primal father and his full, unmediated—in a word, incestuous—enjoyment. We might say, then, that the *fiction* of the father as symbolic agency, as sovereign enforcer of the social contract of reciprocity established by the band of brothers, is forever shadowed by the *fantasy* of a ferocious father whose murder continues to clear the path of and facilitate the psychic growth of beings of language, beings endowed with the capacity for symbolic and 'contractual' action."[5] This father, said to be sovereign, is nonetheless dead as well as a fiction and a fantasy, and, unsurprisingly under these circumstances, makes no further appearance in Santner's book on "the endgames of sovereignty," even though Freud—and we will return to this point in Chapter 10— told us rather clearly that the dead father did not remain dead for very long.

If Freud's various versions of the Oedipus legend function like a veil, what is veiled is indeed the father—perhaps in his obscenity, but, more importantly, in his impossible fragility—and perhaps this fragility is precisely what strikes us as so obscene. In 1902, Otto Weininger puts the matter with desperate bluntness: "fatherhood is a miserable delusion."[6] Miserable and necessary, of course, and everywhere at work, like God, that other grand and miserable delusion that does and does not come to an end at the same time, and for similar reasons.

In the shadow of the dead father and hemmed in by fictions and fantasms that share their designation, fathers live on, continuing their

---

4   Discussing *Totem and Taboo*, Lacan writes, "if this murder is the fruitful moment of debt through which the subject binds himself for life to the Law, the symbolic father is, in so far as he signifies this Law, the dead Father." Jacques Lacan, "On a Question Preliminary to Any Possible Treatment of Psychosis," in *Ecrits: A Selection*, trans. Alan Sheridan (New York: W. W. Norton, 1977), 199.
5   Eric L. Santner, *The Royal Remains: The People's Two Bodies and the Endgames of Sovereignty* (Chicago: University of Chicago Press, 2011), 26.
6   "[D]ie Vaterschaft [ist] eine armselige Täuschung," Otto Weininger, *Geschlecht und Charakter: Eine prinzipielle Untersuchung* (Munich: Matthes & Seitz, 1980), 307.

fathering. Concerning his own children, Freud writes in a well-known passage in Chapter VI of *The Interpretation of Dreams*:

> I held to it that their names ought not to be chosen according to the fashion of the day but be determined in memory of dear persons. Their names make the children into "revenants." And in the end, are children not for all of us the only access to *immortality*?[7]

If children are revenants (we will have to come back to this term later), who is returning in their name? The first sentence above suggests that it is "dear persons," *teure Personen*, the last one that it is, instead, the naming father whose deathlessness becomes the child's responsibility. In isolation, neither claim—naming as commemoration of loved or admired others, children as a path to immortality—is particularly striking or original, but in combination, they set up a tension well worth exploring. Freud names his oldest son Jean-Martin, after Charcot, the neurologist and theorist of hysteria; his second son Oliver, after Cromwell; his third son Ernst, after his teacher Ernst Wilhelm von Brücke. The encounter with Charcot and his work, needless to say, was a milestone in Freud's professional life, and in 1927, he writes of the physiologist von Brücke as "the greatest authority that ever has influenced me."[8] Cromwell does not quite seem to fit in, but elsewhere in the Dream Book, Freud notes that this "great historical personality . . . had attracted me mightily in my boyhood years, especially after my stay in England" (432), and he comments: "It is easily noted how the suppressed megalomania of the father is transferred to his children in his mind; yes, one will gladly believe that this is one of the ways in which the suppressions of the same which has become necessary in life takes place."[9]

To the extent that Charcot, Cromwell, and Brücke in this context appear as men with whom Freud identified to a greater or lesser degree, children, curiously, provide access to immortality not by embodying their father but by returning as their father's ideal selves, his fantasmatic past becoming their and hence also his future. Their

---

7 "Ich hielt darauf, daß ihre Namen nicht nach der Mode des Tages gewählt, sondern durch das Andenken an teure Personen bestimmt sein sollten. Ihre Namen machen die Kinder zu 'Revenants.' Und schließlich, ist Kinder haben nicht für uns alle der einzige Zugang zur *Unsterblichkeit*?" Freud, *Die Traumdeutung*, 468–9.
8 ". . . der größten Autorität, die je auf mich gewirkt hat." Sigmund Freud, "Nachwort zur 'Frage der Laienanalyse,'" in *Studienausgabe*, Ergänzungsband, 344.
9 "Es ist leicht zu merken, wie die unterdrückte Größensucht des Vaters sich in seinen Gedanken auf die Kinder überträgt; ja man wird gerne glauben, daß dies einer der Wege ist, auf denen die im Leben notwendig gewordenen Unterdrückungen derselben vor sich geht." Freud, *Die Traumdeutung*, 432.

names honor admired men and create a benign outlet for the megalomania life has forced the father to suppress—and, one must assume, will force them to suppress in turn. But if we look just a little more closely, it appears that the naming of the child is not a mere consolation for an already suppressed megalomania, as might be expected, but also constitutes one of the very avenues of these suppressions as well as a way to circumvent them. The naming of the child marks identifications, their loss, and their recuperation. When Oliver Cromwell returns as Oliver Freud, the effect is one of great satisfaction—"I had the resolve to use precisely this name if it were to be a son and, deeply satisfied, saluted with it the one just born"[10]—but Freud's subsequent comment makes it clear that this satisfaction comes at a certain price. Declaring the son to be Oliver is tantamount to the admission that his father is not.

At the same time, the loss of the fantasy of *being* Oliver (Jean-Martin, Ernst) may be compensated or outweighed by the both symbolic and quite real power involved in making him return as one's child. Oliver Freud shows up with a curious delay; in the passage cited above, Freud first returns to a dream he had already analyzed roughly 20 pages earlier, a dream concerning his father:

> *After his death, the father played a political role with the Hungarians, he unified them politically,* whereby I see a small indistinct image: *a crowd as in the Reichstag, a person standing on one or two chairs, others around him. I remember that on his deathbed he resembled Garibaldi so much, and I'm glad that this prophecy has come true after all.*[11]

In analyzing this dream—and Oliver does not yet make an appearance in this section—Freud plays on the (etymologically metonymic) homonymy of the German words for chair and for excrement, *Stuhl*, analogous to English "stool," and interprets his father as a "Stuhlrichter," judge of excrement. He remembers that "the most torturous of his sufferings was the total paralysis of his colon (*Obstruction*) over the last weeks" (415), an obstruction that, as we will learn only later, led to Jakob Freud defecating in his bed several times. Interestingly enough,

---

10 "Ich hatte das Jahr der Erwartung über den Vorsatz, gerade diesen Namen zu verwenden, wenn es ein Sohn würde, und begrüßte mit ihm hoch *befriedigt* den eben Geborenen." Ibid., 432.
11 "Der Vater hat nach seinem Tode eine politische Rolle bei den Magyaren gespielt, sie politisch geeinigt, wozu ich ein kleines undeutliches Bild sehe: eine Menschenmenge wie im Reichstag, eine Person, die auf einem oder zwei Stühlen steht, andere um ihn herum. Ich erinnere mich daran, daß er auf dem Totenbette Garibaldi so ähnlich gesehen hat, und freue mich, daß diese Verheißung doch wahr geworden ist." Ibid., 414.

Freud does not mention his father soiling his bed at this point, but remembers a fellow high school student:

> One of my contemporaries who lost his father while he was still in high school, on which occasion I, deeply moved, offered him my friendship, once told me with derision of the pain of a relative whose father had died on the street and had been taken home where one found, while undressing the corpse, that during the moment of death or *postmortally* a *defecation* (*Stuhlentleerung*) had taken place.[12]

Through this double detour—the father of the friend's relative—Freud introduces the image of the defecating father, and the child's mortification at such a sight. One might expect Freud to read his own dream as fulfilling the wish to see his father's lost honor vindicated, but his final interpretation performs a curious displacement: "Now we have penetrated to the wish which embodies itself in this dream: *After one's death to stand before one's children pure* (also: clean) *and great*, who would not wish for that?"[13] Who is dreaming this dream, Jakob or Sigmund Freud? Both? Or the one as the other's revenant?

It is only in the second telling of the dream that Freud explicitly acknowledges his own father's defecation. He repeats the last sentence of the first telling, and adds (some repetition is necessary in the labyrinth):

> (To this, a forgotten sequel.) From the analysis I can now insert what belongs into this dreamgap (*Traumlücke*). It is the mention of my second boy to whom I gave the first name of a great historical personality that mightily attracted me during my boyhood years, especially after my stay in England. I had the resolve to use precisely this name if it were to be a son and, deeply satisfied, saluted with it the one just born. It is easily noted how the suppressed megalomania of the father is transferred to his children in his mind; yes, one will gladly believe that this is one of the ways in which the suppressions of the same which has

---

12 "Einer meiner Altersgenossen, der seinen Vater noch als Gymnasiast verlor, bei welchem Anlaß ich ihm dann tief erschüttert meine Freundschaft antrug, erzählte mir einmal höhnend von dem Schmerz einer Verwandten, deren Vater auf der Straße gestorben und nach Hause gebracht worden war, wo sich dann bei der Entkleidung der Leiche fand, daß im Moment des Todes oder *postmortal* eine *Stuhlentleerung* stattgefunden hatte." Ibid., 415–16.

13 "Hier sind wir nun zu dem Wunsch vorgedrungen, der sich in diesem Traume verkörpert. *Nach seinem Tode rein und groß vor seinen Kindern dastehen*, wer möchte das nicht wünschen?" Ibid., 416.

become necessary in life takes place. The little one gained his right to be included in the context of this dream through the fact that he had been subjected to the same—easily forgivable in the child and the dying man—accident to soil his linens. Compare here the allusion "*Stuhlrichter*" and the wish of the dream: To stand before one's children *great* and *pure*.[14]

It is of course Freud himself who is the judge of excrement, standing on the chair, the stool, one or two of them—it is he who *forgives* both his father and his son for defecating, while dreaming himself first as son, second as father, but always in control of his own stool, clean/pure and great. While the dead Jakob Freud returns as the Garibaldi of the Hungarians, the newborn Oliver now appears as a revenant of Jakob in his excrement, in an association that places him on the deathbed while he is still in his diapers.

If Cromwell (Brücke, Charcot) return as Freud's incontinent little infants, however, megalomania has hardly been suppressed, it has merely taken a little detour. The act of naming is, after all, an exercise of power, and so is the evocation of the dead that makes revenants of Freud's own children. The passage as a whole is rather clear on this: the section that ends with the passage on the naming of his children follows his third reading of the famous self-dissection dream in which Ernst von Brücke himself had told Freud to "prepare" anatomically his own lower body, an activity which he understands to symbolize his self-analysis (438). The section itself presents his second reading of a double dream involving first the appearance of the dead Professor Ernst Fleischl in Ernst von Brücke's laboratory, and then his (dead) friend P. who joins Freud and Fliess for dinner. During the meal P. dissolves into nothing after Freud, realizing that P. is already dead, pronounces, while penetrating him with his gaze, "non vixit," "he did

---

14 "(*Dazu eine vergessene Fortsetzung.*) Aus der Analyse kann ich nun einsetzen, was in diese Traumlücke gehört. Es ist die Erwähnung meines zweiten Knaben, dem ich den Vornamen einer großen historischen Persönlichkeit gegeben habe, die mich in den Knabenjahren, besonders seit meinem Aufenthalt in England, mächtig angezogen. Ich hatte das Jahr der Erwartung über den Vorsatz, gerade diesen Namen zu verwenden, wenn es ein Sohn würde, und begrüßte mit ihm *hoch befriedigt* schon den eben Geborenen. Es ist leicht zu merken, wie die unterdrückte Größensucht des Vaters sich in seinen Gedanken auf die Kinder überträgt; ja man wird gern glauben, daß dies einer der Wege ist, auf denen die im Leben notwendig gewordene Unterdrückung derselben vor sich geht. Sein Anrecht, in den Zusammenhang dieses Traumes aufgenommen zu werden, erwarb der Kleine dadurch, daß ihm damals der nämliche -- beim Kinde und beim Sterbenden leicht verzeihliche -- Unfall widerfahren war, die Wäsche zu beschmutzen. Vergleiche hiezu die Anspielung '*Stuhlrichter*' und den Wunsch des Traumes: Vor seinen Kindern *groß* und *rein* dazustehen." Ibid., 432.

not live," an error in tempus Freud realizes within the dream itself. The last affect Freud relates is again one of great satisfaction: "*I am tremendously pleased about* [P's disintegration], *understand now that Ernst Fleischl as well was only an appearance, a revenant, and find it quite well possible that such a person exists only for as long as one wishes and that he can be removed by the wish of the other.*"[15]

In the first telling, Freud had added a few mysterious sentences in which he notes that he would love to tell his audience the "full solution of these riddles," that is, "the meaning of the dream which is well-known to me," but claims that he cannot "sacrifice consideration for such dear persons to my ambition, as I do in my dream" (409). "Dear persons (*teure Personen*)" reappear later on as the namesakes of Freud's children, but even without that repetition, it is obvious that the dream concerns Ernst von Brücke rather than Ernst Fleischl, and that the dissolution of the "greatest authority" of his life is at stake. Freud himself feels reminded of his own disintegration under von Brücke's gaze. His former teacher had once reprimanded him for coming late to the lab: "What he said was scant and firm; however, the words did not really matter. What overwhelmed me were the terrible blue eyes with which he gazed at me and before which I faded—like P. in the dream, who to my relief reversed the roles."[16] Revenants return as reversals, and, like dreams or the fairies of old, they appear to fulfill wishes, inverting the father's gaze, granting to the dreamer the imaginary power of the father he will never hold in his waking life—for the father's power is real only in its fantasmatic effects on the son, it cannot be experienced by the father himself.

When Freud returns to the dream later on, and once again mentions the satisfaction it gave him, he reflects on the "difficult self-overcoming involved in interpreting and communicating one's dreams. One has to uncover oneself as the only villain among all the noble ones with which one shares life," and he continues, rather cryptically:

> Hence, I find it entirely understandable that the *revenants* exist only as long as one likes them, and that they can be removed by a wish. The revenants, however, are the successive incarnations of my childhood friend; hence I am also satisfied that I have

---

15 "Ich bin ungemein erfreut darüber, verstehe jetzt, daß auch Ernst Fleischl nur eine Erscheinung, ein Revenant war, und finde es ganz wohl möglich, daß eine solche Person nur so lange besteht, als man es mag, und daß sie durch den Wunsch des anderen beseitigt werden kann." Ibid., 409.

16 "Was er mir sagte, war karg und bestimmt; es kam aber gar nicht auf die Worte an. Das Überwältigende waren die fürchterlichen blauen Augen, mit denen er mich ansah und vor denen ich verging—wie P. im Traum, der zu meiner Erleichterung die Rollen verwechselt hat." Ibid., 410.

replaced this person again and again, and a replacement for the one I am now in the process of losing [i.e., Fliess] will find itself. Nobody is irreplaceable.[17]

What have we learned so far about children? They are figures of return as well as of replacement, repositories of selves that are and are not sacrificed to the demands of the reality principle, compensation for the death of beloved friends. Naming them is akin to an identity deposit. Similar to the logic by which the fetish allows the fetishist to both acknowledge and deny castration, the son allows his father to both acknowledge and deny death and replaceability: in other words, time. The son does not merely return as his father, but, perhaps as importantly, as his father's father, inverting a relationship of submission into one of power through the act of naming. The most troubling and perhaps the most extraordinary metonymical equation, however, is that of the child as revenant and the revenant as the figure who can be "removed by a wish." The passage that, in isolation, appeared like a benign and perhaps mildly self-ironical assessment of a father's ambition for his children, acquires a sinister filicidal subtone. Of course, to an extent, naming the son after another is always already a process of erasing his identity, of withholding him from his own time, of smothering his separateness in layers and layers of identities already established and meaningful, and in its most benign intentions a violent inscription on the softest of flesh. Luce Irigaray, questioning Levinas's conception of fatherhood, notes that "the child should be for himself, not for the parent. When one intends to create a child, giving the child to himself appears as an ethical necessity. The son should not be the place where the father confers being or existence on himself, the place where he finds the resources to return to himself in relation to this same as and other than himself constituted by the son."[18] She is right, but she perhaps underestimates the difficulty of "giving the child to himself" in a culture where father-son succession and substitution organize all foundational narratives, and where all the names are already taken.

---

17 "Man muß sich als den einzigen Bösewicht enthüllen unter all den Edlen, mit denen man das Leben teilt. Ich finde es also ganz begreiflich, daß die *Revenants* nur so lange bestehen, als man sie mag, und daß sie durch den Wunsch beseitigt werden können. . . . Die Revenants sind aber die aufeinanderfolgenden Inkarnationen meines Kindheitsfreundes; ich bin also auch befriedigt darüber, daß ich mir diese Person immer wieder ersetzt habe, und auch für den, den ich jetzt zu verlieren im Begriffe bin, wird sich der Ersatz schon finden. Es ist niemand unersetzlich." Ibid., 467.
18 Luce Irigaray, "Questions to Emmanuel Levinas," in *The Irigaray Reader*, ed. Margaret Whitford (London: Blackwell, 1991), 181.

There is nothing new, of course, in drawing attention to paternal violence in its many forms and guises; especially in the wake of Freud, such violence has been taken for granted as one of fatherhood's defining features, engendering and legitimizing patricidal fantasies and acts in turn. The prohibitions against these fantasies and acts are, in fact, rather weak as soon as we enter metaphoric or symbolic realms. If anything, violent rebellion against all fathers has been the norm and often enough the ideal in cultural production (at least) since the Enlightenment, and it surely serves as a privileged (and not necessarily tragic) model of history. But what of the father himself, what is *his* position here? And what is involved in the moment of becoming-father? Isn't the dilemma of fatherhood the encounter with a rival you cannot destroy without destroying yourself?

While Freud reads the oedipal plot as a child's fantasy of patricide, we might be tempted to consider the plot of the subordinate son who displaces his desire in the interest of the patriarchal family as the Laiusian fantasy par excellence. Why else would you choose the six-year-old to embody the Oedipal force? Isn't that the most reassuring rival a man could have? Unlike the infant, the young child is no longer allied with the mother's body whose womb and breasts he had usurped (providing her, at least according to Freud himself, with a phallus he in some regards has stolen from the father), and unlike the young adult, he is socially and materially dependent, physically weak, and sexually insignificant. By stark contrast, the Oedipus of Greek myth comes into view at the two moments in which the promise of fatherhood is most critically threatened by the outbreak of filicidal violence: the birth of the son, which turns the man from lover into father (the moment in which the poet Donald Hall addresses his newborn as "My Son, my Executioner"[19]), and his transition to adulthood in which he gains the very real power to challenge the father physically, sexually, and socially.

Two of Freud's own dreams mark these two moments very clearly— one barely mentions his children, the other one is the closest he comes to an explicitly filicidal fantasy. The first:

An elevation, on it something like an open-air privy (Abort), *a very long bench, at its end a large privy hole. The edge at the very back densely occupied with little piles of excrement of all sizes and stages of freshness. Behind the bench, bushes* ein (Gebüsch). *I urinate onto the bench; a long stream of urine rinses everything clean* (rein), *the pieces*

---

19 Donald Hall, "My Son, My Executioner," in *Fathers and Sons: An Anthology*, ed. David Seybold (New York: Atlantic Monthly Press, 1995), 129.

of excrement come loose easily and fall into the opening. As if something were left over at the end.[20]

Freud happily receives his unconscious's assertion that he is "der Übermensch," Hercules, Gulliver, and Gargantua wrapped into one, and to the extent that he acknowledges the presence of his children in this dream, he comments that "I have discovered the childhood etiology of the neuroses and thus have saved my own children from falling ill."[21] It is very tempting, however, to speculate about a quite different reading. At the time of writing, Freud had six children, born in 1887, 1889, 1891, 1892, 1893, and 1895, "of all sizes and stages of freshness" so to speak. Even if the equation of defecation and birthing becomes prominent in a slightly later stage in Freud's work—he touches upon it in the section of birthing dreams but only develops the theme in the analysis of Little Hans—, the equation of feces and gold and of children and wealth belongs to the *Interpretation of Dreams*,[22] and so does the association of bushes and the female pubes.[23] The word Freud uses for "privy," *Abort*, is also the medical term for abortion, and finally, Freud himself characterizes the location of the dream as follows: "The elevation and the bushes belong to Aussee where my children are staying at this point (gehören nach Aussee, wo jetzt meine Kinder weilen)," (452).

Freud, of course, does not think of the little piles of feces as his children whom he can rinse away with a powerful stream of urine, a penile act of abortion inverting the act of begetting, just as he does not draw a connection between the revenants he can dissolve with his gaze and the revenants he declares his children to be. In general, when Freud talks about himself as father in the Dream Book, he presents himself as an especially benign one rather than as the villain as whom he usually delights in posing. When he dreams of having "to flee my

---

20 "Eine Anhöhe, auf dieser etwas wie ein Abort im Freien, eine sehr lange Bank, an deren Ende ein großes Abortloch. Die ganz hintere Kante dicht besetzt mit Häufchen Kot von allen Größen und Stufen der Frische. Hinter der Bank ein Gebüsch. Ich uriniere auf die Bank; ein langer Harnstrahl spült alles rein, die Kotpatzen lösen sich leicht ab und fallen in die Öffnung. Als ob am Ende noch etwas übrigbliebe." Freud, *Die Traumdeutung*, 452.
21 "Ich habe die Kindheitsaetiologie der Neurosen aufgedeckt und dadurch meine eigenen Kinder vor Erkrankung bewahrt." Ibid., 452
22 "'How many children do you have now?' —'Six.' —A gesture of respect and precariousness. —'Girls, boys?' —'Three and three, that is my pride and my wealth.'" ("'Wieviele Kinder haben Sie jetzt?' —'Sechs.' —Eine Gebärde von Respekt und Bedenklichkeit. —'Mädel, Buben?' —'Drei und drei, das ist mein Stolz und mein Reichtum.'") Ibid., 302.
23 See ibid., 360: "The male genital symbolized by people, the female one by a landscape."

children," in an unusual transitive usage of the German verb *flüchten* (426), he finds in himself only sorrow at the prospect of separation and worry and care for their well-being (427), not a hint of a wish to be free of them. When, in the same dream, two of his sons appear with a father who is not Freud himself (426), he does not reflect on the appearance of another father as a possible inversion of the family romance,[24] or as a variation on the ancient theme of paternal uncertainty, but realizes that he, as a Jewish man, cannot provide them with a *Vaterland*, barred from the metonymy of pater and patria that sustains fatherhood and the state alike.[25] When he dreams that his children's physician falls ill, he does not wonder whether he may be wishing for their illness as well. When he dreams of "my son the myop" (426), he does not ask what there may be to be gained in a son who does not see. The theme of filicide does surface in a passing joke—"A little bit later, a shingle hit my eye: Dr. *Herodes*, Practice Hours . . . I said, 'I hope the colleague isn't a pediatrician'"[26]—but the allusion is safely contained in the history of Jewish persecution: it is always the other father who kills.

Only once in *The Interpretation of Dreams* does Freud come close to acknowledging in himself the Laiusian wish to destroy the child, and that is a passage added much later, in 1919, concerning a son who has entered the privileged arena of masculine power, war:

> *I tell my wife I have news for her, something very special. She is afraid and wants to hear nothing. I assure her that, on the contrary, something that will make her very happy, and begin to tell that our son's officer corps has sent a sum of money (5000 K?), . . . something about acknowledgment . . . distribution . . .* [Freud enters a pantry, and suddenly] *I see my son appear . . . He mounts a basket next to a cupboard as if to place something on top of this cupboard. I call to him; no response. It seems to me that he has his face or his forehead bandaged, he arranges*

---

24 On the theme of inverted family romance, see Marie MacLean, "The Heirs of Amphitryon: Social Fathers and Natural Fathers," *New Literary History* 26, no. 4 (1995): 787–807.

25 "The Jewish question, the worry about the future of the children to whom one cannot give a fatherland, the worry to bring them up in such a way that they can become free to move. [*freizügig* also carries connotations of cosmopolitan, sexually liberated, loose], are easy to recognize in the relevant dream thoughts." ("Die Judenfrage, die Sorge um die Zukunft der Kinder, denen man ein Vaterland nicht geben kann, die Sorge, sie so zu erziehen, daß sie freizügig werden können, sind in den zugehörigen Traumgedanken leicht zu erkennen.") Freud, *Die Traumdeutung*, 427.

26 "Kurz darauf fiel mir ein Schild in die Augen: Dr. *Herodes*, Sprechstunde. . . . Ich meinte: 'Hoffentlich ist der Kollege nicht gerade Kinderarzt.'" Ibid., 428.

something in his mouth, pushes something in. I think: Should he be so exhausted? And does he have false teeth?[27]

Freud, asleep in a night during World War I, realizes that he is dreaming about his son's death: "It is easy to see that the conviction that he has been wounded or killed finds expression in the content of the dream," but when he begins to talk about the element of wish fulfillment that by his own account pervades all dreams, he takes a detour:

> the location of a pantry, the cupboard, . . . these are unmistakable allusions to an accident of my own. . . . The deepening of the analysis then lets me find the hidden impulse that could find satisfaction in the feared accident of the son. It is the envy against youth which the older man believes to have stifled thoroughly in his life, and it is unmistakable that precisely the strength of the painful emotion, should such a calamity really occur, discovers such a repressed wish fulfillment as its solace.[28]

If there is a wish here somewhere, it is no longer the driving force of the dream, it is no longer the forbidden fantasy that pushes through the defenses of our waking, loving mind—wish fulfillment here is at best secondary, solace for a very general pain.[29] In order to consider the

---

27 "Ich sage meiner Frau, ich habe eine Nachricht für sie, etwas ganz Besonderes. Sie erschrickt und will nichts hören. Ich versichere ihr, im Gegenteil, etwas, was sie sehr freuen wird, und beginne zu erzählen, daß das Offizierskorps unseres Sohnes eine Summe Geldes geschickt hat (5000 K) . . . etwas von Anerkennung . . . Verteilung. . . . Plötzlich sehe ich meinen Sohn erscheinen. . . . Er steigt auf einen Korb, der sich seitlich neben einem Kasten befindet, wie um etwas auf diesen Kasten zu legen. Ich rufe ihn an: keine Antwort. Mir scheint, er hat das Gesicht oder die Stirn verbunden, er richtet sich etwas im Munde, schiebt sich etwas ein. Auch haben seine Haare einen grauen Schimmer. Ich denke: Sollte er so erschöpft sein? Und hat er falsche Zähne?" Ibid., 532–3.
28 "die Örtlichkeit, eine Speisekammer, der Kasten . . . das sind unverkennbare Anspielungen an einen eigenen Unfall. . . . Die Vertiefung der Analyse läßt mich dann die versteckte Regung finden, die sich an dem gefürchteten Unfall des Sohnes befriedigen könnte. Es ist der Neid gegen die Jugend, den der Gealterte im Leben gründlich erstickt zu haben glaubt, und es ist unverkennbar, daß gerade die Stärke der schmerzlichen Ergriffenheit, wenn ein solches Unglück sich wirklich ereignete, zu ihrer Linderung eine solche verdrängte Wunscherfüllung aufspürt." Ibid., 534.
29 When Freud does finally and at length reflect on a father's dream, the son is already dead, and the only wishes Freud allows us to imagine are that he has come to life again, or that sleep goes on. It is striking that the dream of the burning child is explicitly framed as the one dream where the usual dream economy of fantasy, wish, and the outside does not apply. Cathy Caruth

dream as wish fufillment at all, Freud must soften death to accident, murderous fantasy to envy, and in yet another double inversion of paternal and filial position, the accident repeats his own while his son appears as an old man with gray hair and false teeth.

Such slides pervade Freud's reflections on his own fatherhood, and perhaps fatherhood and sonhood are simply so intimately bound up with each other that they cannot be kept apart. It is certainly the case that under the influence of Lacan and others, Freud's concept of the oedipal has become generalized to such a degree that the position of any *given* father (in contrast to "the" father, the symbolic one) appears to be subsumed under it. Claude LeGuen suggests as much when he writes: "I would say unequivocally that there is only an Oedipus complex, the Laius complex being only an appendage. But what an appendage!"[30] To be sure, the citations from the Dream Book suggest over and over again that the father is always also and perhaps primarily son—or at least, that he is more ready to present and reflect on himself as a son rather than a father. But why is that? Certainly, sonhood precedes fatherhood biographically—every father has been a son first. And unlike fatherhood, sonhood is not optional, and thus (for all the historical, cultural, and individual differences that apply) amounts to a universal situation. In this light, it is hardly surprising that a father's self-image will be suffused by the remnants of his earlier filial perspective. But at the same time, in any given life, the father precedes his son—he is there first. And the newborn, no matter how deeply embedded in the symbolic his life may already be, will have to come into awareness of his sonhood in encountering a father who is already there (or will be fantasized as always already having been there). Empirical and experiential temporalities collide and intertwine. Paternal subjectivity emerges both as a recuperation of filiality and its fantasms while encountering the other, who by his very appearance moves the father one generation closer to death and appeals to him to assent to this death.

Paternity is contaminated by filiality, but the same is not true in reverse. The son does not recover, in himself, memories of having been a father. His position is clearer, and much easier to inhabit. Oedipus is not Laius, or at least not yet (always not yet). And even Oedipus is not Oedipus, as I will show in the next two chapters—if anything, he is the

---

comments: "Unlike in other dreams, Freud remarks, what is striking in this dream is not its relation to inner wishes, but its direct relation to a catastrophic reality outside." *Unclaimed Experience: Trauma, Narrative and History* (Baltimore: Johns Hopkins University Press, 1996), 94.

30 Claude Le Guen, "The Formation of the Transference: Or the Laius Complex in the Armchair," *International Journal of Psychoanalysis* 55, no. 4 (1974): 512.

figure of father-son duality gone tragic. In Sophocles's tragedy—the version of the Oedipal myth Freud claims as his inspiration—Laius is always already dead, and his death is so constitutive of the myth as we read it that he is not merely dead, it appears as if he has never lived, that death is his existence: *non vixit*.

Section II
The Tragic Father

Two The Laius Complex

Freudian paternity is a space in the shadow of Oedipus, and it is in that shadow space that Laius has lived for a very long time. It has been difficult to catch a glimpse of him there, and you're never quite sure what you see: a corpse, a monster, a *Gschnas*,[1] a reflection, a memory, a fear. Of course, Sophocles introduced him as already invisible, already gone: "Laius, my lord, was the leader of our land before you assumed control of this state," Creon explains.[2] Oedipus responds emphatically that he knows it well (*exoida*), and adds, in the well-known ironical twist, "by hearsay, for I never saw him" (line 105). Laius indeed has been the one we know by hearsay only, the one who never speaks himself. He exerts his power through the speech of others, always evoked, never present. Unlike, say, Hamlet's father, to whom he bears a distant resemblance, he never stakes his claims in his own name. It is Sophoclean Laius, then, who enables all Freudian and Lacanian readings that invest the absent father with tremendous power not despite but because of his death, in a model of paternity that can only be articulated on the basis of oedipal filiality, an afterthought to, a product of sonhood.

But while modernity has had little time for a living Laius, he was once a prominent figure, and it is possible to know at least a little bit more about him. Due to the vagaries of reception, he left few traces in what remains extant of classical literature, but we do know *of* numerous texts that engaged him. Aeschylus's tragedy *Laius* is lost as well as Euripides's *Chrysippus*, a play that probably staged Laius's rape or abduction of his host Pelops's favorite son by the same name. Neither the *Oidipea* nor the *Thebais*, epic poems that presumably had much to say about him, have survived. We have a suggestive but inconclusive remark in Plato's *Laws*, some fragments from the Theban tragedies of Aeschylus, Sophocles, and Euripides,[3] and the following

---

1   See Chapter 10.
2   Sophocles, *Oedipus Tyrannus*, in *The Plays and Fragments*, ed. and trans. with notes by Sir Richard C. Jebb (Cambridge: Cambridge University Press, 1914), line 104. Unless otherwise noted, all subsequent references will be to this edition and translation.
3   Among other scattered sources, see Hans Joachim Mette, *Der verlorene Aischylos* (Berlin: Akademie Verlag, 1963), which contains extant fragments from Aeschylus's *Laius*, and *Tragicorum Graecorum fragmenta*, ed. August

34   The Tragedy of Fatherhood

lines in Pseudo-Apollodorus's *Library*, a mythography from the early Christian era, which, together with other fragmentary evidence, have given rise to the more elaborate constructions that now undergird nearly the entirety of the reception of Laius:

> He [Laius] resided in Peloponnese, being hospitably received by Pelops; and while he taught Chrysippus, the son of Pelops, to drive a chariot, he conceived a passion for the lad and carried him off.[4]

Sir Richard Jebb, in his late nineteenth-century commentaries on *Antigone* and *Oedipus at Colonus*, several times refers to "the curse called down on Laius by Pelops, for robbing him of his son Chrysippus."[5] The entry for Chrysippus in a popular German reference work, *Der kleine Pauly*, refers to "the legend of the abduction of the beautiful Chrysippus" and informs us that "since the Thebans didn't punish the transgression, Hera sends them the Sphinx and has Laius and his house destroyed through Oedipus's fate."[6] The corresponding entry for Laius, oddly enough written by the same scholar, tells us that not Hera, but Pelops "cursed his son's abductor to remain childless or to die by his son's hand."[7] Both entries, however, mention various other versions according to which Chrysippus was killed by his half-brothers Atreus and Thyestes at the instigation of his mother Hippodamia, who hated him,[8] and the Laius entry notes, importantly, that "the curse . . . probably did not originally belong to the Theban legends" (ibid.).

Laius, then, could have been treated along heterogeneous lines, and the very paucity of sources would have put little restraint on the collective imagination. And yet, during modernity, there is hardly

---

Nauck (Hildesheim: G. Olms Verlagsbuchhandlung, 1964). The most complete account of the various texts and fragments in question is still Carl Robert, *Oidipus: Geschichte eines poetischen Stoffs im Griechischen Altertum*, 2 vols. (Berlin: Weidmann, 1915).

4   Apollodorus, *The Library*, trans. Sir James George Frazer, 2 vols. (Cambridge: Harvard University Press; London: William Heinemann Ltd., 1921), 3.5.5.
5   Sophocles, *Oedipus Tyrannus*, 66n. 369.
6   Konrat Ziegler and Walther Sontheimer, eds., *Der kleine Pauly: Lexikon der Antike in fünf Bänden* (Munich: dtv, 1979), 1:1169. My translation.
7   Ibid., 3:454. In the *Phoenician Women*, however, Oedipus merely speaks of "the legacy of curses I received from Laius," and it is unclear which curses Oedipus has in mind, even though the fact that Euripides did write a play about Chrysippus is, of course, suggestive. Euripides, *The Phoenissae*, trans. E. P. Coleridge, vol. 2, in *The Complete Greek Drama*, ed. Whitney J. Oates and Eugene O'Neill, Jr., 2 vols. (New York: Random House, 1938).
8   See also Plutarch, *Moralia*, trans. Frank Cole Babbitt, vol. 4 (Cambridge, MA: Harvard University Press, 2005).

anything at all on him, and certainly nothing remotely comparable to the intense engagement with Oedipus. During the hundreds of years we have spent thinking about Oedipus, the act of patricide has never been far from anybody's mind, whether the readings that have emerged from this history center on the Sphinx or on incest, on knowledge, desire, or fate. Its victim, however, barely appears. For the most part, he is simply the ("the") father and dead by his son's hand, invisible and beyond both analysis and blame—yes, he exposed a newborn infant to what must have seemed certain death, but that story is related without condemnation in a play notably bursting with anger, regret, and reproach. Always-already offstage, it appeared as if he did not need to be imagined, as if "hearsay" could tell us all we needed to know. As one of the purest literary instances of a powerful presence in absence, to Oedipus's modern readers, the figure of Laius needed neither image nor description.

When he finally *does* reemerge from obscurity, he rises as the dark father of a child's worst nightmare. Hugo von Hofmannsthal brings him to life in 1906, in *Oedipus and the Sphinx*, and Laius enters the stage as a nasty old man. Oedipus has just killed the king's herald in self-defense, and Laius, furious at the death of his old servant, will not accept Oedipus's humble offer to make amends, but instead threatens to torture and kill him. Oedipus asks, aghast, "With what murderer's hands do you reach into the world? Who are you?" Laius replies:

> An old man who had to see an old man die
> like a dog under your hands.
> But you shall pay!
> I will send you down, draped in torments
> and amongst the dead he will encounter you
> and will feast on the sight and will bless me for it.[9]

Much can be said about this passage and the play as a whole, but for now, it is enough to note that Hofmannsthal's Laius understands himself to be the voice of an old man, of all the old men. Still alive, he already speaks for the dead, in the voice of a murderous antagonism too virulent to die with them—it is the voice of the father as dreamed in the Freudian dark. Here is how Hofmannsthal has Oedipus see him:

> Your voice is hatred and torment. You never had a child,
> You are of the infertile ones,
> Your sad wife, dust in her hair,

---

9   Hugo von Hofmannsthal, *Oedipus und die Sphinx. Tragödie in drei Aufzügen* (Berlin: S. Fischer, 1906), 56. My translation.

Has lain before the gods night and day—
Let me pass, let me go![10]

Hofmannsthal's vision of Laius is both extraordinary and entirely typical of modern fatherhood: extraordinary because he imagines him at all, gives him the voice he has lacked for so long, even if it is little more than a snarl; thoroughly modern because Laius, even if Oedipus with somewhat heavy-handed irony accuses him of infertility, appears entirely defined by the perspective of the oedipal son who will kill him. He is little more than a pure obstacle on the road to selfhood, and a singularly unappealing one at that.

Pier Paolo Pasolini, too, shows us a deeply disturbing Laius, even though he is now a young man, recently married, and wearing the uniform of the fascists. Stealing into the room where his son is lying in his crib, Laius stares at the infant, his face a mask of petulant rage. On the screen, his thoughts flash in writing: "You are here again to take my place and rob me of all I have. (*looking to Jocasta*) She, the woman I love, already you steal her love."[11] Later, we see him viciously squeezing the infant's feet, soon to be bound tight by ropes, as if not even Pasolini had the nerve to show an actual piercing.

Such fictional treatments seem to join seamlessly with scholarly ones. John Munder Ross, a psychoanalyst, sees in Laius a sadist beset by "pederastic and filicidal inclinations that I believe to be universal among fathers,"[12] and he calls him "one of the prototypic perpetrators

---

10 "Deine Stimme ist Haß und Qual. Du hast nie ein Kind gehabt, / Du bist von den Unfruchtbaren, / Dein trauriges Weib, mit Staub in den Haaren, / Ist Tag und Nacht vor den Göttern gelegen— / Laß mich vorbei, laß mich fort!" Ibid., 56–7.

11 *Oedipus Rex*, directed by Pier Paolo Pasolini (1967; New York: Water Bearer Films, 2003), DVD. In the original screenplay, Laius is listening to his "inner voice": "Here he is, the child who is gradually going to take your place in the world. Yes, he will hound you away and take your rightful place. He will kill you. He is here for no other reasons. He knows it. The first thing he will rob you of is your wife, your sweet wife who you believe lives only for you. While instead there is love between this fellow here and her; and you are well aware that she returns it, that she is betraying you. Through love of his mother, this fellow will murder his father." *Oedipus Rex: A Film by Pier Paolo Pasolini*, trans. John Mathews (New York: Simon and Schuster, 1971), 20. In light of this passage, it is rather interesting to see Pasolini write in the introduction to the script that "Freud . . . carries no more weight in the film than an amateur would have given him"—a claim that, if anything, goes to show that our imagination of the father has been conditioned by Freud's narratives to such an extent that his influence has become invisible. Ibid., 9.

12 John Munder Ross, "The Darker Side of Fatherhood: Clinical and Developmental Ramifications of the 'Laius Motif,'" *International Journal of Psychoanalytic Psychotherapy* 11 (1985): 117.

of child abuse."¹³ Elsewhere, Ross names Laius as "an embodiment of a veritable web of paternal disease and its terrible consequences, offering himself as a prototype or paradigm of the 'bad father.'"¹⁴ For Martin Bergmann, he is "the father of pederasty about whom nothing favorable can be said."¹⁵ Marie Balmary, who returns to Laius in the context of her reading of Freud's relationship to his father, relies on Pierre Grimal's *Dictionnaire de la mythologie grecque et romaine* when she renders the story as follows: "Laius was very young when his father, King Labdacus, died, and he had to flee when the regent was killed. He sought refuge with King Pelops. 'There he developed a passion for young Chrysippus, Pelops's son, and thus, by some accounts, he conceived unnatural passions. Laius ran off with the young man and was cursed by Pelops. . . . Chrysippus, from shame, committed suicide,'" and she continues:

> Such is the origin of the curse of the Labdacidae. . . . It is neither Oedipus's desire, nor blind destiny, that constitutes the profound motive behind the tragic events that will befall him. At the origin is the fault committed by Laius; the abduction and homosexual violation of the young son of his host and the suicide that follows constitute the mainspring of the Oedipean myth.[16]

As they say, important if true. But none of the better-known texts—say, Homer's *Odyssey*, Sophocles's *Oedipus the King*, or Euripides's *Phoenician Women*—mentions the story when they talk about Oedipus, and we have already seen that the Chrysippus motif may well be a late addition to the Theban saga. Euripides, provided his *Chrysippus* did lay blame on Laius for the whole Theban mess, is famous for rationalizing the tragic myths his dramatic predecessors had told, and he may have introduced the Chrysippus motif to motivate more plausibly the downfall of the Labdacidae—it is, in any case, impossible to tell. While Plato's *Laws*[17] and a smattering of other sources do link the name of

---

13 John Munder Ross, *What Men Want: Mothers, Fathers, and Manhood* (Cambridge, MA: Harvard University Press, 1994), 95.
14 John Munder Ross, "Oedipus Revisited: Laius and the Laius Complex," *Psychoanalytic Study of the Child* 37 (1982): 169–200.
15 Martin S. Bergmann, *In the Shadow of Moloch: The Sacrifice of Children and Its Impact on Western Religions* (New York: Columbia University Press, 1992), 298.
16 Marie Balmary, *Psychoanalyzing Psychoanalysis: Freud and the Hidden Fault of the Father*, trans. and intro. Ned Lukacher (Baltimore: Johns Hopkins University Press, 1982), 8.
17 "If we were to follow in nature's steps and enact that law which held good before the days of Laius, declaring that it is right to refrain from indulging in the same kind of intercourse with men and boys as with women, and adducing

Laius to pederasty (which hardly translates into "child abuse" in the Greek context), most of the extant sources concerning the rape and abduction of Chrysippus belong to the Christian era, and it is entirely unclear whether (and, I suspect, rather unlikely that) the earlier ones we no longer have carried the same tone of condemnation we find in Balmary or Ross.

Hofmannsthal and Pasolini are self-consciously, even aggressively modern: they reimagine the old story as a new one, and the results are stunning. The psychoanalytically oriented critics, on the other hand, insist that Laius has *always* been lurking in the shadows, that the ancient story is the same one as the one they want to tell. In other words, they want us to believe that Laius never was a tragic hero. There is, in those accounts, no reflection on the specifically modern desire that drives their readings, including a very modern heteronormativity that, rather scandalously, far too often fails to distinguish between pedophilia, pederasty, and homosexuality.

Certainly, "all versions belong to the myth," as Lévi-Strauss insisted, but myths evolve, and when and how they evolve matters. The darkening of Laius may or may not have some early roots—it is impossible to tell from the sparse philological evidence—, but it becomes all pervasive in the twentieth and twenty-first centuries. Surely, no scholar would dare call Oedipus "one of the prototypic perpetrators of elder abuse" without being accused of perpetrating some serious myth abuse in turn—for while Oedipus's story has undergone near constant reevaluation, its tragic structure has never been in doubt. Laius, by contrast, consistently had it coming. Framed as a child rapist and a child murderer, his figure has no defense against the banal moralizations of contemporary therapeutic discourse. As the *New York Times*, in its habitual ignorance of the most basic tenets of philological scholarship, puts it: "Laius may have got what he deserved because he tried to murder his son and was a pederast to boot. Although Sophocles's drama and Freud's theory focus on the son's guilt and thus suppress the father's history of abusing children, that does not change the legend. Long before Oedipus was born, Laius raped Chryssipus, who

---

as evidence thereof the nature of wild beasts, and pointing out how male does not touch male for this purpose, since it is unnatural,— in all this we would probably be using an argument neither convincing nor in any way consonant with your States." Plato, *Plato in Twelve Volumes*, vols. 10 and 11, *Laws*, trans. R. G. Bury (Cambridge, MA: Harvard University Press; London: William Heinemann Ltd., 1967–68), 10:836c. It is striking that this passage has led many scholars to claim that Laius *invented* pederasty—surely, it implies at best a shift in legal thinking.

was King Pelops's son. In other words, Laius had a 'Laius complex.' He wanted to murder his son."[18]

While the reception of Oedipus is driven by recurrent movements of identification, the stories lately told about Laius, by contrast, conspicuously *block* empathy. Precisely when criticism deems itself most critical of Freud, it repeats its fundamental move most faithfully: we are all Oedipus, and none of us is Laius. But if there seems to be a need to exonerate Oedipus from crimes for which he himself insisted he was responsible, it may bespeak a specifically modern guilt that here manifests itself not in any questionable Freudian elevation of the father, but in the disavowal of his humanity. In those accounts, Laius is no longer "the dead father, the father who, after his death, returns as his Name, that is, as the embodiment of the symbolic Law/Prohibition"[19]— his name returns only to justify his killing over and over again, as a marker of the son's innocence, his enduring victimhood. We are encountering, as it were, the Passion of the Oedipus.

Bergmann argues that the sacrifice of children is as surely part of our cultural heritage as the patricidal urges to which Freud was so attuned,[20] and David Lee Miller suggests that "the motif of filial sacrifice is the most striking feature shared by the canonical texts of English literature, along with their classical and biblical antecedents," adding: "Why do Western patriarchies so persistently imagine sacrificing their sons?"[21] It is indeed a powerful motif that raises urgent questions concerning the structure and imagery of patriarchy and fatherhood alike, but we should not forget that the three most important narratives of filial sacrifice all imagine the son who survives: Isaac does *not* die on the Mountains in Moriah; Oedipus does *not* die on Mount Kithairon; and Jesus, who does die on Mount Golgotha, in a fashion, is resurrected again to live forever.[22] In this regard, the foundational narratives central to our Greek and Judaeo-Christian cultural inheritance is the boy who lives, despite the odds, his survival a precondition of the story that turns into history.

If fantasies of patricide and of filicide are inextricably linked, as I, too, believe they are, then whose fantasies are they, and what

---

18 Sarah Boxer, "How Oedipus Is Losing His Complex," *New York Times*, December 6, 1997; http://www.nytimes.com/1997/12/06/theater/how-oedipus-is-losing-his-complex.html
19 Slavoj Žižek, *The Ticklish Subject* (London: Verso, 2000), 315ff.
20 Bergmann, *Moloch,* 298.
21 David Lee Miller, *Dreams of the Burning Child: Sacrificial Sons and the Father's Witness* (Ithaca, NY: Cornell University Press, 2003), 1.
22 The same is also true for Cronus and Zeus, powerful gods who both survive their fathers' filicidal strategies, and for Iphigenia, who survives Agamemnon's sacrifice.

ambivalent needs, desires, and anxieties feed them? Ever since Georges Devereux's influential 1953 paper, "Why Oedipus Killed Laius,"[23] those psychoanalysts who have paid attention to him have focused on what Devereux, in another paper, called his "cannibalistic impulses."[24] But according to the remaining fragments of Aeschylus's *Laius*, it is Oedipus who takes his father's blood into his mouth, not vice versa. What do we make of that? Is it a gruesome staging of their consanguinity, or is it its rejection? In the light of ample semiotic evidence of the interchangeability of bodily fluids, does the father's blood stand in for the mother's milk, only to be rejected as nurturance? Or is it the father's sperm that is tasted and spat out? What if the son is the one with the "cannibalistic impulses," incorporating the father's body, just as Christians will drink the blood of the son for millennia to come?

Over the course of this book, I will argue that our thoughts and feelings regarding fatherhood have been deeply shaped by two deeply conflicting grand traditions, one ancient Greek or Athenian, the other biblical. The distinction between Jerusalem and Athens emerges as that between a world in which there is an original father who, being fatherless himself, grounds and limits the power of all fathers after him, and a world in which the highest paternal power—Zeus—is always also a son whose revolt succeeded.[25] This is not to say that Greece does not have its share of filicidal narratives. In fact, those stories abound, but there is a striking difference. Tantalus serves his son Pelops to the gods—but Pelops is resurrected and Tantalus is severely and eternally punished, sentenced to unquenchable desire. Laius has Oedipus exposed on Kithairon—but Oedipus survives, kills Laius, and ends up as Athens's highly revered guardian corpse. Agamemnon sacrifices Iphigenia to the military interest of the state—but Iphigenia is saved and Agamemnon murdered by his wife. In the divine realm, both Uranus and Cronus attempt to kill their children, but ultimately, neither of them succeeds, and both lose their power in the process. If Genesis, in the story of the binding of Isaac, grounds actual and symbolic fatherhood in a story of averted filicide—more on that in the next chapter—demanded and practiced by a paternal deity that alone can lift the command at the last moment, Greek mythology installs

---

23 Georges Devereux, "Why Oedipus Killed Laius," *International Journal of Psychoanalysis* 34, no. 1 (1953): 134–41.
24 Georges Devereux, "The Cannibalistic Impulses of Parents," *Psychoanalytic Forum* 1 (1966): 114–30.
25 Certainly, the New Testament introduces a son as well, and Christianity has been read as a "son religion" often enough, but Jesus is nothing *but* son; he never becomes a father in turn, and it is precisely for that reason that he can serve as a figure for Christian identification.

Zeus through a story of accomplished patricide,[26] a theme noticeably absent from the Bible.[27]

The different structures have eminently political implications. Monotheism and its regimes rely on a paternal triad in which god, king, and father are both strictly analogous and subjected to each other in a descending hierarchy—the power of God establishes and trumps the demands of the king who, as the representative of the nation, in any crisis overrules the rights of the father. The political history of ancient Greece and especially Athens, in marked contrast, is characterized not by the personal struggle of paternal rulers competing for legitimacy, but by rivaling models of political organization that successfully challenged the principle of monarchy long before such a thing becomes possible again in the Christian West. Certainly, Olympus is nothing if not a patriarchy, but regime change is always possible.

Laius's modern detractors, who rely unhesitatingly on the most obscure versions of the myth, often postdating the main narrative they are said to illuminate, tend to ignore entirely a very suggestive passage in an easily accessible canonical text: Aeschylus's *Seven against Thebes*, which precedes and informs the Sophoclean Oedipus whose version of the story has dominated reception.

Anyone I have ever asked why Laius had Oedipus exposed—and I have asked hundreds of people by now—has given me the same answer: because an oracle told him that his son would kill him. This is the story that shapes all comparisons of Laius and Abraham, but it is *not* the story Aeschylus tells:

> Indeed I speak of the ancient transgression, now swift in its retribution. It remains even into the third generation, ever since Laius—in defiance of Apollo who, at his Pythian oracle at the earth's center, said three times that the king would save his city if he died without offspring. Ever since he, overcome by the thoughtlessness of his longing, fathered his own death, the parricide Oedipus, who sowed his mother's sacred field, where he was nurtured, and endured a bloody crop. Madness (*paranoia*) united the frenzied (*phrenôleis*) bridal pair.[28]

---

26 Zeus does not and cannot kill Cronus, since Cronus is immortal, but immobilizing him under a mountain seems close enough.

27 There is only a single story of patricide in the Bible, and it is exceptionally obscure: Sennacherib, an exceedingly cruel and, worse, idolatrous king, is killed by his sons, whom he had meant to sacrifice to his false gods (2 Kings 19:36–7 and Isa. 37:37–8). Importantly, not the patricides, but their brother ascends to his throne.

28 Aeschylus, *Seven against Thebes*, in *Aeschylus*, ed. and trans. Herbert Weir Smyth, 2 vols. (Cambridge, MA: Harvard University Press; London: William Heinemann, Ltd. 1926), 1: lines 742–57.

Laius has to choose not between his son and his god, like Abraham, nor between his son's life and his own, as *opinio communis* insists, but between his son and his city. To my knowledge, Peter Szondi is the only major critic who has stressed the tragic implications of this passage and linked it to the ironic structure of Sophocles's Oedipus,[29] recognizing that Laius's dilemma is a variation of the quintessentially tragic logic: the very act thought to avert catastrophe will make it happen more surely.

In the Christian era, most political thought preceding the early Enlightenment (and much of that beyond) conceives of kingship and fatherhood as parallel and analogous modes of benign and legitimate power, but the analogue is, of course, much older than that. Even Aristotle, one of the model's earliest challengers, claims that "the relationship of father to sons is regal in type, since a father's first care is for his children's welfare. . . . [T]he ideal of kingship is paternal government."[30] Laius, however, must choose when paternity and paternal government emerge as mutually exclusive. To beget an heir, as heroic kings are expected to do in order to ensure the continuity of the city and its rule, would destroy the city instead. Under Apollo's injunction, King Laius must sacrifice both his sexual desire and his desire to leave behind an heir; he is called upon to let go of the path to immortality sons are said to offer, to accept the finitude of his own life and body, to die *gennas ater*, without something he had engendered, made, created, so that the city can survive without him and without his.

Apparently, he took the oracle seriously enough, but he might not have trusted its message—according to Aeschylus, it had to be repeated three times, as if Laius wanted to make sure what it said, as if it could not possibly have said *that*. His eventual surrender to desire is portrayed as a single event, a moment whose madness is doubly stressed: *paranoia* brought together a pair of crazed (*phrenôlês*) newlyweds. Laius does violate a divine command, but even if Greek culture valued sexual continence, marital sex does not usually make the cut of unforgivable transgressions.

Allow me to stress this: in Aeschylus's version, superseded in nearly every mythographic account of the curse by Sophocles's corrective

---

29 Commenting on the same passage in Aeschylus, Szondi writes: "In order to have descendants, he shall forego them, for the heir, which otherwise saves the dynasty from going under, would here occasion the downfall himself." Peter Szondi, "Analysen des Tragischen," in *Schriften I* (Frankfurt: Suhrkamp, 1978), 213. My translation.

30 Aristotle, *Nicomachean Ethics*, ed. and trans. Horace Rackham (Cambridge, MA: Harvard University Press; London, W. Heinemann, Ltd., 1934), 1160b. Unless otherwise noted, all subsequent references will be to this edition and translation.

interpretation, the oracle does not predict that the son will kill his father, but instead that the city will fall if Laius does not die childlessly. It is not a matter of protecting his own survival. For the sake of the city, the son must die before he dies. Time must turn. The king must not be a father anymore. And hence, nothing less than the very nature of rule is at stake.

Just as the biblical account of Abraham's sacrifice did not show him as struggling, the extant Greek passages that refer to Laius's (and/or Jocasta's) decision do not suggest that exposing Oedipus was a difficult choice for him or for them. But the brief passage in *Seven against Thebes* bespeaks at the very least a resistance on his part, and it is certainly phrased in such a way as to suggest that he had to make an active choice. Like Hans Joachim Mette, who collected, edited, and commented the few fragments of *Laius* there are, I like to imagine that the lost *Laius* recounted scenes in which Laius and Jocasta agonized over the decision to abandon Oedipus in the wilderness, similar to Aeschylus's portrayal of Orestes struggling with his decision to kill Klytaemnestra.[31] Even if indirect infanticide carried not nearly as heavy a prohibition as it does now, it is not as clear that the choice would have been as easy as modern commentators assume.[32] Ancient texts, especially the Homeric epics, tell prominent stories of doting fathers,[33] and even if Greek culture did not know the adoration of the infant or the romanticized childhood of late Christianity, I suspect that Laius's dilemma would not have been the stuff of tragedy in the first place if it did not entail a stark conflict.

Unlike Abraham, Laius is not called upon to wield the knife himself, and while there is, as I mentioned, an account of Oedipus taking his slain father's blood in his mouth and spitting it out again,[34] no corresponding motif appears in the accounts of Laius. One might wonder whether Oedipus's exposure could not be read as a gesture of

---

31 Such scenes, if they existed, had to be recapitulations, since it appears as if the *Laius* began with Laius's journey to Delphi. See Mette, *Der verlorene Aischylos*, 345.

32 Cf., for instance, Erik Erikson: "We take it for granted that King Laius knew what he was doing—for could he not count on the authority of the Oracle when he left his baby boy to die, taking no chances with the possibility that a good education might have proved stronger than the oracular establishment?" "Reflections on the Dissent of Contemporary Youth," *International Journal of Psychoanalysis* 51, no. 1 (1970): 22.

33 See Luigi Zoja, *The Father: Historical, Psychological and Cultural Perspectives*, trans. Henry Martin (East Sussex: Brunner-Routledge, 2001), which includes moving chapters on Hector and Odysseus (83–114).

34 Cf. Mette, referring to the Byzantine "Etymologicum Magnum," *Der Verlorene Aischylos*, 35.

ambivalence. Laius's ultimate mistake may not have been his drunken coitus with Jocasta, but his decision—despite the high stakes—not to make sure of Oedipus's death, as he surely could have done, but to leave him to his fate on Kithairon, or in the hands of a servant with a soft heart. Perhaps the king wavered, perhaps he was tempted to let the city go to hell in order to let this infant live, perhaps he decided to give fate a small chance, giving those awful scales a nudge, tipping the balance.

Perhaps not. Exposure was, after all, the accepted infanticidal procedure, designed, probably, to forestall the pollution that would ensue from the actual murder of a blood relative, even an unnamed infant who would not have counted as fully human yet.[35] In any case, Laius, again very much unlike Abraham, loses: his son and his fatherhood, his life, the city. Choosing the welfare of the city over the welfare of his child surely must be read as a sacrifice to the political— but like so many of Greece's filicidal offerings (and in stark contrast to Roman political myth), the sacrifice fails. The city does not survive but disintegrates after Oedipus curses his sons Polyneices and Eteocles to die in fratricidal bloodshed, and Creon, the last king of the cycle, loses his own son Haemon to suicide after he has condemned Antigone to death. Political paternity does not fare well in Thebes, or in the Thebes presented on the Athenian stage.

Of all the stories we have been told about Laius, this, then, is the oldest one we have: father of the city and father of a son, he is forced to choose between the two, chooses the city, loses both, and dies by the hand of the son he thought he could not allow to live. His story is far more compelling than the one about the child molester, the nasty old man, the prototypical "bad father" (to cite Ross again), far more intelligent politically, and far more durable in the end. What is at stake in the story of Laius is nothing less than the fate of the mediation between family and state, a mediation that has always depended on paternity as the junction between a domestic and a public sphere imagined as both separate and in harmony. This book investigates the tragic failure of that mediation, along with the echoes of that failure elsewhere.

---

35 For an in-depth account of infant exposure, see Cynthia Patterson, "'Not Worth the Rearing': The Causes of Infant Exposure in Ancient Greece," *Transactions of the American Philological Association* 115 (1985): 103–23.

Three   Oedipus Patêr

The first two chapters were devoted to oedipalization as the erasure of fatherhood. The most stunning effect of that process was the erasure of Oedipus *as* father. But Oedipus's paternity may well be the central theme of Sophocles's play, hidden in plain sight.

More than a century after Freud's first commentary on *Oedipus the King*, reading the play as a comment on the structure of the family is habitual, almost automatic, at least for most nonclassicists.[1] And yet, within the very long history of its reception, this is a fairly recent association. Neither Aristotle, whose *Poetics* first identified it as the best of tragedies, nor any of the play's famous pre-Freudian German readers—such as Schiller, Schelling, Hölderlin, Hegel, or Nietzsche—used *Oedipus the King* to reflect on the family. This silence is especially striking in light of Hegel's influential comments on *Antigone*, which explore the conflict of family and state at great length. It is equally striking in an aesthetic context where the domestic tragic drama (*bürgerliches Trauerspiel*) had long reigned as the most successful modern model of tragedy, so that the family and its conflicts were very much dramatically present. *Oedipus the King*, however, continued to be understood in the light of human identity, of the conflict between divine and human, fate and will, or necessity and freedom. And when Freud finally discovered the family in the play, he reinvented Oedipus as the universal son.

In contrast to both traditions, the idealist and the psychoanalytic one, I want to show that not only Laius, but Sophocles's Oedipus is a paradigmatic father, and that his fatherhood pervades the play. It is important to note that the twentieth-century focus on his filiality cannot be laid at Freud's feet alone, even though Freud is certainly responsible for much of the silence that has swallowed the father's voice, and not just in *Oedipus the King*. Oedipus-the-son, however, also owes much to both explicit and implicit conflations with two other famous sons, Hamlet and Jesus, neither of whom are fathers,

---

1   As Jean-Pierre Vernant argues, with only a little exaggeration: "Freud's interpretation of tragedy in general and *Oedipus Rex* in particular has had no influence on the work of Greek scholars. They have continued their research just as if Freud had not spoken." Jean-Pierre Vernant and Pierre Vidal-Nacquet, "Oedipus without the Complex," in *Tragedy and Myth in Ancient Greece*, trans. Janet Lloyd (Sussex: Harvester Press, 1981), 70.

and both of whom are childless not by accident, but in accordance with the logic of their respective figures. But before and beyond any specific omissions and contaminations, Oedipus's fatherhood fell prey to the very hermeneutic passion the play engenders. The vast majority of the seminal readings are driven by various modes and gestures of identification, from Aristotle to Freud and beyond. A superb modern translation, by the poet Stephen Berg in collaboration with the classicist Diskin Clay, cuts to the chase in this regard when it renders a line in the fourth stasimon that speaks of Oedipus's decline as an example, a pattern (*paradeigma*), thus:

we are you
we are you, Oedipus[2]

It is, I suspect, the pervasive self-reflexivity Sophocles imposes on Oedipus that has in turn generated such a wealth of self-reflexive readings. In consequence, Oedipus is who we are or who we fear to be, he belongs to the gods who abuse us as well, to the shape of time we inhabit along with him, the desires we, too, suppress, or the fullness of meaning that eludes us like him. Whether he is the victim of fate, irony, desire, or politics, the champion of human freedom or the exemplary figure of its inexorable loss, his obsessive use of the word "I" always appears to echo in his readers' collusive "we, too"—an identification that is no less striking for being concealed behind the vocabulary of the general or the universal,[3] and an effect that has often prevented the exploration of Oedipus's very specific position within a very specific historical and mythological constellation.

No other tragic hero, with the possible exception of Hamlet, has engendered such empathy, and it is, indeed, very difficult to avoid the vocabulary of universalism, or at least the sense that *Oedipus the King* marks structures or logics that must be negotiated again and again, even if their content may significantly differ from era to era. In the twentieth

---

2 Sophocles, *Oedipus the King*, trans. Stephen Berg and Diskin Clay (New York: Oxford University Press, 1978), 78.
3 Cf. Bernard Knox's preface to his study of *Oedipus the King*: "This book is essentially a study of the Sophoclean play, *Oedipus Tyrannus*, in terms of the age which produced it, an attempt to answer the question, 'What did it mean to them, there, then?' But it suggests also an answer to the question, 'What does it mean to us, here now?' And the answer suggested is: the same thing it meant to them, there, then. For in this case, the attempt to understand the play as a particular phenomenon reveals its universal nature; the rigidly historical method finds itself uncovering the timeless. . . . The play needs only to be seen clearly as what it was, to be understood as what it is." Bernard M. W. Knox, *Oedipus at Thebes* (New York: W. W. Norton, 1957), 1–2.

century, the oedipal logic became the logic of the family as the site of desire's socialization. Freud radically secularized the play's central conflict, which until then had largely been perceived as decidedly metaphysical, in order to effect this tremendous reversal. To do this, however, he had to perceive it as a collective dream, the documentation of a fantasy as opposed to an extreme representation of what is. Oedipus, figure of the collective I, now became the exception, the man who does what is by necessity denied to all of us, the one who actively transgresses against a collective and universal rule (i.e., the prohibition against incest and patricide) rather than the one who suffers the concrete and extreme manifestation of a collective fate (e.g., the time-bound impermanence of human fortune). To be sure, identification is still the key here, and the old distinction between will and necessity continues to be at work in the disguise of the pleasure and reality principles, but it is a retrospective identification, in Freud's prose almost a wistful one. Oedipus (at least the Oedipus of the transgressions) is the "I" we left behind in order to become who we are: in the context of Freudian masculinity, you must have overcome Oedipus in order to become a father, and the Freudian father, as I will show in Chapter 6, keeps himself covered. Thus, redefining Oedipus as the universal (male) child effectively blocks not only reflection on the Sophoclean text itself; it also removes from sight two figures intimately related to Oedipus-the-king: Oedipus's own father, Laius, always already offstage, and Oedipus at Colonus—the other Oedipus, the one who lives on and returns to the very metaphysical realm that Freud so successfully erased from the story.[4] Last, and not the least importantly, Freud's universalist gesture blends out the play's complex relationship to what precedes it, that is, the way in which it must have functioned as a political commentary at a certain moment in Greek, or rather Athenian, history.

Hegel was one of the play's first readers to insist on its historicity. In one of his early lectures on the *Philosophy of World History*, Hegel conceptualizes the moment of Oedipus as a moment that reveals what is at stake in the transition from Egyptian to Greek culture:

> A sphinx, the Egyptian image of riddle itself, appeared in Thebes, it is said, and posed a riddle with the words: "What is that which

---

4   Cf. a recent study by the German classicist Wolfgang Bernhard, *Das Ende des Ödipus bei Sophokles: Untersuchung zur Interpretation des "Ödipus auf Kolonos"* (Munich: Beck, 2001). Bernhard, working against the weight of a long tradition that idealizes Oedipus's death, portrays Oedipus in a far harsher light, focusing on his evasions, his hatred, his filicidal curse, and the abject terror of the final death scene. In correcting several centuries of obfuscating glorification, however, he may end up understating the ambivalence of his death, in which the sacred and the abject intertwine.

walks on four legs in the morning, on two at noon, and on three in the evening?" The Greek Oedipus, it is said, solved the riddle and cast the Sphinx off the cliff by saying that this was the human. This is true; the riddle of the Egyptian is the mind (*der Geist*), the human, the consciousness of his own proper nature. But this old solution by Oedipus, who thus showed himself as one who knows, is in him coupled with the most monstrous ignorance about himself and what he does. The dawn of spiritual clarity in the old regal house is still linked to horrors committed out of ignorance. It is the old patriarchal rule, to which knowledge is heterogeneous and which is thereby dissolved.[5]

The notion that tragedy stages moments of world-historical change is crucial to the idealist theory of tragedy, displacing the aesthetics of pity that had characterized Enlightenment reflections concerned primarily with the emotional effects of tragedy. It is only fitting in this context that *Oedipus the King*, the perfect tragedy, is associated with the dawn of *Geist* itself, with self-knowledge in its general form: "it is not the particular human who should recognize his specificity, but the human *in general* should recognize himself."[6]

Hegel's assertion that the Oedipus myth concerns "the human in general" (*der Mensch überhaupt*) is immediately plausible as long as

---

5 "Eine Sphinx, das ägyptische Gebilde des Rätsels selbst, sei in Theben erschienen und habe ein Rätsel aufgegeben mit den Worten: 'Was ist das, was morgens auf vier Beinen geht, mittags auf zweien und abends auf dreien?' Der Grieche Ödipus habe das Rätsel gelöst und die Sphinx vom Felsen gestürzt, indem er aussprach, dies sei der Mensch. Dies ist richtig; das Rätsel der Ägypter ist der Geist, der Mensch, das Bewußtsein seines eigentümlichen Wesens. Aber mit dieser alten Lösung durch Ödipus, der sich so als Wissender zeigt, ist bei ihm die ungeheuerste Unwissenheit gepaart über sich selbst und über das, was er tut. Der Aufgang geistiger Klarheit in dem alten Königshause ist noch mit Greueln aus Unwissenheit verbunden. Es ist die alte patriarchalische Herrschaft, der das Wissen ein Heterogenes ist und die dadurch aufgelöst wird." G. W. F. *Hegel, Vorlesungen über die Philosophie der Weltgeschichte*, auf Grund der Handschriften, ed. Georg Lasson, vol. 3, bk. 2 (Hamburg: Felix Meiner, 1976), 510. My translation.

6 "Es ist nicht der partikuläre Mensch, der seine Besonderheit erkennen soll, sondern der Mensch überhaupt soll sich selbst erkennen." G. W. F. Hegel, *Vorlesungen über die Philosophie der Geschichte*, Werke, vol. 12 (Frankfurt am Main: Suhrkamp, 1970), 272. While Hegel explicitly only refers to the story (*Erzählung*) of Oedipus, it is obvious that he is thinking of Sophocles's tragedy, the first extant articulation of the myth that centers on the process of self-knowledge. It should also be noted here that Hegel, in the *Aesthetics*, suggests a more nuanced view of the particularity of Greek tragic heroes, placing them exactly between modern "characters" and "abstractions." G. W. F. Hegel, *Aesthetics: Lectures on Fine Art*, 2 vols., trans. T. M. Knox (Oxford: Clarendon Press, 1975), 1209.

we keep in mind (as Hegel certainly did) that any articulation of this universal human is historically, culturally, and politically bound, not just in its specific contents but in its relations to other universals and specifics. Oedipus's encounter with the Sphinx, to which Sophocles's text refers mostly implicitly, does indeed bring to the fore an aspect of human existence that could not be more universal or more fundamental—its self-conscious subjection to time.

Hegel's more specific suggestion that the new form of general knowledge fails only because it is still contaminated by a previous form of equally general ignorance is all the more intriguing in this context because Hegel links this contamination explicitly to *patriarchal* rule, that is, to the blindness of fatherhood that thinks of itself as the model of political rule. At the same time, the conflict in *Oedipus the King* arises out of the discrepancy between general knowledge and *particular* ignorance; more pointedly, it is precisely the divergence of general and particular self-knowledge that is at stake. Oedipus does not stand under the imperative to recognize "the human in general"—*that* he did before he even enters the stage. He is called upon to experience his particularity. But it is precisely the tension between the particular and the general that constantly threatens and undermines the construction of both social and symbolic fatherhood.

Stressing Oedipus's particularity is not to suggest that he is an individual in the modern sense, defined by his idiosyncrasies; he is rather, as Hegel said about Antigone, a figure of particularity itself. Oedipus, who recognizes the human in the sequence of infancy, adulthood, and old age has yet to learn how very specific indeed *his* infancy, manhood, and age will be shown to be,[7] and when recognition sets in, the chorus will say that he has been discovered by "time which sees all" (*ho panth' horôn chronos,* 1213)—for while life may progress toward the future, knowledge, proceeding in retrospect, loops back toward what was. In *anagnorisis*, the past is no longer past (Hölderlin, to my knowledge, was the first to reflect on the strangeness of tragic time, the way in which it refuses "to rhyme," as he put it[8]).

---

7   It is striking, for instance, that Oedipus has been three-legged at all stages: they pierced his feet and tied his two legs together when he was an infant, and he is already walking with a stick, presumably because of this old injury, when he encounters Laius at the crossroads. His name, it is true, contains the *-dipous* (two-footedness), but language has never been as treacherous as in *Oedipus the King*.'

8   "die Zeit, weil sie in solchem Momente sich kategorisch wendet und Anfang und Ende sich in ihr schlechterdings nicht reimen läßt." Friedrich Hölderlin, "Anmerkungen zum Oedipus," *Werke, Briefe, Dokumente,* nach der kleinen Stuttgarter Hölderlin-Ausgabe, ed. Friedrich Beißner, selected and with an afterword by Pierre Bertaux (Munich: Winkler, 1963), 624.

This chapter, too, is concerned with speculations about historical transitions, the tension between the general and the particular, the subsistence of the old within the new, with general structures that manifest themselves in a specific failure, and, above all, with the dissolution of "the old patriarchal rule." Oedipus's downfall has nearly always been linked to transgression, but this transgression, I will argue, is not (as has been suggested variously) that he killed his father, nor that he committed incest with his mother, nor that he killed the Sphinx and all she may stand for, nor that he challenged the gods, nor that he knew both too much and too little, even though he was, of course, guilty of all these things, and they all matter. As I will argue, his central flaw, to mimic the traditional language of literary history, is the flaw of fatherhood, both specific to him or his story and universal, that is, doubly unavoidable, or, in the Aristotelian terminology, necessary.

Oedipus, then, to repeat, will here appear neither as the universal subject of idealism and the many readings directly or indirectly indebted to it, nor as the quintessential son of psychoanalysis, but as the tragic figure of fatherhood, a position that has been thoroughly and conspicuously obscured in the reception of the play. This reception does not merely illustrate the construction of the invisibility of the father; to a significant extent, reading Oedipus *has been* that construction—the status of *Oedipus the King* in intellectual history is unparalleled by any literary work. Jean-Joseph Goux, for instance, writes:

> Implicitly for Sophocles and explicitly for Hegel, Oedipus is the prototypical figure of the philosopher, the one who challenges sacred enigmas in order to establish the perspective of man and self. This Oedipean configuration impresses upon all of philosophy, from its origins to the various overturnings of idealism, the filiarchal demand that has continuously been carving out a place for itself in that philosophy.[9]

Goux, who despite his critical reading of Freud is deeply influenced by and rather faithful to psychoanalytic figures of thought, accepts that Sophocles's Oedipus is a filial figure. For him, as for so many others who take their cues from the alleged monomyth of the hero, the story of male identity exhausts itself in initiation and conquest, be it the conquest of the monster or the princess. Goux forcefully insists on the singular nature of Oedipus's story, on the many ways in which Oedipus is not the hero who kills, marries, and disappears (either into death or the happily-ever-after). However, Oedipus is also a special

---

9   Jean-Joseph Goux, *Oedipus, Philosopher*, trans. Catherine Porter (Stanford, CA: Stanford University Press, 1993), 3.

case because his relationship to his children is as important as, perhaps even more important than, his relationship to his father, his adversaries, or his heroic deeds. The exclusive focus on Oedipus's sonhood does not merely bespeak a certain critical neglect; in some cases, most noticeably in Freud, it has been actively construed *against* the Sophoclean text. This is not to suggest that Oedipus is not a son or even "the" son in some regards, but rather to insist that Sophocles stages him as both father *and* son, that it is precisely this doubleness that matters—to the play and to everything that follows in its wake.

"Children!" he says when he first appears on stage, "youngest brood of old Cadmus." Or at least something like that: *ô tekna, Kadmou tou palai nea trophê* (line 1). The line is full of ambiguities, and perhaps it is a mistake to try and resolve them as translators have done by necessity and commentators by inclination. There is *nea*, for instance—*neos*, young, youthful, recent. Sir Richard Jebb, in 1887, translates it as "latest born," and adds in his commentary: "not 'young,' for *tekna* includes the old men."[10] Siegfried Melchinger, by contrast, suggests that Oedipus is not even addressing the adult men, but "only the 'tekna,' the 'nea trophe'. . . ; it is the sight of the children by which the priests try to affect the confounded king."[11] But to Oedipus, they are all his children. His stance implies that he sees himself as their collective father, a father even to the oldest of them. His rhetorical gesture is purely paternal, both thoroughly benign and dangerously inappropriate. To put it more generally, Oedipus does not understand time very well, at least not yet. Soon, he himself will be addressed as *teknon*, which demonstrates clearly enough that *teknon* determines an intersubjective position here, not age.

Nea follows in hard junction on *tou palai* (of old), announcing on the stylistic level the catastrophic encounter of youth and age, past and present that is to follow. And then there is *trophê*, a strange word here—it usually means "food, nourishment." Jebb translates, "My children, latest-born wards of old Cadmus," and, perhaps too eager to tame the text, comments, "trophê = *thremmata* (abstract for concrete). . . . . Cadmus, as guardian genius of Thebes, is still *tropheus* of all who are reared in the *dôma Kadmeion*."[12] But what if they are, indeed, old Cadmus's newest nourishment rather than his *thremmata*, his nurslings—or rather both? After all, fatherhood has always embodied the tension between and the interdependence of "abstract" and "concrete." What if the *tropheus* (one who rears or brings up, a foster-father) is also the one who, like Cronus (and *chronos*, time—even though the two are not etymologically

---

10 Jebb quoted in Sophocles, *OT*, 5 n1.
11 Siegfried Melchinger, *Das Theater der Tragödie: Aischylos, Sophokles, Euripides auf der Bühne ihrer Zeit* (Munich: C. H. Beck, 1974), 174.
12 Jebb quoted in Sophocles, *OT*, 5 n258.

related, their near-homophony is surely at work here), devours his offspring? To be sure, filicide is written all over the myth, in Laius's two failed attempts to kill his son (once knowingly, once unknowingly) as well as in Oedipus's deadly curse of his own Eteocles and Polyneices. Cadmus may be the guardian genius of Thebes, but he is other things as well: a Phoenician, the mythical inventor or quasi-historical messenger of the alphabet, another figure of world-historical change through knowledge, and the one who sowed the dragon's teeth from which countless warriors sprang only to kill each other. These tales would be well known to an audience as steeped in myth as the Athenians whom Sophocles is addressing (just as the Athenians would remember that Thebes, in submitting to the Persians, had betrayed the Greek city-states' devotion to political autonomy that defined itself in no small part through its opposition to the barbarian model of absolute kingship).

The name of Cadmus, standing simultaneously for a ferocious and mindless civil war, the founding of a powerful, imperial polis, and the introduction of the alphabet, foreshadows the multiple identity of Oedipus, solver of the human riddle who will become Athens's guardian corpse, but only after he curses his sons to die by each other's hand—in a repetition of the massacre that preceded the founding of Thebes, itself the result of a highly irregular birth. It is Euripides who, in the *Phoenician Women*, insists on the Cadmeian origin of the double fratricide between Polyneices and Eteocles. There, Euripides mentions the "sown men" numerous times, and the name of Cadmus appears no fewer than 15 times. Sophocles, by contrast, keeps Cadmus in the background (there are only three more occurrences of the name after the first line), as a faint rumbling of the past, present but hard to hear.

When he speaks his opening line, Oedipus does not know that he, too, is a descendant of both Cadmus and the sown men: offspring, perpetuator, and prey of that history that inextricably intertwines knowledge, politics, and fratricidal bloodshed.[13] Since he assumes himself to be both a foreigner and the legitimate king, he can represent himself as nothing but the father, the one-who-knows. In Thebes, he is nobody's son, it seems, belonging by origin neither to the city nor to any family within it, and it is this status as an outsider that allows him to assume a stance of pure paternity, that is, a paternity unfettered by a simultaneous filiality. For a while (a short while on stage, but for quite some time by historical implication), Oedipus inhabits a subject position to which everybody else is *teknon*, child. The term, appearing 16 times throughout the play, not counting related verbs and

---

13 Oedipus is the son of Laius, son of Labdacus. Labdacus is the son of Polydorus, born of the marriage between Cadmus and the goddess Harmonia, and Nicteis, daughter of the sown man Chtonius.

participles, will be repeated almost obsessively around the anagnorisis. Before knowledge becomes explicit, first the old shepherd (1030) and then the chorus (1098) address Oedipus as their *teknon*. In the fourth stasimon, directly following the revelation, Oedipus becomes the begotten begetter (*teknounta kai teknoumenon*) and *Laeion teknon* (child of Laius). The messenger who brings the news of Jocasta's suicide shortly thereafter speaks of her as one who had "borne a husband of her husband, children of her child" (*ex andros andra kai tekn' ek teknôn tekoi*, 1250). Oedipus's peripeteia, then, can be seen as the violent reversal from father to child, a movement heavily emphasized in the last scene when Creon orders him to "now let go of the children" (1801).

Toward the end, his fatherhood comes into view once more at the very moment where its loss is completed. The dialogue closes with Creon's harsh and apparently unmotivated admonition to "not wish to be powerful (*kratein*) in everything," and the chorus, in its final words, addresses its famous "count no man happy" speech to a polis now no longer comprised of *tekna*, but, in a slight shift, "inhabitants of the fatherland (*patra*) of Thebes" (1522–4).

Creon's use of *kratein*, intimately linked in political discourse to *kurios* (power or authority), is a crucial detail here. The term (root of the English -cracy suffixes) is at the center of Greek debates concerning political power,[14] and it would appear to come at a fairly incongruous moment only as long as we fail to see that the play explores, negotiates, and undermines the ancient association of power and paternity. Creon does not allow Oedipus to lay claim to his daughters because it is not just Oedipus-the-king whose destruction needs to be staged here, it is Oedipus-the-father—that is to say, the king *as* the father.

Seth Benardete argues that Oedipus's first words "suggest that he understands himself as father only in a metaphorical sense and is blind to the literal meaning of generation,"[15] but that formulation clouds the issue more than it illuminates it. Oedipus clearly understands himself to be the literal father of Eteocles, Polyneices, Antigone, and Ismene as well—Creon mentions how much joy (*terpsis*) Oedipus has always taken in his children (1477). It is certainly true, and has been widely acknowledged, that the plague points to a disturbance in generation and procreation: the buds won't open, the breeding of cattle has stopped, and the women give birth to dead children. It is also true that, again Benardete, the "play moves from the question of who killed Laius to that of who generated Oedipus" (72). But what follows is not that

---

14 The term appears 19 times in the *Politics*, 23 times in the *Laws*, and 21 times in the *Republic*.
15 Seth Benardete, *The Argument of the Action: Essays on Greek Poetry and Philosophy*, (Chicago: University of Chicago Press, 2000), 72.

Oedipus is blind to sexual generation, or blind to literal fatherhood. It means, first of all, that he is unaware of the particular circumstances of his fathering (in the double sense), and, second, that he does not understand himself *as son*. The crisis of generation is a crisis of begetting; the question as of yet unanswered is not simply, what does it mean to be Oedipus?, or what does it mean to be a man?, but what does it mean to be or become a father, literally and metaphorically?

The answer—that paternity implies filiality, that there is no such thing as a father who is not also a son—appears obvious, perhaps even banal, but it is of tremendous importance, both to the tragedy and to the political structure of fatherhood itself. This becomes clear when Oedipus, briefly before the revelation, at the climax of both his power and his delusion, proclaims his conviction that he is, in all important regards, self-generated:

> But I, who hold myself son of Fortune that gives good, will not be dishonored. She is the mother from whom I spring, and the months, my kinsmen, have marked me sometimes lowly, sometimes great. Such being my heritage, never more can I prove false to it, or keep from searching out the secret of my birth. (1080ff.)

Insisting that what defines him are his intelligence, his knowledge, and his victory over the Sphinx, he attempts to render the circumstances of his biological birth irrelevant, something about which only a woman would care. At this point, Merope and Polybus, his social parents whom he believes to be his biological ancestors, are dead. Hence, Oedipus's self-image—"I, of myself" (*egô d' emauton*)—is now that of a fully self-created man who owes his existence to the good fortune that enabled his heroic acts. If there is a mother (*tuchê* can but need not be deified), she is a goddess who does not procreate sexually.

Ironically, the fantasy of being self-begotten, without a father, has its truth in the much-noted fact that Oedipus is both Jocasta's son and husband, hence, in the structure of nuclear kinship, indeed in the position of his own begetter. In the Freudian paradigm, this simultaneity bespeaks a universal erotic desire for the mother, but in Sophocles's text, it emerges as something different: the desire for the self, autonomous and unbeholden to genealogy, be it matrilineal or patrilineal. Such a reading is not, needless to say, wholly incompatible with the Freudian one; for psychoanalysis, passing through the oedipal stage is the main or indeed the only route to subjectivity, and there, too, selfhood can be most severely threatened by the reemergence of the past. In this regard, it is not a question of replacing or correcting Freud's general account of what it means and what it costs to grow up, but to tease out those aspects both of the Sophoclean play and the oedipal logic that Freud either neglects or actively conceals from view. I will return to that in Chapter 6.

Fathering your children within your mother means to be in two places at once; it means to defy the logic of succession that governs father-son relationships and the transfer of power along those lines. To be your children's oldest brother is to be your own heir, your own successor. It is, in other words, a strategy of defeating time (as is the attempt to thwart an oracle that predicts the future—after all, if it could be thwarted, it would cease to be the future). Hölderlin, one of the relatively few commentators who have dwelled on this passage, suggests in his *Annotations to the Oedipus* that "towards the end the speeches are dominated by the insane (*geisteskrank*) questioning for a consciousness."[16] But why is *Geist* ill here? What exactly ails it? The main terms that structure the dilemma are knowledge/ignorance, past/present, power/powerlessness, procreation/self-determination, ego/polis, and human/divine,[17] but these pairs do not map onto each other in any optimistic fashion. The movement, at first glance, appears contradictory: from self-ignorance to self-knowledge, but thereby also from power to powerlessness, from autonomy to heteronomy, from foreigner to native and from native to outcast, from wise man to blind man, from kingship to abjection, from everybody's father to a man violently separated even from his biological children. His trajectory, the chorus says, is not contingent, but paradigmatic—and we need to assume, I think, that it is paradigmatic not merely according to the all-too-general injunction to count no man happy before his death. Neither, however, does it appear fair to conclude that knowledge itself is to blame, even though Oedipus's self-knowledge does well enough, and indeed overperforms, as an insight into the fundamental heteronomy of both desire and power. In this sense, the height and depth of Oedipus's misfortune, the grandeur as well as the illness of his spirit, consist in the fantasy of an absolute autonomy that would render null and void the circumstances of birth and all it stands for.

Of all the play's modern readers, Jean-Pierre Vernant has insisted most eloquently on the nature of Attic tragedy as the antecedent of political philosophy, as the "passage between mythic thought and

---

16 "Zuletzt herrscht in den Reden vorzüglich das geisteskranke Fragen nach einem Bewußtsein." Hölderlin, "Anmerkungen," 622.
17 The reader may miss male/female in this list, but the male-female distinction is far less important here than the distinction between several modes of masculinity.

philosophic thought, between Hesiod and Aristotle."[18] Christian Meier, with a focus on Aeschylus, has analyzed important aspects of that relationship in detail,[19] and Hellmuth Flashar, in a recent monograph on Sophocles, takes Sophocles's political impact for granted.[20] In an echo of Hegel, Vernant suggests that "this whole form of tragedy was invented, so to speak, both to call the City into question within a well-defined context, and also . . . to call into question a certain image of man, and I would even say to indicate a change in man."[21] He clarifies, further on, that there

> is tragic man because human action has become properly human. . . . But, on the other hand, human action has not attained so much autonomy that man can feel himself to be the unique, exclusive source of his action. There is the fundamental fact that the act takes on its meaning only when it has been detached from man and inserted in a religious, cosmic order which transcends man. (286)

I agree that it is human autonomy that is at stake in *Oedipus the King*, but I am less sure that this play conceives of its limitations as predominantly imposed by a religious or cosmic order. Sophocles's enduring reputation as "pious" may rest mainly on *Oedipus at Colonus*, a play overtly concerned with metaphysical events (and strikingly "untragic" according to most criteria of the tragic in play). Meier notes with a puzzlement I share that the "political references" that are conceded to Aeschylus and Euripides are "mostly denied" to Sophocles,[22] but

---

18 Jean-Pierre Vernant, "Greek Tragedy: Problems of Interpretation," in *The Structuralist Controversy*, ed. Richard Macksey and Eugenio Donato (Baltimore: Johns Hopkins University Press, 1970), 289.
19 Christian Meier, *Die politische Kunst der griechischen Tragödie* (Munich: Beck, 1988).
20 "Tragedy is 'political' in the broadest sense. It is civic theater on the soil of Attic democracy; it is bound to acts of political self-representation; in the tragic plot's recourse to mythos, it challenges the citizens to reflect on political thinking, acting, and deciding. Its poets, especially Sophocles, were 'politically' active as citizens of this polis." Hellmuth Flashar, *Sophokles: Dichter im demokratischen Athen* (Munich: Beck, 2000), 8. My translation. Goux writes: "The autonomy of the son gives birth to philosophy. If this new mode of thought is one of the major factors in the Greeks' break with the past, it is because it corresponds to an antipatriarchal agitation that can be detected in other characteristic features of Greek civilization, including the establishment of democracy." *Oedipus, Philosopher*, 141. I agree that Sophocles's play is antipatriarchal, but Oedipus is anything but the figure of the autonomous son.
21 Vernant, "Greek Tragedy," 284.
22 Meier, *Die politische Kunst*, 186.

he himself considers only *Ajax* and *Antigone*. As in *Antigone*, the gods are hardly present in *Oedipus the King*. True, they are evoked by the chorus and the characters several times, but in a rather perfunctory way. Creon asserts that Oedipus's exile is the will of the gods, but it is Oedipus himself who had asked for it first and Oedipus who, in his role as the sovereign who can spontaneously lay down the law, had earlier proclaimed exile as the punishment for Laius's murderers. The last lines, possibly a later emendation but surely the appropriate place for a religiously inflected final message, do not mention the gods at all:[23]

> Dwellers in our native land of Thebes, see to what a storm of cruel disaster has come Oedipus here, who knew the answer to the famous riddle and was a mighty man, on whose fortune every one among the citizens used to look with envy! So that one should wait to see the final day and should count none among mortals fortunate, till he has crossed the bourne of life without suffering grief.[24]

The closing stresses once again the way in which human fortune is dynamic, subject to time; more specifically and more importantly in this context, it emphasizes the instability of political might and, in its address, contrasts the powerful individual to the polis as collective. *Oedipus the King* appears far more concerned with social order than with religious order. It is a critique not so much of tyranny (in the Aristotelian sense that is all too often projected onto the play), but of a model of individual sovereignty, be it grounded in merit *or* in blood. It is precisely the best of kings who needs to be destroyed here, the superior individual who, in the terms of Aristotle's *Politics*, must either be declared *pambasileus* (absolute sovereign of the city)— or ostracized. The tragedy's political purpose, then, is to privilege *patria* over paternity, the fatherland over the father, in a radical yet metonymic slide that once again both invokes and destabilizes the father's power—thus opening a political space in the modern but also in the Aristotelian sense, as I will argue in the sixth chapter.

---

23 By contrast, the last lines of Sophocles's *Women of Trachis* read: "Do not be left behind in the house, maiden; you have lately seen terrible deaths, and many sufferings unprecedented, and none of these things is not Zeus" (1275ff.); Heracles's last words in *Philoctetes* invoke "mighty Fate (*Moira*)" and "the all subduing god who has decreed this" (1466ff.); in the last lines of *Antigone*, the chorus exhorts the audience to "not be impious towards the gods" (1350ff.). All references are to *Sophocles: Works*, ed. and trans. Hugh Lloyd-Jones, Loeb Classical Library 20–1, vol. 2 (Cambridge, MA: Harvard University Press, 1994).
24 Sophocles, *OT*, in *Sophocles: Works*, 1524–30.

Four "I Must Do What I've Been Told": Abraham and the Conditions of Unconditional Paternity

If Athenian tragedy of the fifth century ritually performed the sacrifice of the father to the polis, its great counterpart, the Bible, sacrifices the son to the nation. And genre matters here. Tragedy: a multitude of embodied voices, individual and collective, conflicting, converging, conflicting. The Bible: one disembodied voice, narrating continuity—at least, that is the text's gestus, though certainly not its history.

The previous chapters were dedicated to making visible two tragic fathers of whom we lost sight: Laius, because he is always already dead, and Oedipus, because he is always the son. But there is another reason why in modernity, neither of them have appeared as paternal subjects: the position of the universal father had long been taken by Abraham, the most famous and the most revered filicide of all time, father of faith, father of monotheism, father of fathers, mythical ancestor of Jews, Christians, and Muslims alike. Abraham, it appears, is the paradigmatic figure of fatherhood coalesced into a position of unassailable power, the one where metaphysics, politics, and the family mesh, the standard bearer, as it were, of the paternal triad.[1] This is how Leon R. Kass, who reads his story as a narrative about "educating father Abraham," sees it:

> Abraham, the new man, is to be the founder of a new nation steeped in God's new way, which this nation is to carry as a light unto all the nations of the world. The new way entails rightful conduct toward and rightful relations with members of one's household, members of the tribe, strangers and members of other nations, and the divine.[2]

---

1   This is not to suggest that the differences between the reception of the Abraham narrative do not differ significantly between the various traditions. See Jon D. Levenson's *Inheriting Abraham: The Legacy of the Patriarch in Judaism, Christianity, and Islam* (Princeton, NJ: Princeton University Press, 2012), which argues on behalf of strong distinctions between the respective figurations.
2   Leon R. Kass, "Educating Father Abraham: The Meaning of Fatherhood," *First Things* 48 (December 1994): 32.

Whether we share Kass's affirmative reading or not, it is safe to say that there is no equivalent of such fatherhood in Athenian culture. Robert Paul reminds us that, conversely, "scholars have frequently noted that while Oedipus provides a paradigm for the Hellenic strain of Western culture, he has no counterpart in the Hebraic strain."[3] While the stories may be incompatible, they are not, however, incomparable: "Instead, in the Judeo-Christian tradition, of comparable but different significance is the incident known as the *Akedah*, the 'binding' of Isaac by his father, Abraham, who has been ordered by God to offer Isaac as a sacrifice, as described in Genesis 22" (ibid.). As we have seen, shifting the focus from Oedipus to Laius may well move them a bit closer, and Paul himself argues:

> the Hellenic and Judeo-Christian traditions are more alike than different, and . . . these two stories are no exception. In every tale concerning the succession of a junior male to senior status—a deed that inevitably implies an "oedipal" rebellion—a previous episode of the story portrays a senior male attempting (unsuccessfully, of course) to kill that junior male. The filicidal attempt represents the hostile and jealous side of the ambivalent senior male–junior male relationship, while the survival of the junior male represents the offsetting nurturant and preserving dimension. (Ibid.)

Fair enough, but neither the Oedipal myths nor the *akedah* and their respective rich cultural afterlives are adequately summed up as "senior male unsuccessfully tries to kill junior male who will displace him." We would need to forget or bracket an extraordinary amount of detail to equate these stories: Oedipus himself curses his sons to die by each other's hand, that is to say, he is as much filicidal father as patricidal son, and he, in turn, will not be replaced by *his* "junior males." More to the point, Laius and Abraham fare rather differently. It is hard to know what to make of Paul's reminder that "Oedipus is rescued by a shepherd [while] Isaac is rescued by a sheep," but it is certainly not true that "like Abraham, Laius binds Oedipus in response to a divine decree—the Delphic oracle—and prepares to hand him over to death" (54). The oracle at Delphi did not issue commands, it issued prophecies. And that difference is decisive, since it erases from Greek myth and its tragic formulations the question of obedience, which is crucial to so many readings of Genesis.

The *akedah* is generally held to be a terrible story. Kierkegaard famously feared and trembled when he imagined Abraham, but the

---

3 Robert A. Paul, *Moses and Civilization: The Meaning behind Freud's Myth* (New Haven, CT: Yale University Press, 1996), 54.

enormity of the tale is a much older topos. A fourteenth-century Jewish commentator, Bachya ben Asher, wrote that "[t]his act was not like any other, this trial was not like any other, and nature cannot bear it, nor the imagination conceive it."[4] Miller comments:

> Evidently the intolerability of the story is its point: if Abraham sacrificed himself, he would win sympathy and admiration but not horror (from the Latin *horrere*, to tremble). The thought of killing Isaac arouses more pathos. The emotion it leads to is not quite tragic—not only because the killing is averted but also because the feelings it arouses, even in prospect, are not pity and terror but pity and horror. We can be terrified by what a protagonist like Oedipus does or suffers unknowingly; we are horrified by what a protagonist like Abraham *intends to do*. "Then Abraham reached out his hand and took the knife to kill his son" (22:10). We are meant not to empathize with Abraham but to recoil from his incomprehensible will. (19)

Is it as incomprehensible as all that? As we will see, it all depends on whether you read the *akedah* as an event of extreme singularity with all the deviance characteristic of all narratives of origin, or as cultural matrix, affirming paternal power over life and death as patriarchal political power. To be sure, there is a tremendous affective gap between killing your son with a knife you hold in your own hand and sending your sons into war to be killed by the knives of others, but in either case, the father yields to the demands of what is said to be greater and more valuable than he, his son, and his love for him, or that which commands a greater love and a more complete loyalty,[5] and this demand on fatherhood is articulated over and over again, in the story of Abraham, of Laius, and of countless others after them.

Laius and Oedipus fall, while Abraham is exalted. And yet, I suggest that we are not looking at a simple inversion. Abraham's paternal power—at its extreme in filicide—is both affirmed and denied, established and overruled by the divine *Übervater* who renders Abraham's own power to second order. Abraham, like all human fathers and like Oedipus before him, is here both father and son, subject and subjected, and this specific dichotomy, one of many that constitutes and strains

---

4   Bachya ben Asher, *Commentary on the Torah*; quoted in Miller, *Burning Child*, 19.
5   The theme of the father who sacrifices his sons to the state will deeply engage early modern writers who, long before Oedipus rises to his present paradigmatic status, work through it via the figure of Brutus.

fatherhood, is related as a purely structural fact, not as an affective rift. Here is Erich Auerbach's famous commentary:

> On the third day, he lifted up his eyes and saw the place from afar. That gesture is the only gesture, is indeed the only occurrence during the whole journey, of which we are told; and though its motivation lies in the fact that the place is elevated, its uniqueness still heightens the impression that the journey took place through a vacuum; it is as if, while he traveled on, Abraham had looked neither to the right nor to the left, had suppressed any sign of life in his followers and himself save only their footfalls.[6]

This "process which has no present" (7) has no interiority, either; Abraham looks neither right nor left nor inward, "thoughts and feeling remain unexpressed, are only suggested by the silence and the fragmentary speeches" (9). Isaac is nothing but the son, and, as Auerbach points out, there is no "characterization of Isaac as a person, apart from his relation to his father and apart from the story; he may be handsome or ugly, intelligent or stupid, tall or short, pleasant or unpleasant" (10). He draws a surprising conclusion: "Only what we need to know about him as a personage in the action, here and now, is illuminated, so that it may become apparent how terrible Abraham's temptation is, and that God is fully aware of it" (8). By what logic would the loss of a generic child be worse than the loss of a particular child to which the father has a particular bond? Auerbach's commentary reveals that it is the threat to *fatherhood* that is at stake here, not the loss of a child.

If the point of the story is to "make apparent" how terrible Abraham's temptation is, why is it that there is no mention of any terror, any conflict, any fear? Where is the terror located in the text? "And they came to the place which God had told him of; and Abraham built an altar there, and laid the wood in order, and bound Isaac his son, and laid him on the altar upon the wood. And Abraham stretched forth his hand, and took the knife to slay his son" (Gen. 22:9-10 KJV).

What makes the story terrible is precisely the fact that it is told as if it were not. It is not the basic structure of the plot that prevents the story from being tragic, but its telling, its *discours*. Genesis 22 does not show us an Abraham who struggles; he does not rebel as he rebels against God's plan to incinerate Sodom and Gomorrah; he never pitches his own will against the will of God or of a powerful other. Abraham has no antagonist, and the agon is the one element tragedy cannot do without. Where it might have been, there is a gap:

---

6 Erich Auerbach, *Mimesis: The Representation of Reality in Western Literature*, trans. Willard R. Trask (New York: Doubleday/Anchor, 1957), 7.

> And He said, Take now thy son, thine only son Isaac, whom thou lovest, and get thee into the land of Moriah; and offer him there for a burnt offering upon one of the mountains which I will tell thee of. And Abraham rose up early in the morning, and saddled his ass, and took two of his young men with him, and Isaac his son, and clave the wood for the burnt offering, and rose up, and went unto the place of which God had told him. (Gen. 22:2-3 KJV)

The story does not merely take place in a vacuum, it creates one: right between the first and the second sentence cited above. Ben Asher, Kierkegaard, Auerbach, Miller and countless others all respond to the powerful appeal to fill in the terrible blank, to supplement if not a revolt, then at least evidence of a nearly unbearable inner struggle, at the very least a question. But there is none—Abraham rises, saddles his ass, collects Isaac, and sets off. It is only God's voice that speaks of Abraham's love, that articulates the sharpest dissonance: take your only son whom you love and kill him.

Auerbach contrasts the Bible in general and the *akedah* in particular with the *Iliad* and Odysseus's homecoming—but not with the myth of Laius. With a different focus and from within a very different conceptual and ideological framework, Leo Strauss, too, insists on the fundamental incompatibility between "Athens and Jerusalem," those

> two roots [of Western civilization], which are in radical disagreement with each other. . . . This radical disagreement today is frequently played down, and this playing down has a certain superficial justification, for the whole history of the West presents itself at first glance as an attempt to harmonize, or to synthesize, the Bible and Greek philosophy. . . . These attempts at harmonization were doomed to failure for the following reason: each of these two roots of the Western world sets forth one thing as the one thing needful, and the one thing needful proclaimed by the Bible is incompatible . . . with the one thing needful proclaimed by Greek philosophy . . . To put it very simply and therefore somewhat crudely, the one thing needful according to Greek philosophy is the life of autonomous understanding. The one thing needful as spoken by the Bible is the life of obedient love.[7]

To Strauss, Abraham is an emblematic figure in this regard, the one who "unhesitatingly obeys" an "unintelligible command," whereas

---

7   Leo Strauss, "Progress or Return?" in *The Rebirth of Classical Political Rationalism: An Introduction to the Thought of Leo Strauss: Essays and Lectures by Leo Strauss*, ed. Thomas L. Pangle (Chicago: University of Chicago Press, 1989), 245–6.

Socrates's response, faced with an equally unintelligible demand by Apollo, "consists not in unhesitating obedience, but in examining an unintelligible saying of Apollo" (251–2). Strauss is intent on creating a sharp distinction between the Bible and Greek *philosophy*, but Greek literature and mythology, with their many stories of revolt against paternal heroes and deities, may offer similar and indeed more compelling comparisons. Consider Oedipus, who, faced with the oracle that tells him that he will kill his father and sleep with his mother, chooses neither to believe nor not to believe (when either response would have saved him), but to challenge its force through action. A divine oracle is not the same as a divine command, but precisely for that reason it may carry an even greater and certainly a different force, rendering any rebellion a challenge not to divine will but to divine *knowledge*.

Strauss pushes the distinction further into the realm of politics and metaphysics. He first refers to Maimonides's contrast between philosophy which "teaches the eternity of the world" and the Bible which "teaches creation out of nothing," and then elaborates: "The root of the matter, however, is that only the Bible teaches divine omnipotence, and the thought of divine omnipotence is absolutely incompatible with Greek philosophy in any form" (252).

While that may be so, monotheist theology has, though not without strain, found ways to incorporate and assimilate Greek philosophy. Greek tragedy, however, may well provide the sharper contrast with and the greater challenge to biblical narratives, particularly when they appear to come very close to each other. To be sure, until the twentieth century, Laius and Abraham appeared to have little in common; in fact, I have not found any earlier text that mentions them in the same breath. In this sense, Martin Bergmann had history on his side when he claimed that the "very idea of comparing Abraham, 'the father of faith,' with Laius, the father of pederasty about whom nothing favorable can be said, is bound to evoke misgivings."[8]

Clearly, however significant classical reception and in particular the reception of Athenian tragedy has been to the cultural formation of the modern West, Greek myth has not been coded to carry the same gravity or elicit the same reverence as a foundational biblical passage. But more specifically, the *akedah* has always been read as a narrative of *sacrifice*, that is, a killing in the service of the sacred, whereas Laius has simply been "the father who on learning from an oracle that his son would kill him, sent the infant away to die from exposure."[9] As we

---

8 Bergmann, *Moloch*, 298.
9 Henry Hanoch Abramovitch, *The First Father Abraham: The Psychology and Culture of a Spiritual Revolutionary* (Lanham, MD: University Press of America, 1994), 3.

have seen, though, Oedipus is very much a sacrifice as well, and twice so—a sacrifice not to the gods or a god, but to the city. Conversely, the *akedah* hardly lacks a political dimension. While, in Bergmann's words, Abraham's "willingness to sacrifice Isaac symbolized a victory of his sonhood over his fatherhood" (199), Abraham's metaphysical sonhood also grounds his social and political fatherhood, and his submission to the command to kill his son has imbued that fatherhood with a strange moral power that long remained impervious to challenge. And yet, as many of the most reverent commentaries uneasily grant,[10] admiring Abraham entails a willingness to admire and condone blind obedience to a brutal and senseless command issued by a paternal deity that does not explain itself. By contrast, Laius's failed sacrifice of his son destabilizes him and leads to both his death and his political failure.

Among the many differences in play, the manner of the child's survival may well be crucial. In Genesis, both the command to kill and the command *not* to kill issue from the same source, the deity who can both contain and resolve the rift within fatherhood because, unlike human fathers and the gods of polytheism, he is nobody's son and he cannot be killed or disempowered in turn. In commanding both murder and mercy, he grounds the nation he had promised to Abraham, but he may also have named its price—the sacrifice of the sons which every state has reenacted in war after war ever since.[11]

While the analogy between father and king, and their potentially lethal powers, is old, the analogy between the sacrifice of Isaac and the power to send young men to war belongs to the twentieth century. Wilfred Owen's "The Parable of the Old Man and the Young," in 1918, may have been the first text that explicitly reconfigured Isaac as a representative of the political sacrifice of a generation:

> Then Abram bound ~~his son the youth~~ the youth with belts and straps
> And ~~built~~ buildèd parapets ~~of earth and wood~~ and trenches there,
> And stretchèd forth the knife to slay his son.
> When lo! an angel called him out of heaven
> Saying, Lay not thy hand upon the lad,
> Neither do anything to him. ~~thy son~~ Behold,

---

10 See Kierkegaard, Strauss, and Wellisch, to name a few.
11 In a letter to the NY times editor, an Albert S. Cain wrote, apropos Iraq and an op-ed piece that had suggested that the United States found a foreign legion: "We are a peaceful people, but not a cowardly people. We defend ourselves, when needed, with our own flesh and blood." "Who Should Fight America's Battles?" *New York Times*, February 24, 2003, Section A: Editorial Desk, 16.

> A ram, caught in a thicket by its horns;
> Offer the Ram of Pride instead of him.
> But the old man would not so, and slew his son,
> And half the seed of Europe, one by one."[12]

The manuscript shows that Owen had originally called the poem "The Parable of the Old Man and His Son," and Owen strikes out the word "son" twice more while sharpening the juxtaposition between the archaic—"built" becomes "buildèd"—and the modern—"earth and wood" become the "trenches" of World War I. Filiality is thus both generalized and becomes a feature of youth, while the story of filicide averted becomes the story of mass death—not as repetition of the *akedah*, but as the *failure* to repeat. In this regard, Owen appears to accept the widespread reading of the *akedah* as commanding the end of human sacrifice.

In 1969, Leonard Cohen releases *Songs from a Room*, including "The Story of Isaac," which takes up the theme, but Cohen, as well, insists on a distinction between the biblical Abraham, who retains his mythical gravity, and those who would kill in his name:

> You who build these altars now
> to sacrifice these children,
> you must not do it anymore.
> A scheme is not a vision
> and you never have been tempted
>
> by a demon or a god.
> You who stand above them now,
> your hatchets blunt and bloody,
> you were not there before,
> when I lay upon a mountain
> and my father's hand was trembling
> with the beauty of the word.[13]

Against the same cultural backdrop, Bob Dylan releases the laconic "Highway 61 Revisited," where Abraham, now "Abe," does not elicit

---

12 Wilfred Owen, "The Parable of the Old Man and the Young" (1918). In *Complete Poems and Fragments*, ed. Jon Stallworthy (New York: W. W. Norton, 1994). Manuscript facsimile at http://www.oucs.ox.ac.uk/ww1lit/collections/item/4542
13 Leonard Cohen, "The Story of Isaac," *The Lyrics of Leonard Cohen*. London: Omnibus Press, 2009.

even a hint of reverence. In this most radical of the three lyrical acts of reception, obedience turns from faith to craven submission:

> Oh God said to Abraham, "Kill me a son"
> Abe says, "Man, you must be puttin' me on"
> God say, "No." Abe say, "What?"
> God say, "You can do what you want Abe, but
> The next time you see me comin' you better run"
> Well Abe says, "Where do you want this killin' done?"
> God says, "Out and Highway 61"[14]

Yet more recently, Carol Delaney puts Abraham "on trial," arguing that "[although] the nation-state is a modern invention, the roots of the idea return us to religion on specifically to Abraham," who was promised "all the land that thou seest, to thee . . . and to thy seed, forever (Gen. 13:5)."[15] After arguing that the story of Abraham, in which paternal power is "symbolically allied with divine power" has grounded the "man's prerogative . . . to take life—both of animals and other humans," her *j'accuse* closes with an earnest appeal:

> I ask that people consider deeply the question that motivated this book: Why is the willingness to sacrifice the child, rather than the passionate protection of the child, at the foundation of faith? I ask that people imagine how our society would have evolved if protection of the child had been the model of faith. If I have not completely convinced you with my analysis of the Abraham story, I hope I have at least, raised a reasonable doubt. (252–3)

It seems to me that this is a rather naïve question: is is precisely *because* the child is most cherished that its killing can function as the supreme test of faith. In that sense, it is curious that all these texts imply that in some way the *akedah* legitimizes, or has been used to legitimize, filicidal violence in the broadest sense, and all of them—with widely varying degrees of nuance and sophistication—assume the oedipal position, as it were. All of them speak *to* or *about* fathers symbolic and real, in protest and revolt.

Pre-Freudian Abraham, however, while certainly *the* most prominent embodiment of an all-inclusive paternity spanning from sexual to familial to political and metaphysical, had embodied not the tension

---

14 Bob Dylan, "Highway 61 Revisited," *Bob Dylan: Lyrics, 1962–2001*. New York: Simon & Schuster, 2004.
15 Carol Lowery Delaney, *Abraham on Trial*, 249.

between old and young or father and son but between reason and revelation, selfhood and submission. Abraham could be the figure of that conflict precisely because of the pervasive horror of the impending slaughter: "nature cannot bear it, nor the imagination conceive it." The act of cutting your son's throat with a knife is so intolerable, the reception agrees, that *only* the most faithful and the most devoted man would accede to it, a man so faithful, so devoted that his inner life at that moment can be neither imagined nor represented. He is, in other words, not representative of fathers but the very opposite, representative of a faith that has overcome the "natural ways of fathers and son"[16] in sacrificing fatherhood itself—and sacrificing it twice, for he had already sent Ishmael, his firstborn, away on Sarah's insistence.

Modern thought before Freud circles around that theme. In the *Conflict of the Faculties* (1798), Kant uses the *akedah* as his prime example illustrating the problem of revelation: "If God should really speak to man, man could still never know that it was God speaking. It is quite impossible for man to apprehend the infinite by his senses, distinguish it from sensible beings, and recognize it as such. But in some cases man can be sure the voice he hears is not God's. For if the voice commands him to do something contrary to moral law, then no matter how majestic the apparition may be, and no matter how it may seem to surpass the whole of nature, he must consider it an illusion."[17] And in an acerbic footnote, he adds some helpful advice to Abraham:

> As example may serve the myth of the sacrifice which Abraham wanted to perform by slaughtering and burning his only son (the poor child, unwittingly, himself carried the wood). Abraham should have answered to this alleged divine voice: "That I ought not kill my good son is entirely certain; but that you, who appears to me, are God, of that I am not certain and cannot become certain," even if it boomed down from the (visible) sky. (Ibid.)[18]

---

16 Kass, "Educating Father Abraham," 33.
17 "Denn wenn Gott zum Menschen wirklich spräche, so kann dieser doch niemals wissen, daß es Gott sei, der zu ihm spricht. Es ist schlechterdings unmöglich, daß der Mensch durch seine Sinne den Unendlichen fassen, ihn von Sinnenwesen unterscheiden und ihn woran kennen solle.—Daß es aber nicht Gott sein könne, dessen Stimme er zu hören glaubt, davon kann er sich wohl in einigen Fällen überzeugen; denn wenn das, was ihm durch sie geboten wird, dem moralischen Gesetz zuwider ist, so mag die Erscheinung ihm noch so majestätisch und die ganze Natur überschreitend dünken: er muß sie doch für Täuschung halten." Kant: AA VII, *Der Streit der Fakultäten*, 63.
18 "Zum Beispiel kann die Mythe von dem Opfer dienen, daß Abraham auf göttlichen Befehl durch Abschlachtung und Verbrennung seines einzigen

Clearly, this is a bad faith argument (pun intended). But that aside, it is important to note that to Kant, who refuses to conceive of an irrational or suprarational God or entertain the possibility of condoning an ethical choice countermanded by reason, filicide is so clearly and unambivalently and so self-evidently wrong that no divine voice, should there be one, could command it without immediately losing its credibility in the very instance.

Hegel, a year later, offers an even more damning reading of Abraham. In the disturbingly anti-Judaic (and less disturbingly anti-Kantian) *Spirit of Christianity and Its Fate*, Abraham appears as the world-historical figure of alienation following a prehistorical state of harmony between nature and humanity. In Hegel's relentlessly secularizing reading, Abraham leaves the land of his birth in search of full independence, in the desire to become the *Oberhaupt* himself, and to leave behind all ties of love.[19] For Hegel's Abraham, the world after the flood is a fully hostile place, to be mastered and subjugated by his "Ideal"—Hegel refuses to name it "God"—, a nature without any participation in the divine. Thus protected and entirely separated from the world, Abraham

> could love nothing; even the only love he had, his love for his son, and hope of descendants, the only way to expand his being, the only form of immortality he knew and hoped for, could press upon him, could disturb his wholly detached soul and produce a disquiet which once went so far that he wanted to destroy this love as well, and he was calmed only by the certainty of the feeling that this love was only as strong as to leave him the capacity to slaughter the beloved son by his own hand.[20]

Sohnes (das arme Kind trug unwissend noch das Holz hinzu)—bringen wollte. Abraham hätte auf diese vermeinte göttliche Stimme antworten müssen: 'Daß ich meinen guten Sohn nicht töten solle, ist ganz gewiß; daß aber du, der du mir erscheinst, Gott sei, davon bin ich nicht gewiß und kann es auch nicht werden', wenn sie auch vom (sichtbaren) Himmel herabschallte." Ibid.

19 "um ein ganz selbständiger, unabhängiger Mann, selbst Oberhaupt zu sein, ohne beleidigt oder verstoßen zu sein, ohne den Schmerz, der nach einem Unrecht oder einer Grausamkeit das bleibende Bedürfnis der Liebe kundtut, die, zwar verletzt, aber nicht verloren, ein neues Vaterland aufsucht, um dort zu blühen und ihrer selbst froh zu werden." G. W. F. Hegel, *Frühe Schriften*, vol. 1 of *Werke* (Frankfurt am Main: Suhrkamp, 1986), 277.

20 "Nur lieben konnte er nichts; selbst die einzige Liebe, die er hatte, die zu seinem Sohne, und Hoffnung der Nachkommenschaft, die einzige Art, sein Sein auszudehnen, die einzige Art der Unsterblichkeit, die er kannte und hoffte, konnte ihn drücken, sein von allem sich absonderndes Gemüt stören und es in eine Unruhe versetzen, die einmal so weit ging, daß er auch diese Liebe zerstören

The unremitting bleakness of this passage is only matched by its daring. Hegel is the only one before the quasi- and pseudo-Freudians of the late twentieth century who rewrites the *akedah* as a volitional act occasioned by no command—not as an act of aggression, but as an act of liberation for a soul that does not wish to love and yet, it is implied, has been compelled to love by Isaac's very existence, the guarantee of nothing but (and nothing less than) Abraham's futurity. If for Kant, the slaughter of the son is simply in conflict with the most basic certainties of practical reason, for Hegel, it belongs to the realm of the deepest alienation both from the human sphere of relationality and from nature. Ironically, Hegel's Abraham merges with Kant when obedience to the moral law emerges as scarcely less alienated than Abraham's search for loveless autonomy.[21]

Reason fares little better in Kierkegaard's famous reading—both anti-Hegelian and deeply indebted to Hegel—where Abraham appears as the knight of faith who attains complete selfhood in an absurd act of absolute obedience. Kierkegaard's dialectic moves from the aesthetic, a stage of immediacy that is shattered by reflection and language, to the ethical, a quasi-Kantian state where decision becomes possible in relation to a universality that cannot distinguish between the ethical and the divine spheres. Authentic selfhood, however, depends on the recognition of God's otherness and the self's dependence—in an act of faith, individuality must reemerge from universality:

> Faith is precisely this paradox, that the individual as the
> individual is higher than the universal, is justified over
> against it, is not subordinate but superior-yet in such a way,
> be it observed, that it is the individual who, after he has been
> subordinated as the individual to the universal, now through
> the universal becomes the individual who as the individual is
> superior to the universal, for the fact that the individual as the
> individual stands in an absolute relation to the absolute.[22]

Since God, for Kierkegaard, is "wholly other," and since to be wholly other, the divine cannot be constrained by ethics that govern the relationship between humans, communion with the divine can only

---

wollte und nur durch die Gewißheit des Gefühls beruhigt wurde, daß diese Liebe nur so stark sei, um ihm doch die Fähigkeit zu lassen, den geliebten Sohn mit eigener Hand zu schlachten." Ibid., 279.

21 See Mark C. Taylor, "Journeys to Moriah: Hegel vs. Kierkegaard," *Harvard Theological Review* 70, nos. 3/4 (July-October 1977), 305–26.

22 Søren Kierkegaard, *Fear and Trembling*, trans. Walter Lowrie (Princeton, NJ: Princeton University Press, 1970), 66.

proceed in utter solitude: "intercourse with God is in the deepest sense and absolutely non-social."[23] In other words, Hegel's alienation becomes Kierkegaard's fulfillment—a reading made possible or bearable, one suspects, only by the fact that Abraham's hand is stayed by the same voice he absurdly obeys: "by faith he got Isaac."

It feels wrong, almost reprehensible, to rush through these rich and endlessly suggestive texts without lingering over their nuances and implications, but none of them are particularly engaged with the question of paternity—and that is fascinating in itself. Rather, paternity, for all the differences that emerge in that sequence of radical revisions, is, in all of them, that which we already know and are meant to agree upon. Kant, Hegel, and Kierkegaard do not agree on a single thing, and yet they are united in the basic assumption that the bond between father and son is self-evidently compelling, in need of being neither articulated nor analyzed. Abraham's story, however it is told, emerges as deeply significant only against that backdrop: Abraham matters not because he acts like a typical father *but because he does not*.

Before Freud, then, filicidal sacrifice is the extreme of human action, an act unimaginable, utterly alienated, absurd, or beyond reason. The impact of its threat is such that it signals, in many interpretations, the end of *all* human sacrifice.[24] After Freud, Abraham's act—and the binding *is* an act, even if the sacrifice itself is averted in the vast majority of readings[25]—appears as the blueprint for child abuse, intergenerational violence, a manual for the masters of war and exploitation. In between, there is silence: Freud had absolutely nothing to say about Abraham—which is both stunning and entirely appropriate in a theory built around the silence of the father.

Twentieth-century Abraham and twentieth-century Laius have come to resemble each other only once they have been stripped of their tragic and metaphysical dimension. They owe their late kinship to a fundamental shift in the way in which we imagine mythical narratives to do their cultural work, but in most regards, that shift is a *post*-Freudian, *not* a Freudian one. When Freud declared the oedipal transgressions that had horrified Greek and modern audiences to be representations of repressed desires, horror and desire themselves emerged as uneasily joined, and in consequence, every taboo came under suspicion of masking a wish, every

---

23 Kierkegaard, "The Lilies of the Field and the Birds of the Air," in *Christian Discourses*, trans. Walter Lowrie (New York: Oxford University Press, 1962), 334.
24 See Thomas Naumann's essay, "Die Preisgabe Isaaks: Genesis 22 im Kontext der biblischen Abraham-Sara-Erzählung," which argues forcefully against this common conception. In *Opfere Deinen Sohn: Das "Isaak-Opfer" in Judentum, Christentum und Islam* (Tübingen: Francke, 2007), 19–50.
25 For a contemporary articulation of this persistent anxiety, see the film *The Believer* (2001), written and directed by Henry Bean.

story of its breach an indication of violent impulses barely restrained. We would do well, however, to remember that Freud's story is a story of reconciliation, of patricide and incest averted—and, after that patricide that initiates the possibility of culture in *Totem and Taboo*, universally averted in the history of civilization as he writes it. In other words, it lifts the taboo only to reaffirm it. Oedipus as the figure of desire only serves as a model for societal structures *ex negativo*, even if *oedipality*—as the imperative to defer gratification in a never-ending chain of substitutes for an unobtainable original object of desire—emerges as a powerful model of both the achievements and the misery of civilization. That model's paternity is purely symbolic, incorporated—or rather, perhaps, ex-corporated—in the dead father of *Totem and Taboo*.

Critics of Laius, Abraham, and Freud are certainly correct to point out that the ferocious and abusive father is not just fiction of fantasy, that filicide is more common than patricide, and that fathers, as psychic beings, harbor their fair share of aggression toward their children,[26] be it by universal necessity, cultural norm, or idiosyncratic inclination. And yet, these revisions suffer from a fundamental misunderstanding regarding the relationship between divine, political, and familial/ spermal articulations of fatherhood. On the one hand, the paternal triad is indeed a structure of cross-legitimization, a flexible set of analogies in which the respective powers of paterfamilias, king, and monotheos repeat and amplify each other. Remarkably, Genesis makes that transition explicit, telling the story of how Abram, "high father," becomes Abraham, "father of nations," marking the difference between them with the addition of a single Hebrew letter, and exacting, as the price of political paternity, all the foreskins to come. Thus, the transition from spermal to political fatherhood is violently cut into the very organ of male reproduction, and fatherhood is expanded from those you have sired to those under your power. Note how the biblical account moves from fathering offspring, "seed," to fathering kings and conquering territory, and from fathering both children and nations to submission to the monotheos:

> Neither shall thy name any more be called Abram, but thy name shall be Abraham; *for a father of many nations have I made thee.*

---

26 Recently, Iris Levy published a brief overview of the history of that "Laius Complex," a "latter vicissitude" (Levy, 227) of the Oedipus complex. Devereux had called it "an appendix." But like the theories of Marie Balmary and Carol Delaney, who also take Freud to task for ignoring Laius's aggression, all of these revisions indeed remain deeply beholden to the Oedipal paradigm and just as deeply dependent on a demonized Laius and his "loathsome character" (Delaney, 219).

> And I will make thee exceeding fruitful, and I will make nations of thee, *and kings shall come out of thee*. . . . And I will give unto thee, and to *thy seed* after thee, *the land* wherein thou art a stranger, all the land of Canaan, for an everlasting possession; *and I will be their God*. And God said unto Abraham, Thou shalt keep my covenant therefore, thou, and thy seed after thee in their generations. This is my covenant, which ye shall keep, between me and you and thy seed after thee; Every man child among you shall be circumcised. And ye shall circumcise the flesh of your foreskin; and it shall be a token of the covenant betwixt me and you. And he that is eight days old shall be circumcised among you, every man child in your generations, *he that is born in the house, or bought with money of any stranger, which is not of thy seed*. (Gen. 17:8-13; emphases added)

To be sure, then, the story of Abraham is nothing less than the story of the construction and affirmation of the paternal triad—importantly enough, linked to the divine generative power of naming, for fatherhood has always been established by the word. At the same time, however, Genesis *also* marks the immense struggle to establish universal paternity, inscribed through multiple acts of retrospectivity, *Nachträglichkeit*, for that is the hallmark of fatherhood as well.

First, philological research has established that Abraham is the youngest of the biblical patriarchs, his story, it appears, designed to fill a gap of origin, possibly to contribute to the unification of separate tribes that eventually become personified. And stories of origin are not just stories of crisis, rupture, and exception, but they everywhere tend to be stories of deviant reproduction in particular. The God of the Bible is the one who creates a world out of nothing and man out of mud, the God of the virgin birth and the reanimation of the dead. And while the Greek gods tend to procreate sexually, Greek mythology has its number of irregular births as well: Aphrodite is born from the foam of Uranus's severed genitals; Athena springs from Zeus's head fully formed; Dionysus gestates in Zeus's thigh; Athens's mythical king Erichthonius is born from Hephaistos's sperm spilled on the soil; Poseidon's grandson Cadmus sows dragons' teeth and reaps warriors. It appears as if the capacity to procreate otherwise is the very hallmark of divinity and divine intervention, both in Jerusalem and in Athens.

The story of Abraham is no different, marked, as it is, by repeated instances of incest and transgression. Sarai is Abram's half sister, is captured for Pharaoh's harem and nearly raped a second time by Abimelek; Lot's daughters seduce their drunk father without his knowledge. The birth of Isaac is miraculous, as it is biologically impossible: "Abraham and Sarah were already very old, and Sarah was past the age of childbearing."

Second, the imagery of God as father—so crucial to the equations and associations of the twentieth-century readings I discussed—may belong to the Old Testament, but it has surprisingly little prominence in a theology that is far more invested in presenting God as unknowable. Thus, he is rarely addressed as father and frequently carries maternal attributes. The paternal God, in other words, is very much a retrospective construct as well. Consider, for example, the KJV translation of Deuteronomy 32.18: "Of the Rock that begat thee thou art unmindful, and hast forgotten the God that formed thee." The New Revised Standard Edition, by contrast, offers as the more accurate translation this: "You were unmindful of the Rock that bore you; you forgot the God who gave you birth" (literally, I have been told, "writhed in labor pains with you"). Procreating "otherwise," as I have called it, almost as a rule means erasing the maternal, and while that is true in countless narratives of foundational deviant birth, securing the paternal triad requires that mothering needs to be written out of the story in the philological register as well.

Third, the story itself sees Abraham-become-father three times (four times if we include his quasi-paternal relationship to his nephew Lot). First, when he impregnates Hagar, who bears Ishmael, who is then banned and only returns to bury Abraham. Second, when the previously "barren" Sarah finally gives birth to Isaac, miraculously. Third, when Isaac, already bound upon the altar and facing death (another motherless event), is substituted by the ram.

Abraham's fatherhood, then, is indeed anything but "natural." On the contrary, his story is a story of fatherhood's fragility, marked throughout by failure, improbability, and impending loss. The cultural labor that goes into the construction of the paternal triad is immense, and immensely visible once we start to look. Abraham's strength is, it appears, his knowledge of paternity's contingency. Leonard Cohen again:

> He said, "I've had a vision
> and you know I'm strong and holy,
> I must do what I've been told."

This father, then, the father of fathers, is the paradoxical figure of a helpless violence. His act, the act imagination cannot conceive, marks the son as the one we must not imagine killing—and yet, we have not been able to avert our eyes from this scene. Here is the irony: while our gaze is fixed on the sacrifice that does not happen, we blind ourselves to all the murders that *do* occur all around us. With Kant, we intone,

"That I ought not kill my good son is entirely certain." But we will not kill him because there is always a substitute—we can kill, or be complicit in the killing, of other people's children; if the killing of the primal father instituted the command to take only the women of others, the binding of Isaac commands us to only kill the children of others. As Derrida writes in *The Gift of Death*,

> the smooth functioning of . . . society, the monotonous complacency of its discourses on morality, politics, and the law, and the exercise of its rights, are in no way impaired by the fact that, because of the structure of the laws of the market that society has instituted and controls, because of the mechanisms of external debt and other similar inequities, that same "society" puts to death or allows to die of hunger and disease tens of millions of children without any moral or legal tribunal ever being considered competent to judge such a sacrifice, the sacrifice of others to avoid being sacrificed oneself.[27]

So, no, the *akedah* does not function as the master narrative that allows us to sacrifice our children. It is the master narrative that allows us to sacrifice, or to silently accept the sacrifice of, the children not our own.

---

27 Jacques Derrida, *The Gift of Death*, trans. David Willis (Chicago: University of Chicago Press, 1996), 86.

Section III
The Political Father

Five Aristotle and the Body of the Father

Here is another difference between the fathers of Jerusalem and the fathers of Athens: in the entire Bible, there is not a single case of paternal uncertainty. Nobody ever wonders who his father is. Nobody ever wonders whether his son is really his son. And instead of dual fathers, we actually find dual mothers: Hagar and Sarah, or the two mothers of Solomon's circle. This is all the more striking seeing the text's strong investment in paternal lineage. Or perhaps it is precisely *because* paternal lineage is so crucial to the larger narrative that even the specter of paternal uncertainty would be a threat? What is certain is that neither prudishness nor a surfeit of virtuous characters can account for the absence of the theme—sexual misbehavior, sexual crimes, and highly sexualized narratives and imagery abound. Fatherhood itself, however—and this I take to be a central message of Abraham's story—is not confirmed by the sexual relations, which serve merely as its condition, but by a spiritual event commemorated by an inscription into the male flesh. It is, more bluntly, a contract: originally a contract between God and men, afterwards, a contract between men and men, or men and boys.

Athens, by contrast, struggles with the question of sperm, and the nature of the paternal body—or more precisely the question of the somatic component of paternity—is a subject of considerable theoretical concern. We know that the concept of fathering was a contested one, even though, again, we don't know most of the texts that we know *of*. We do, however, have Aristotle's biological writings, or at least a version of them, and they make for fascinating reading—far more fascinating, in fact, than most of the brief summaries one is likely to encounter suggest.

In the introduction to *Homo Sacer*, Giorgio Agamben comments on the relationship between the Greek terms zôê and *bios* as follows:

> The Greeks had no single term to express what we mean by the word "life." They used two terms that, although traceable to a common etymological root, are semantically and morphologically distinct: *zo*, which expressed the simple fact of living common to all living beings (animals, men, or gods), and *bios*, which

indicated the form or way of living proper to an individual or a group.¹

Later on, Agamben cites Michel Foucault's assertion that for "millennia, man remained what he was for Aristotle: a living animal with the additional capacity for political existence."² Central to both thinkers' argument is a passage at the beginning of the *Politics* that expands on the distinctions between various forms of communal living:

> men also come together and maintain the political community in view of simple living, because there is probably some kind of good in the mere fact of living itself (*kata to zên auto monon*). If there is no great difficulty as to the way of life (*kata ton bion*), clearly most men will tolerate much suffering and hold on to life (*zên*) as if it were a kind of serenity (*euêmeria*, beautiful day) and a natural sweetness.³

Agamben argues that in "the classical world," despite the potential value of life as zôê, "simple natural life is excluded from the *polis* in the strict sense, and remains confined—as merely reproductive life—to the sphere of the *oikos*, 'home'" (2).

Even though the distinction between *zôê* and *bios* that Agamben develops here is not quite as consistent in Greek texts (as he himself notes), the Aristotelian passage is indeed suggestive. If political community depends on the transformation of *zôê* into *bios* or *eu zên* (the good, i.e., meaningful life as opposed to mere organic existence), then "bare life" needs to be organized through a process of progressive signification in an ascending hierarchy of communal associations. Politics, as the most meaningful organization of human *zôê*, is what most clearly distinguishes human life from the life of other animals by surpassing that which they have in common.

While there is *zôê* without *eu zên*, however, there can be no human association without either *zôê* or *bios*. And even though Agamben is correct in pointing out that Aristotle goes to some length in insisting on the difference between *oikos* and *polis* and between the modes of authority that govern either, the latter appears to be far more intimately

---

1 Giorgio Agamben, *Homo Sacer: Sovereign Power and Bare Life*, trans. Daniel Heller-Roazen (Stanford, CA: Stanford University Press, 1998), 1. In order to keep the context of Agamben's remarks intact, I am quoting the translation given there.
2 Ibid., 3. The reference is to Michel Foucault, *La volonté de savoir* (Paris: Gallimard, 1994), 188.
3 *Pol.* 1278b; quoted in Agamben, *Homo Sacer*, 2.

linked to and dependent on the former than the argument cited above suggests. More importantly, once reproduction is framed by the *oikos*, reproduction is no longer "mere" reproduction. It is not through the *polis* but through the *oikos* that zôê accrues its cultural meaning, and that transformation can no more be "excluded" from the *polis* than its individual households. When Aristotle, then, begins his enterprise in the *Politics* with a critique of those who do not see the difference between *oikia* and *polis* (more on that in the next chapter), he does not claim that these various forms of beneficial association (*koinônia*) are distinct realms in every respect. Rather, after announcing that understanding the state will mean to analyze "the elements of which it is composed," Aristotle continues:

> The first coupling together of persons then to which necessity gives rise is that between those who are unable to exist without one another: for instance the union of female and male for the continuance of the species (and this not of deliberate purpose, but with man as with the other animals and with plants there is a natural instinct to desire to leave behind one another being of the same sort as oneself). (*Pol.* 1252a)

The dynamics of reproduction condition the first constitutive union of the state, and the polis is merely the highest form of *koinônia*, a term that may have had clear sexual connotations.[4] There is, in Aristotle, then, a progression from coupling without deliberation (i.e., without *proairesis*, a term that also connotes specifically political course of action) to the political association of the state, from the urge to procreate which is shared by humans and trees to the specifically human construction of community that begins not in coitus but when male and female join in a union that exceeds sexual congress.

The passage cited above suggests that the first step in the protohistorical transformation of zôê into *bios*, of bare life into meaningful life, consists in the hierarchic organization of reproduction, an organization that depends first of all on the distinction between male and female, *thêlus* and *arsên*, terms that are generic enough to cover biological, grammatical, and metaphorical gender. This does not mean, however, that the *oikia* is not already a quasi-political space, or that, within it, reproduction could still be seen as "mere" reproduction. The household is comprised of husband, wife, children, and slaves and combines no

---

4 In Euripides's *Bacchae*, Agave is asked by Kadmos: "What son did you bear to your husband in the house?" Agave responds: "Pentheus, from my union (*koinônia*) with his father." Euripides, *The Bacchae*, in *The Tragedies of Euripides*, trans. T. A. Buckley (London: Henry G. Bohn, 1850), 1275–6.

fewer than three different forms of power relations: husband/wife, father/children, and master/slave. There is a considerable distance between traveling flower pollen and this highly complex social unit, and it is rather striking that so many of Aristotle's commentators do not see the need to focus on the conceptual leap involved here. While he does not elaborate on it, Aristotle draws attention to the tremendous difference between sexual forms of coupling that are "necessary" for most species to survive and the coupling that is not necessary in that restricted sense,[5] the one that then gives rise to the institution of the *oikia* that includes the couple, its children and its slaves, and other private property. It is here, after all, that the *zoon* becomes *politikon*, laying claim to a nature of its own.

It goes almost without saying that the gender difference grounds everything to follow. As Aristotle stresses at the very beginning of the *Politics*, it is exactly the distinction between forms of rule that is at stake in defining the *polis* against other unions, and although Aristotle condemns as barbaric those who think the male-female relation is analogous to the master-slave relation, the rule of the male is never in question—whereas slaves can in principle be set free and cease to be slaves, women cannot cease to be women. True, the husband-wife relationship is "political" (1259b) and purports to follow the aristocratic model of rule by merit, but merit accrues to the male without fail: while male rule may be either just or unjust, as the specific case may be, it is permanent, and Aristotle does not question it either in principle or practice. A woman can either have the good fortune of being ruled aristocratically or the bad fortune of being ruled oligarchically, oligarchy being to aristocracy what tyranny is to kingship.[6]

The male-female couple, while linked to reproduction, precedes the making of the child, and unlike the father-child relationship, which remains prepolitical (see Chapter 6), male-female relations are political precisely *because* of their reproductive potential. What is at stake here is the moment in or rather the process by which the nondeliberative

---

5   Cf. *Rhetoric*, 1357a: "For most of the things which we judge and examine can be other than they are, human actions, which are the subject of our deliberation and examination, being all of such a character and, generally speaking, none of them necessary." Aristotle, *Rhetoric*, in *Aristotle in 23 Volumes*, trans. J. H. Freese, vol. 22 (Cambridge, MA: Harvard University Press; London: William Heinemann Ltd., 1926).

6   The closest analogy to modern thought, presumably, is the rule of the adult over the child: even though it can be just or unjust, and even though we all know adults who are morally and intellectually inferior to the average ten-year-old, nobody—or nobody who gets taken seriously—has ever suggested that children should rule the family if their parents prove to be inferior to them in virtue or intellect.

coupling of the organic world as a whole—coitus or noncoital modes of reproduction without conscious purpose, sexuality without political meaning—acquires *proairesis*, that is, futurity, meaning, and telos. And that is nothing less than the invention of fatherhood:

> With the advent of the couple, procreation on the part of the male became as universal as it is for the female: the rule, from that point forward, is for all males to generate offspring. In this sense, the birth of human society represents a revolution in the lives and status of males: it marks the beginning of the male's achievement of a function as an individual."[7]

In this light, the family is not merely the very foundation of the *polis*, diachronically and synchronically—in producing the father, it also gives rise to the male citizen qua individual, that is, the political citizen without whom Athenian democracy is unthinkable.

The father is the only figure who simultaneously belongs to both *polis* and *oikos*, whereas the son is the only one who can diachronically cross the line dividing them. To be sure, the status of head-of-household implies more than paternity, but it's worth stressing that Aristotle here, quite casually, declares proairetic reproduction to be both the foundation and the raison d'être of the household. When Davis writes that, "while we may be drawn to the naturalness of the origin of the polis, that is, sex, we cannot help remembering that poleis do not grow like flowers. They are instituted,"[8] he falls into the old naturalization trap—before the institution of the *polis*, there is the institution of the *oikos*, and Aristotle knows it, even if Davis does not. As Peter Simpson points out, "the households enter the city and its rule through the man who is their head, and the citizen is part of the city as a man who heads a household (the man, in other words, is not a citizen as a mere individual, but as representing a household)."[9] Conversely, and more importantly, it is only the household that makes him a citizen: the institution of fatherhood, as the joint between domestic and public life, is of central importance both to the citizen and to the city. As Eva C. Keuls points out, "Thucydides makes it clear that, in the Athenian conception, citizens without legitimate sons are not full-fledged members of the

---

7 Zoja, *The Father*, 32.
8 Michael Davis, *The Politics of Philosophy: A Commentary on Aristotle's "Politics"* (Lanham, MD: Rowman & Littlefield, 1996), 2.
9 Peter Simpson, *A Philosophical Commentary on the Politics of Aristotle* (Chapel Hill: University of North Carolina Press, 1998), 133.

community . . . It is even possible that a man without male issue was denied a voice in the Senate."[10]

Athenian fatherhood, however, is indeed only politically relevant to the extent to which it concerns *legitimate* children, or rather sons—it is not merely the capacity to beget male children that counts, but the act of begetting male children within a particular cultural framework. Fundamentally, of course, fatherhood is always already the result of institutionalization, since, unlike at least *one* form of maternity (and the one traditionally seen as its dominant denotation), paternity as a physical relation between two bodies does not admit of direct observation. While the physical link between the biological mother and child can be witnessed during birth,[11] there is no such obvious link between the male body and the child fathered: not every coupling leads to pregnancy, and few births can be traced back to a specific act of coupling.

If we want to retain Agamben's terms, fatherhood is the realm where *zôê* and *bios* cannot be distinguished, since fatherhood is foremost an effect of signification. Paternity's biological aspect, while crucial, is nonetheless always asserted in retrospect—when the woman *is* pregnant or *does* give birth, the father *did* beget. His position defines and is defined by social and political relations that designate his body as having been there. Even before paternal certainty can become an issue, the relationship between coitus, pregnancy, and birth itself needs to be constructed. Fatherhood, in other words, needs institutions to legitimize not simply the sons but *itself*. In other words, it needs a theory.

The most famous and the most influential passages of Aristotle's *Generation of Animals* are just that, a theory of reproduction that fabricates the bodily grounding of fatherhood. As Thomas Laqueur has pointed out, "for Aristotle reproductive biology was essentially a model of filiation."[12] In a laconic formulation of great elegance, Aristotle defines the male and the female as follows: "by a 'male' animal we mean one which generates in another, by 'female' one which generates in itself."[13] Not that masculinity itself here is defined *as* its

---

10 Eva C. Keuls, *The Reign of the Phallus: Sexual Politics in Ancient Athens* (New York: Harper and Row, 1985), 100.
11 At this point in history, we can no longer speak of "the" biological mother, seeing that reproductive technology has led to a differentiation of genetic and gestational mother, but that distinction, needless to say, is an extremely recent one—with tremendous theoretical and potentially political and cultural consequences.
12 Thomas Laqueur, *Making Sex: Body and Gender from the Greeks to Freud* (Cambridge, MA: Harvard University Press, 1990), 30.
13 Aristotle, *Generation of Animals*, trans. with an introduction by A. L. Peck, Loeb Classical Library 366 (Cambridge, MA: Harvard University Press, 1942), 716a.

relation to procreation. And this relation is tenuous since, for men, reproduction always proceeds at a distance. Myths, fairy tales, and the laws concerning adultery have always reminded us that women can never be sequestered sufficiently to rule out sexual rivals, and the very possibility has condemned fathers to search for traces of their bodies in the shapes of their children.

Hence, one of the central problems of paternity is resemblance—a notoriously treacherous category. In the *History of Animals*, Aristotle gives a list of the potential troubles involved in a passage that makes it abundantly clear that he does not, as some commentators allege on somewhat slim evidence, see the womb as the mere vessel of a child formed by its father's semen:

> While children mostly resemble their parents or their ancestors, it sometimes happens that no such resemblance is to be traced. But parents may pass on resemblance after several generations, as in the case of the woman in Elis, who committed adultery with a negro; in this case it was not the woman's own daughter but the daughter's child that was a negro.[14]

It is not the specific shape of any given child a father contributes, but the movement by which shape comes about. The form the child takes is as much determined by the mother's history as by that of the father:

> As a rule the girls have a tendency to take after the mother, and the boys after the father; but sometimes it is the other way, the boys taking after the mother and the girls after the father. And they may resemble both parents in particular features. . . . Some women have a tendency to produce children that take after themselves, and others children that take after the husband; and this latter case is like that of the celebrated mare in Pharsalus, that got the name of the Honest Wife. (Ibid.)

The translator's jocular choice of "honest wife" is rather grating; her name is Dikaia, based on the adjective *dikaios* or a poetic version of *Dikê* itself, that is, just, in keeping with the way things ought to be. Needless to say, the very fact that this horse became famous enough to make an appearance not just in the *History of Animals* but also in the *Politics* (1332a) attests to her exceptional nature. Aristotle knows full well that most horses and most women are not nearly as accommodating. In

---

14 Aristotle, *History of Animals*, trans. D'Arcy Wentworth Thompson, in *The Complete Works of Aristotle*, ed. Jonathan Barnes, vol. 1, Bollingen Series 71:2 (Princeton, NJ: Princeton University Press, 1984), 586a.

reproductive (as in other) matters, justice is the exception rather than the rule.

The moment the semen leaves the male body, carrying with it the abstract principle of movement (sentient *psychê* contained in the *pneuma*, which will soon evaporate), the process of formation is out of the father's control. Deviations from Dikaia's ideal—such as children who are born female, do not resemble their fathers, their parents, or even human beings—manifest not merely the interference of the feminine, as in many other historical accounts of procreation, but the failure of male semen to fully master the matter that is menstrual blood. Aristotle's comments on the process are complicated and somewhat contradictory, and they have often been misconstrued. Thus, Valeria Fenucci claims that "Aristotle had famously argued that women contributed nothing to generation other than the womb in which the fetus develops."[15] Zoja affirms that Aristotle, "the master of 2,000 years of Western thought," believed that the "female produces no seed: the seed comes only from the father."[16] Keuls writes that "Aristotle was one of the fiercest misogynists of all times, obsessed with the need to prove that women play no genetic part in reproduction."[17]

Very little of this, however, is borne out by Aristotle's biological treatises. Aristotle certainly does regard the male contribution to procreation, not only as crucial to conception (who would have argued with him there), but also as superior, just as he clearly regards the male body as superior to the female one.[18] However, according to him, it is *men* who contribute nothing to generation but one very specific, immaterial component, namely, "sentient soul," soul that is *aisthêtikos*. As A. L. Peck notes in the introduction to the Loeb edition of the *Generation of Animals*:

> we must consider what exactly Aristotle meant by Form and Matter in this connexion. In the first place, we must realize that the Form is not bare Form, nor is the Matter bare Matter: this, indeed, is a fundamental doctrine of Aristotle. Form is not found apart from Matter. . . , nor is Matter found which is not to some extent "informed"; and Aristotle can say . . . that Matter in its

---

15 Valeria Fenucci, "Introduction: Genealogical Pleasures, Genealogical Disruptions," in *Generation and Degeneration: Tropes of Reproduction in Literature and History from Antiquity to Early Modern Europe*, ed. Valeria Fenucci and Kevin Brownlee (Durham/London: Duke University Press, 2001), 5.
16 Zoja, *The Father*, 121.
17 Keuls, *The Reign of the Phallus*, 100.
18 See Laqueur for an excellent analysis of the way in which female bodies are both radically different from and an inferior version of male bodies (*Making Sex*, 28–43).

ultimate stage is identical with Form. . . . Hence, the meaning of the statement that "the male supplies the Form" can only be that the male supplies that part of the Form known as sentient Soul: everything else, including nutritive Soul, can be, and is, supplied by the female.[19]

In this regard, it is indeed suggestive that Aristotle sees a need to explain why women cannot generate by themselves, while the question of men reproducing without women does not even come up: "Granted that the female possesses the same Soul [as the male] and that the residue provided by the female is the material [for the fetation], why has the female any need of the male in addition? Why does not the female accomplish generation all by itself and from itself?" (*Gen. An.* 741a). The answer is, of course, that only the male body can concoct seed into its purest and highest state in which it contains that sentient soul, without which any matter would be like "a dead body or a dead limb" (ibid.), but the discussion implies that the father's contribution is quite intangible. In fact, as far as Aristotle is concerned, what is material about it dissolves soon after conception. Like fatherhood itself, semen is something of an abstraction, and because of that, both highly privileged *and* quite elusive. There are important political implications here, at least by analogy. Laqueur suggests that

> Sperma, for Aristotle, makes the man *and* serves as synecdoche for citizen. In a society where physical labor was the sign of inferiority, sperma eschews physical contact with the catemenia and does its work by intellection. The *kurios*, the strength of the sperma in generating new life, is the microcosmic corporeal aspect of the citizen's deliberative strength, of his superior rational power, and of his right to govern. Sperma, in other words, is like the essence of citizen. Conversely, Aristotle used the adjective *akuros* to describe both a lack of political authority, or legitimacy, and a lack of a biological capacity, an incapacity that for him defined woman.[20]

Important if true—but the Periclean laws barred from citizenship children born to Athenian men and foreign women, and Aristotle notes in the *Politics* that "citizenship is limited to the child of citizens on both sides, not on one side only" (1275b). Clearly, then, legitimacy is carried exclusively by neither sperm nor female matter but results only from their mingling. More importantly, while Athenian society indeed

---

19 A. L. Peck, introduction to Aristotle, *Gen. An.*, xi–xiii.
20 Laqueur, *Making Sex*, 54ff.

disdained physical labor, *ponos*, the same is not true of work as *ergon*, a category of vital importance to Aristotle. Hannah Arendt has analyzed the distinction in great detail,[21] but in this context it might suffice to point out that *ergon* is the word Aristotle uses in the *Politics* when he says that "the ruler must possess intellectual virtue in completeness (for any work, taken absolutely, belongs to the master-craftsman, and rational principle is a master-craftsman)." *Ergon*, however, which unlike *ponos* is also a category of making (*poiêsis*), may be precisely what the father lacks when it comes to procreation. To the extent to which fatherhood is linked to resemblance, it is a process of mimesis without *poiêsis*, and as mimesis, as we have seen above, it is at best haphazard. The perfect child—a male replica of its father—relates to actual children like the *Poetics*' beautiful animal relates to the "creature a thousand miles long" that is history.[22]

Paternity, then, is characterized by the absence of both labor *and* work; in the *Nicomachean Ethics*, where poets are said to love their poems as if they were their children, and overly much, Aristotle notes: "Now to receive a benefit seems to involve no labor, but to confer one (*poieô*) is work (*ergôdês*). This is why mothers love their children more than fathers, because parenthood costs the mother more trouble (it is more *epiponos*) and the mother is more certain that the child is her own."[23] True, then, the man is not degraded by the *ponos* of pregnancy and childbirth; neither, however, is he involved in the creation of the child as a poet is involved in the making of a poem or a craftsman in the exercise of his *technê*: "sperma as artisan works in a flash, more like a genie than like a shoemaker who sticks to his last."[24] The kind of soul that is analogous to the *technê* of the craftsman is not the sentient, but nutritive soul, the kind of soul that the female seed possesses as well:

> Now the products which are formed by human art are formed by means of instruments, or rather it would be truer to say they are

---

21 Cf. Hannah Arendt, *The Human Condition* (Chicago: University of Chicago Press, 1958).
22 "It is not the function of the poet to relate what has happened, but what may happen—what is possible according to the law of probability (*eikos*) or necessity (*anankê*). The poet and the historian differ not by writing in verse or in prose. . . . The true difference is that one relates what has happened, the other what may happen. Poetry, therefore, is a more philosophical and a higher [more serious] thing than history: for poetry tends to express the universal, history the particular" (1451b). The distinction notwithstanding, Aristotle the natural historian at times places as much emphasis on what *ought* to happen as on the way things actually turn out.
23 Aristotle, *Nic. Eth.* 1168a.
24 Laqueur, *Making Sex*, 42.

formed by means of the movement of the instruments, and this movement is the activity, the actualization, of the art, for by "art" we mean the shape of the products which are formed, though it is resident elsewhere than in the products themselves. The *dunamis* of the nutritive Soul behaves in the same way. (*Gen. An.* 740b)

In the end, this lack of male work—as *ergon* and *poiêsis*—may be more important to the tenuous quality of paternity than the absence of paternal certainty.[25] Even though *mater certissima pater semper incertus est* (or, in its contemporary version, "momma's baby, papa's maybe") is one of the perennial themes in the history of fatherhood, it merely conceals a more general deficiency that cannot be filled by the strictest rules enforcing female monogamy. Greek fatherhood is a physical relation,[26] but not enough of one—it always needs to be construed culturally, solidified institutionally, and practiced socially. In other words, fatherhood is not the principle of the household, but its product.

---

25 At the same time, the shadow of paternal uncertainty indeed hovers over Aristotle's reflections as well. In Book 8 of the *Nicomachean Ethics*, he had already pointed out that "parents know their offspring with more certainty than children know their parentage," and after adding some other differences between paternal and filial affection, concluded that "these considerations also explain why parental affection is stronger in the mother" (1161b).

26 This, it bears stressing, is in distinction to Roman law and Roman social practice, where adoption, even the adoption of grown men, was a frequent and commonplace political strategy. It is interesting to note that the uncoupling of body and law coexists and perhaps gave rise to the most radical expansion of paternal power in the West. In a different vein, Malinowski's account of the Tobrianders, who, he said, were unaware of the biological aspects of fatherhood, demonstrates that the institution of fatherhood does not need to ground itself in a theory of sperm. Cf. Bronislaw Malinowski, *The Father in Primitive Psychology* (New York: W. W. Norton, 1927).

Six   Paternity and the Perfect City

How does fatherhood enter political theory? When Oedipus is led off the stage, blind, bleeding, and childless, the city is on its own again, just as it was when Laius failed to return—a *patria* without *patêr*. Certainly, we know that Creon will take over, but we also know that he, too, will fail, and that he, too, will fail as father and as king. Since *Antigone* was written before *Oedipus,* we might say that he already has failed, even though his case will be, or has been, yet a different one. All three of them, however, are ensnared by what I call the Laius Complex—the multiple overdetermination of a paternity that turns tragic when its constitutive elements fail to align.

Walter Nestle famously claimed that tragedy began when myth was assessed from the point of view of the citizen,[1] but tragedy did not offer solutions to the acute conflicts it imported and presented to the polis. As Vernant and Naquet argue, it neither affirmed nor rejected the present, but publicly and critically called it into question and into dialogue with the historical and mythical past.[2] Mark Griffith argues that tragedy's "brilliant dynasts" offered the Athenian citizenship an opportunity to "reinforce their continuing and deep-seated faith in the cultural and political value of those great families,"[3] but the ban of the father, as *Oedipus the King* stages it, instead appears to bespeak both a sense of liberation and a deep-seated anxiety (probably the two affects that reliably accompany any significant cultural change). Sophocles's dramatic patricide imbues the power shift from *patêr* to *patria* with its full gravity, and the play's last lines ring with both programmatic and pessimistic force. *Oedipus at Colonus* will entomb Oedipus-the-father, a more successful filicide than Laius had been, in Athens: as a sacred corpse, to be sure, but as a corpse nonetheless.

When philosophy takes over where tragedy leaves off, it inherits, along with a host of other dilemmas, the problem of the paternal trope—both in its appeal and in its potential to undermine the city.

---

1   Attributed by Vernant, Jean-Pierre, and Pierre Vidal-Naquet, *Myth and Tragedy in Ancient Greece*, trans. Janet Lloyd (New York: Zone Books, 1988), 33.
2   Vernant and Vidal-Naquet, *Myth and Tragedy,* 33f.
3   Mark Griffith, "Brilliant Dynasts: Power and Politics in the 'Oresteia,'" *Classical Antiquity* 14, no. 1 (April 1995): 129.

It is Plato's *Republic* that, perhaps unsurprisingly, offers both the most radical and the most unlikely solution. Since fatherhood—as meaningful biological fact, as social practice, and as political master trope—is so central to social and political institutions and the affect sustaining and threatening them, any theory of fundamental political change will have to fundamentally rethink its political function, and it may well be that the figure of the father can serve to distinguish radical and reactive thought, or revolution and reform. If so, movements of reform and reaction will seek to contain, replace, or reestablish the father, while radical politics will be tempted to erase his position altogether. The former would seek to redistribute power, the latter to change its very structure. And invariably, the second one will reap scorn and indignation, imbued with the rhetoric of common sense.

This is, in a nutshell, the relationship between Plato's *Republic* and Aristotle's *Politics*. The *Republic*'s famous call for equality of the sexes is one of its most striking features, and it has engendered passionate scholarly discussion. It is instructive to see how Socrates arrives there: by dismissing as insignificant what has traditionally been seen as the bedrock principle of gender differentiation, "the most important bodily difference within the human race,"[4] that is to say, distinctions in reproduction:

> If it appears that the male and the female sex have distinct qualifications for any arts or pursuits, we shall affirm that they ought to be assigned respectively to each. *But if it appears that they differ only in just this respect that the female bears and the male begets*, we shall say that no proof has yet been produced that the woman differs from the man for our purposes, but we shall continue to think that our guardians and their wives ought to follow the same pursuits.[5] (Emphasis added)

Since no such "distinct qualifications" can be clearly established, Socrates claims, begetting and bearing do not produce a gendered division of labor or a split between *polis* and *oikia*: the sexed body has been unlinked from social organization. If men are to have no political privileges, women, beyond infancy, likewise have no privileged place in the nurturing and rearing of children. All citizens relate to the state alone, and to other citizens merely qua citizens.

---

4   Leo Strauss, *The City and Man* (Chicago: University of Chicago Press, 1978), 117.
5   Plato, *Republic*, trans. Paul Shorey, in *The Collected Dialogues of Plato*, ed. Edith Hamilton and Huntington Cairns, Bollingen Series 71 (Princeton, NJ: Princeton University Press, 1989), 454d–e.

90   The Tragedy of Fatherhood

The heated debates concerning the existence, extent, and discursive status of Plato's "communism" or "feminism"[6] have at times overshadowed Socrates's closely related but in the end even more radical proposal—in the interest of the just state, which can be unified only if its ruling class foreswears private property, he abolishes the guardians' parenthood. It is abundantly clear that Plato is fully aware of the scandalous nature of the idea. Here is Socrates's suggestion:

> In this matter, then, of the regulation of women, we may say that we have surmounted one of the waves of our paradox. . . . "It is no slight wave that you are thus escaping." "You will not think it a great one," I said, "when you have seen the one that follows." "Say on then and show me," said he. "This," said I, "and all that precedes has for its sequel, in my opinion, the following law." "What?" "That these women shall all be common to all the men, and that none shall cohabit with any privately; and that the children shall be common, and that no parent shall know its own offspring nor any child its parent." *"This is a far bigger paradox than the other, and provokes more distrust as to its possibility and its utility."* "I presume," said I, "that there would be no debate about its utility, no denial that the community of women and children would be the greatest good, supposing it possible. But I take it that its possibility or the contrary would be the chief topic of contention." "Both," he said, "would be right sharply debated." (*Rep.* 457c–e)[7] (Emphasis added)

He was quite right, of course, and Socrates's suggestions *have* been sharply debated ever since.[8] Julia Annas argues that "Plato's proposal

---

6   In general, the proposed arrangements are not meant to benefit individuals or cater to their desires, but should benefit the state, which, in assigning women to the household, deprives itself of potentially valuable human resources. In other words, Plato's argument may contain "feminist" ideologemes, but it is certainly not indebted to any concern for women's rights, happiness, or emotional and intellectual fulfillment, and to call him "the Western world's first feminist" (Keuls, *The Reign of the Phallus*, 402) strikes me as a bit of a misreading. Note that a system that, in principle, includes polyandry as well as polygyny, is consistently referred to as the collective ownership of women and children.
7   Cf. also *Rep.* 423e, where Socrates suggests to Adimantus that the dissolution of the family will reasonably follow from everything said: "'For if a right education makes of them reasonable men they will easily discover everything of this kind—and other principles that we now pass over, as that the possession of wives and marriage, and the procreation of children and all that sort of thing should be made as far as possible the proverbial goods of friends that are common.' 'Yes, that would be the best way,' he said."
8   Cf. the essays collected in *Feminist Interpretations of Plato*, ed. Nancy Tuana (University Park: Penn State University Press, 1994), especially Natalie Harris

that the sexes share the same way of life is truly revolutionary. It is the point at which he goes furthest in claiming that ideal justice would require society to be unimaginably different from the existing society."[9] In the light of the extreme gender segregation that characterized Athens, this is a highly plausible comment. At the same time, we might consider that many of Socrates's suggestions concerning the equal status of women gradually *have* been put into practice over the course of history, and it remains an open question, or a matter of perspective, whether society has become "unimaginably different" as a result. Socrates's proposal to end parenthood, by contrast, is still as radical and as politically unviable as ever, and it has startled even Plato's greatest admirers. Here is Leo Strauss, surely one of the most congenial readers of the *Republic*:

> We are disappointed to see that while Socrates takes up the question of whether communism regarding women and children is possible, he drops it immediately. It looks as if it were too much even for Socrates to prove that possibility, *given the fact* that men seem to desire naturally to have children of their own. Since the institution in question is indispensable for the good city, Socrates thus leaves open the question of the possibility of the good city, i.e. of the just city, as such. And this happens to his listeners, and to the readers of the *Republic*, after they have brought the greatest sacrifices—such as the sacrifice of *eros* as well as of the family—for the sake of justice.[10]

The passage appears to bespeak genuine exasperation. Men's "natural" desire to have "children of their own" is so strong that "not even" Socrates can hope to convince his interlocutors—or his readers, including, apparently, Strauss himself—that the abolition of parenthood is possible. And since Socrates has declared it indispensable to the just city, the abolishment of parenthood leads, paradoxically, to the abandonment of justice. Socrates's proposal is so obviously outrageous, runs so deeply counter to Athenian society in particular and human desire in general, we learn, that it chiefly demonstrates the very

---

Bluestone, "Why Women Cannot Rule: Sexism in Plato Scholarship"; Elizabeth Spelman, "Hairy Cobblers and Philosopher-Queens"; and Gregory Vlastos, "Was Plato a Feminist?" See also Sarah B. Pomeroy, *Goddesses, Whores, Wives, and Slaves* (New York: Schocken, 1975), as well as Dorothea Wender, "Plato: Misogynist, Paedophile, and Feminist," *Arethusa* 6 (1973): 75–90.
9 Julia Annas, *An Introduction to Plato's Republic* (New York: Oxford University Press, 1981), 182.
10 Leo Strauss, *The City and Man*, 117.

futility of searching for the perfectly just state; its price is higher than anyone is willing to pay. Stanley Rosen amplifies:

> I accept the following view from Leo Strauss . . . , [that] the political function of the *Republic* is to show that the perfect solution to human political problems is impossible. . . . If you think through what is necessary to have a just city, you will end up with the city which is unjust in the sense that it doesn't take into its account the deepest desires of its citizens. So, from that standpoint, the *Republic* is a political satire.[11]

Certainly, Rosen mentions the abolition of the family as only one example among others in order to argue "that the consequences of attempting to have a perfectly just city are terrible" (ibid.), but Strauss's outburst above constitutes a clear break in his reading of the *Republic* in *The City and Man*—after having brought "the greatest sacrifices" just by *listening* to the proposal. While justice poses many demands that may seem "terrible," the demand to give up children "of one's own" is, it appears, the most terrible of them all, and no argument to support it can be made, not even by the most persuasive of men.

Strauss's reaction is instructive, the more so because his reasoning is somewhat questionable on two counts: first, the remainder of this chapter builds precisely to the condition of the possibility of the community of women and children: the philosopher king, of all monarchic models the one that embodies, as it were, the "complete abstraction from the body" (115). And second, Socrates does not really *need* to produce an argument here because he has already given it—ending the practice of privately owned children is the logical analogue to the previously proposed noble lie in which the guardians lose their parents, being persuaded that they have only imagined them, that they were born of the soil of the city, their only mother.[12] In addition—and Aristotle will have to say more

---

11 Tongdon Bai, "Plato, Strauss, and Political Philosophy: An Interview with Stanley Rosen," *Diotima: A Philosophical Review* 2, no. 1 (2001); available from www.holycross.edu/_diotima/n1v2/rosen.htm

12 "And yet I hardly know how to find the audacity or the words to speak and undertake to persuade first the rulers themselves and the soldiers and then the rest of the city, that in good sooth all our training and educating of them were things that they imagined and that happened to them as it were in a dream; but that in reality at that time they were down within the earth being molded and fostered themselves while their weapons and the rest of their equipment were being fashioned. And when they were quite finished the earth as being their mother delivered them, and now as if their land were their mother and their

about this—, children "of one's own" are merely a special case of the convention of private property, which Socrates had already abolished at this point in the construction of the perfect city, its "possibility" affirmed by his interlocutors. For Plato, both property and its subspecies parenthood are conventions, however entrenched they may be. For Strauss and Aristotle (and countless others), the desire for fatherhood, as distinct from the desire for sexual intercourse, is unquestionably and self-evidently natural.

This doesn't mean that Strauss is necessarily wrong on the larger point. It is quite possible that the *Republic* does indeed name the price of justice, and that those who agree with Plato that justice requires the sacrifice of *erôs* would also agree with Strauss or Rosen that justice costs too much. Strauss's perspective is intriguing, but so are its implications. Logically, the abolition of fatherhood—and it is fatherhood, not motherhood, that is at stake when the family is defined as a property relationship[13]—can only serve to discredit the idea of perfect justice if it is, indeed, just. Strauss, after taking Socrates to task for failing to discuss whether parenthood *can* be abolished, does not take the time to consider any further whether it *ought* to be.

Aristotle, however, does, and at considerable length. In the *Politics* (1261b–62b) he responds, and his criticism of his teacher is so uncharacteristically vehement that Davis calls it, ironically enough, "intellectual parricide."[14] It appears, then, that at least Plato's most prominent disciple did not take it to be a piece of obvious satire or a trap for those who are overly concerned with justice. Before exploring that passage,

---

nurse they ought to take thought for her and defend her against any attack and regard the other citizens as their brothers and children of the self-same earth." *Rep.* 414d–e.

13 This is not to say that the abolition of motherhood has not shocked readers as well. Sinclair tellingly comments that Plato "sees that living in cities answers a human need, yet refuses to his best citizens a place for the far deeper need of a child for its own mother or a woman for her child." Sinclair, *Greek Political Thought*, 157.

14 Davis, *Politics of Philosophy*, 35. It should be pointed out, however, that in his critique, Aristotle is careful to refer to *Socrates*'s ideas or to the state as *described* by Plato. This fact can serve as evidence for Strauss's thesis, but it also suggests that Aristotle could not trust his readers to make the same distinctions between Socrates and Plato, a description and an endorsement. Cf. also Davis's assertion that "[Aristotle] seems not so much to criticize the *Republic* as his own selective abridgement of Book 5. Furthermore, despite his own coupling of Socratic speeches with mimes (*Poetics* 1447b9–11), here Aristotle seems to treat them as though they were altogether contextless and unironic." Ibid., 34.

however, a look at the *Politics'* relationship to paternity more generally is in order.[15]

One of the book's tasks, I maintain, is to resolve the conflicts that necessarily arise in a society that must seek to destroy the symbolic link between governance and fatherhood while retaining the latter as a central institution of communal life. At first glance, this may not appear to be its most important project, but it is striking that there is no definition of the political here that does not in some way involve the delimitation of literal or symbolic paternity. Over the course of the *Politics,* Aristotle will explicitly connect the status of the household, the status of religion, the question of kingship, and the source of the law to the logic of paternity. The household is under the uncontested dominance of the father, who rules women, children, and slaves. The father's rule is monarchical, and, conversely, the king rules in a paternal fashion. The gods, in turn, have been fashioned in the image of the father, and the earliest communal law is the law the father lays down. In this respect, the *Politics* appears to support Freud's claim that fatherhood is the locus of "authority out of whose omnipotence all other social authorities have developed over the course of human cultural history." Here, too, it is impossible to speak of power without speaking of the father. Aristotle, however, says something else as well: it is impossible to speak of the political without constraining his power.

As was true for tragedy, the choice presented to Athenian philosophy was not one between hereditary kingship and democracy—the period between the eighth and the fourth centuries BCE knew a tremendous number of alternative regimes. Aristotle, like Plato before him, distinguishes between the rule of one (monarchy and tyranny), the rule of the few (aristocracy and oligarchy), and the rule of the many (democracy), but within each of these, there was room for often significant variations, and T. A. Sinclair points out that Aristotle "thought it worth his while to examine the government of 158 [city-states] in detail."[16]

Athens had not known the kingship of the tragic past for centuries, even though it had known (and sometimes thrived under) tyrants. Why, then, does Aristotle, too, devote so much space to discussing

---

15 There has been quite a bit of controversy regarding the "book" character of the *Politics,* with some scholars arguing for its cohesion, others focusing on the apparent incompatabilities of its sections and suggesting that it is actually a conflation of two separate treatises. I will here proceed as if it were a single monograph, since that is the (mostly implicit) assumption guiding most of its reception.

16 T. A. Sinclair, *A History of Greek Political Thought* (Cleveland and New York: Meridian, 1968), 5.

it? The general idea that politically qualified (i.e., free male) citizens "share equally in ruling and being ruled (*Nic. Eth.* 1134b)," to use Aristotle's formulation, appears to have been rather well entrenched in practice and widely accepted (though certainly not by Plato); it was, in any case, far *less* controversial than during the beginnings of the democratization of modern Europe. It is all the more suggestive that paternity—and Aristotle makes it abundantly clear that the king's appeal *is* the appeal of the father—appears to have remained such a powerful and cherished model of benign, natural, and hence legitimate authority. Some scholars, like Sinclair, see the continuous fascination with monarchic rule in a cynical light: "the able and unscrupulous popular leader was both abhorred and admired, and Thrasymachus spoke no more than the truth about his fellow countrymen when he said (Plato *Repub.* I 344) that their detestation of a tyrant's injustice was due not to fear of committing his crimes but to fear of suffering them." The literature of the time may also suggest, however, that the desire *for* the monarch runs as deep, perhaps deeper, than the desire to *be* him. True, while monarchy was not much of a political option, it certainly was part of the cultural vocabulary of power, and tragedy's intense dialogue with the royal city makes symbolic fatherhood appear as one of the deepest reservoirs of what Ernst Bloch called nonsynchronism, *Ungleichzeitigkeit*: "Times older than the present continue to affect older strata; here it is easy to return or dream one's way back to older times. . . . In general, different years resound in the one that has just been recorded and prevails."[17]

Different years, different centuries, different images and desires, and certainly different semiotic structures. Christian Meier, like Vernant, draws attention to the fact that "the extraordinarily daring politics of the Athenians" had to imply far-reaching "consequences in that layer which Max Weber called nomological knowledge,"[18] and he insists that the shift involved a "mental enterprise of politics" (53) that manifests its tremendous exertions in the cultural life of the period. Radical political reconfigurations, however, involve changing the Law beyond any legal reforms—they need to reconceptualize both the position and the source of the Law, not just its political and its theoretical grounding, but also, and just as importantly, the affective cathexes of the citizenry. Thus, political education, the formation of the citizen, emerges as

---

17 Ernst Bloch, "Nonsynchronism and the Obligation to Its Dialectics," trans. Mark Ritter, *New German Critique* 11 (1997): 22. Bloch's essay, "Ungleichzeitigkeit und Pflicht zu ihrer Dialektik," was originally published in *Erbschaft dieser Zeit* (Zürich: Oblecht & Helbling, 1935).
18 Meier, *Die politische Kunst*, 43–5.

an issue of central concern in both Plato and Aristotle.[19] The process involves the reinterpretation of mythology, as in tragedy, the writing of new foundational texts, as in Plato's *Republic* and Aristotle's *Politics*, and the reconfiguration of an understanding of justice (be it as *dikê*, *themis*, or *nomos*) in which the law still appears to be founded, legitimized, and hallowed both by tradition and timeless divine origins.

Aristotle is fully aware that Athens now houses politics' dead father, but unlike Plato, he is unwilling to take seriously the possibility of laying *familial* fatherhood to rest—precisely because Plato wants to do so in the service of a monarchy more monarchical than any monarchy ever conceived. Both imply, it appears, that the link between the father of the family and the father of the city, that source of tragic mayhem, must be severed, but their solutions are diametrically opposed. While Plato slowly builds up to his own great unlinking, the *Politics*, after asserting that all communities aim at some good, takes the necessity to distinguish between paternal and political power as *its very starting point*:

> Those then who think that the natures of the statesman (*politikos*), the royal ruler (*basileus*), the head of an estate (*oikonomikos*) and the master of a family (*despotês*) are the same, are mistaken. (1252a)

Again, in the light of roughly two centuries of regimes with a wealth of complicated institutions that do not remotely resemble the organization of a household under a single head, this is a curious beginning, and I suspect that it attests to the great resilience of a political semiotic long superseded in political practice. Aristotle is evoking Plato's *Statesman* here, where the Athenian Stranger, using identical terms, asks whether "we [shall] then assume that the statesman, king, master, and householder . . . are all one, to be grouped under one title?"[20] and goes on to postulate a *technê* of ruling that would, indeed, be the same for all—Plato, after all, is the programmatic philosopher of sameness. For Aristotle, however, political theory begins by correcting a mistake—the mistake of his teacher (assuming that the Stranger articulates Plato's

---

19 I do not mean to reproduce what Sinclair calls the "vague impression that Greek Political Thought began with Plato and ended with Aristotle" (*Greek Political Thought*, 2), but, needless to say, Plato and Aristotle are the two most important political theorists of Greek antiquity, and it is their reception that will be at stake in the following chapters.
20 Plato, *Statesman*, in *Plato in Twelve Volumes*, trans. Harold N. Fowler, vol. 12 (Cambridge, MA: Harvard University Press; London: William Heinemann, Ltd., 1921), 258e.

thoughts on the matter), but also the mistake allegedly at the very center of a fundamental and widespread misunderstanding of the political.

Aristotle does not yet mention the father by name, but that is hardly necessary. The following paragraph that grounds the *oikos* in reproduction and male dominance (see the preceding chapter) will very clearly establish that it is the rule of the father that haunts properly political understanding and threatens Aristotle's own conception of a polity commensurate with the *zoon politikon*.

If the desire for the father runs through political thought as strongly as Aristotle's opening suggests, accounting for no less than the fundamental misconception of the city, Aristotle's undertaking is complex. He postulates a sharp distinction between the household, *oikos*, in which the father's power will remain preserved and perhaps even enhanced, and the *polis*, in which the dream of paternal power cannot and must not be embodied. In order to ground and legitimize the father's position in the home, however, Aristotle takes recourse to a model of nature which threatens to be so attractive that it runs the risk of vindicating the barbarian practice of kingship. Conversely, many of the arguments that are mustered against monarchic rule would seem to apply to the father as well, weakening the theoretical support for his oikonomic supremacy. To be sure, the postulated qualitative difference between governing a household and governing a city would go a long way toward solving these conundrums, but Aristotle never quite delivers on his promise to explain in which way they differ. He will, however, repeatedly argue that paternal kingship is the best of regimes *in principle*. Or at least in light of some principles. Davis, somewhat polemically, sums up:

> The first three books, which culminate in Aristotle's teaching about kingship, have as their underlying theme the fact that the best regime is not really a regime. Its citizens are not really human. Books 4–6 have as their underlying theme that the best regime is not best. . . . Books 1–3 show that it is unjust for the best men not to rule. Books 4–6 show that it is unjust for them to rule.[21]

Provided the king is chosen because of his superior virtue, monarchy

> does seem to embody the theoretical goal of the best political order—the coincidence of wisdom and power. We have seen that Aristotle indicates his awareness of the difficulty with this "best" solution by likening this sort of king, the *pambasileus*, to the father

---

21   Davis, *Politics of Philosophy*, 97.

of a family. Yet Book 1 is devoted in large part to the argument that the kind of rule existing within the family is incomplete and not really political at all. (Ibid.)

It is not clear, however, whether Book 1 really does contain any *argument* of this sort, though I agree that it is implied. True, Aristotle *asserts* the difference several times, but in the end, we only know that "the government of a household (*oikonomikê* . . . *archê*) is monarchy (*monarchia*) (since every house is governed by a single ruler), whereas statesmanship (*politikê* . . . *archê*) is the government of men free and equal" (*Pol.* 1055b). Thus, the distinction between the household and the *polis* emerges as the distinction between a community that is by definition monarchic, the *oikos*, and one that is by definition not, the political community of free and equal citizens. Of course, then, the household cannot be political simply because its members, with the exception of the male head, are not and cannot be citizens, and their relationship to the father is unequal. In that light, yes: no matter how many times Aristotle may praise the king, we know by the middle of Book 1 that a king's subjects—and that would include the philosopher king's subjects—, would be akin to women, children, or slaves, even if he were the best of kings. The inferiority of women, children, and slaves, in turn, is so deeply ingrained in Athenian culture that the analogy may well be understood to undercut a priori any endorsement of the monarchy that will follow. Conversely, however, it is clear that the political citizen, the one capable both of ruling and of being ruled, is only produced by the difference between man and woman, free and unfree, father and son: he is, as we have seen, a product of the *oikos*.

Needless to say, it is the last of these distinctions that is of interest to me here, the relationship between father and son: it will emerge as the only politically relevant one precisely because it is not permanent. The slave will always remain a slave because Aristotle's slaves are generally slaves by nature, not by conquest, and women are, well, women—governed politically in principle, but not, to be sure, in practice. Of the *oikonomikos*'s three types of subjects, then, only the son can become a political citizen in turn. The father-son relationship is the link between *oikos* and *polis*, the only domestic relationship that meets, temporalized, the criterion of the political: that the one ruled can take the place of the one ruling.

In the logic of biblical monotheism, paternal power has a firm grounding in (monarchic) divine power, but for that reason, as we have seen, it comes at the price of an enduring filiality. The Athenian father-citizen, by contrast, is not subjected to a paternal principle but to a law that is not simply the Law of the Father, even while it remains, for all purposes, a law of fathers. Greek politics, however oppressive according to contemporary standards of justice, becomes truly "daring" when it departs from the tragic supposition, however tentative, ambivalent, or circumscribed, that there is a realm where *themis*, *dikê*, and *nomos* coincide.[22] Aristotle's general pessimism with regard to the very possibility of a perfect city entails a dim view of any attempts of grounding the political in either tradition or religion. This means that he has to let go of what Foucault, in *The Order of Things*, has analyzed as the premodern thinking of and in similarity and analogy. The German classicist Olof Gigon, in his excellent introduction to the *Politics*, calls it "the very old equation" that parallels "the cosmos, the state, and the individual"[23]—the very equation that not only finds its most powerful instantiation in the paternal triad of god, king, and father but also informs Plato's political writings in a slightly different version (the good, the philosopher king, the *logistikon*). Aristotle takes care of the metaphysical point of the triangle in one paragraph:

> The village according to the most natural account seems to be a colony from a household, formed of those whom some people speak of as "fellow-sucklings," sons and sons' sons. It is owing to this that our cities were at first under royal sway and that foreign races are so still, because they were made up of parts that were under royal rule; for every household is under the royal rule of its eldest member, so that the colonies from the household were so too, because of the kinship of their members. . . . This explains why all races speak of the gods as ruled by a king, because they themselves too are some of them actually now so ruled and in other cases used to be of old; and as men imagine the gods in human form, so also they suppose their manner of life to be like their own. (*Pol.* 1252b)

The last sentence is admirably concise, exposing the principle of cosmic harmony as a metaphoric operation superimposed on a historical process that is itself grounded in the (allegedly) natural organization of the household: Zeus, like the paternal head god of other religions, is a

---

22 All three of the terms are translated as justice, right, or ethical custom; as Vernant has shown, it is futile to attempt to systematize the vocabulary of justice at the time, since the meaning of the terms is in flux precisely because of the revolution in legal, social, and political thought. Usually, of the three, *themis* is most closely related to divine or ancestral law, that is, furthest removed from written statutes, whereas *nomos* is most closely associated with positive laws.

23 The citation is from Gigon's introduction to a German edition of the *Politics*. Aristoteles, *Politik*, übersetzt und herausgegeben von Olof Gigon (Munich: dtv, 1973), 15. My translation.

representation of the king whose power is an extension of the father's authority in primitive or barbarian societies. "All races" (*genoi*), then, do not merely confuse the household and the city, but the city and the cosmos.

Monotheism places all its stakes in grounding the father and hence the paternal triad in divine power, and in the process declares the Ur-Father bodiless. Aristotle, well aware of the triad's appeal, erases its metaphysical origin by declaring it an afterthought and replaces it with *phusis*, that is, the biological father. In regrounding order in "nature" rather than in the divine, however, Aristotle runs the risk of blurring the sharp distinction between fatherly and kingly rule for which he had argued at the beginning—at first glance, the succession from father to master to king appears a bit *too* natural to be easily superseded. There is an interesting subtext here, as Davis notes:

> Also strange is Aristotle's account of the fact that cities were originally ruled by kings. He points out that households, from which the first cities grew, are ordinarily ruled monarchically by the eldest. This is sensible enough, but for evidence he quotes Homer (*Odyssey* 9.114–15): "And each lays down the law to children and even spouses" (1252b24). The context is the description of the lives of the Cyclopes. Aristotle cites as the prototype for monarchic rule beings known more for cannibalism than anything else.[24]

It is a bit less strange once we realize that Aristotle, as so often in the *Politics*, implicitly refers himself once again to Plato. In the *Laws* (680a–e), the Athenian Stranger, citing the exact same Homeric passage, presents the life of the Cyclopes as an example of the first stage of political association in which there is no need for a legislator, "for those born in that age of the world's history did not as yet possess the art of writing, but lived by following custom and what is called patriarchal law." In ironic contrast to the *Odyssey*, the Stranger describes the arrangements of the Cyclopes as rather idyllic, since they "live under a patriarchal government and a kingship which is of all kingships the most just."

That said, it is indeed rather striking that this "most just" of all kingships is to be found among mythical one-eyed semihumans of questionable repute. If traditional kingly rule appears as natural as the father's rule, then nature may well be somewhat more suspect than most Aristotelians tend to believe. Since it is safe to say that Aristotle is not recommending Cyclopian political arrangements, the city, in order to become political, must leave nature behind *precisely to the*

---

24   Davis, *Politics of Philosophy*, 17.

extent that patriarchal rule is said to be natural.[25] It is the very universality of paternal rule and its metaphysical back-up systems that would present a near-insurmountable obstacle to a theory that sees the *polis* as something that would grow teleologically in the Aristotelian sense, that is, according to "its own internal principle of motion propelling it towards its mature and well-functioning form" (Yack, 90). Such *teloi*, however, are unpolitical: as Yack points out, "Aristotle denies that any existing polis is well-ordered" (ibid.); he holds out no utopian promise of the perfect city to come.

In this light, Aristotle's famous formula of the *zoon politikon* marks not the way in which human life is political by nature, but, perhaps more significantly, the way in which politics and nature conflict—man is not an animal that is also political but an animal that is, however, political.[26] This is not to say that Aristotle does not place most of his stakes in human nature, but that it is precisely the political in the human that opens up its nature to indeterminacy. And in order to conceive of this human indeterminacy as a form of freedom, the city cannot be subjected to the gods. Hence the link between the Cyclopes, the gods, and the kings: if religious traditions that support paternal power are a secondary primitive fiction—and no matter what we are supposed to think of the Cyclopes, they are most surely figures of a barbarian past—then it is not "the desire for freedom *in its most extreme* form" that "will *ultimately* lead to a revolution against the gods,"[27] as Davis argues—in Aristotle, the gods are bracketed where the political begins, in the apparently modest claim that the household and the city must be kept apart.[28]

This leads to a new problem: Aristotle seeks to undermine a very powerful analogy, but without destabilizing the family, which he

---

25 I side with Yack, who argues here against a long scholarly tradition that there are no "adequate grounds for concluding that Aristotle thinks of the polis as a substance with its own nature." Bernard Yack, *The Problems of a Political Animal: Community, Justice, and Conflict in Aristotelian Political Thought* (Berkeley: University of California Press, 1993), 92 n.9. The book includes a list of some of the relevant literature.

26 Gigon points out that "it is profoundly wrong to say of the ancient Greek that for him human and civic existence coincided, as it were, and that he could not have conceived of an existence outside of the state. Nothing is more false. Or more precisely: such an impression may lean on an illustrious text, namely our Aristotle's endlessly quoted sentence that man is by nature a "'political being.' . . . It is mostly overlooked that Aristotle, far from expressing a general Greek opinion, mounted a thesis of his very own" (14).

27 Davis, *Politics of Philosophy*, 93.

28 Using very different evidence, Robert C. Bartlett has demonstrated how "Aristotle denies the claimed superiority of divine legislation." Robert C. Bartlett, "Aristotle's Science of the Best Regime," *American Political Science Review* 88, no. 1 (1994): 143.

sees as essential to the city. Thus, while Davis observes that "much of Book 1 is . . . concerned with *linking* the polis to what seems the most obviously natural of human associations—the household or oikia,"[29] Simpson stresses Aristotle's argument for "the primacy of the city."[30] Both are correct—the city needs the household more than the household needs the city, but in order to become political in Aristotle's sense, the community subordinates the natural household. They must be shown to be both alike and not alike, and both moves are essential. Also esssential, however, is the nature of nature, as it were. If paternal power, grounded in neither religion nor tradition, draws its legitimacy from the natural as the physical, the problematic nature of the father's body makes things far more complicated than many scholars have assumed.

But let us return to Aristotle's response to Plato. He marshals a significant number of sometimes conflicting reasons why the abolition of kinship in the service of the city's unity is a very bad idea.

— he denies that the greatest unity of the state is desirable, for "if the process of unification advances beyond a certain point, the city will not be a city at all for a state essentially consists of a multitude of persons . . . so that even if any lawgiver were able to unify the state, he must not do so, for he will destroy it in the process" (*Pol.* 1261a). What is at stake here is not just Plato's vigorously antidemocratic insistence on fixed social and political hierarchies but his general objection to unruly multiplicity in all registers, an objection that informs his aesthetics and his metaphysics as well as his politics. Where Plato abhors mobile and multiple subjects, Aristotle declares them to be the condition of governance among free people: "it is only just, whether governing is a good thing or a bad, that all should partake in it, and for equals thus to submit to authority in turn imitates their being originally dissimilar; for some govern and others are governed by turn, as though becoming other persons; and also similarly when they hold office the holders of different offices are different persons" (*Pol.* 2161b).

— he next denies that Platonic unity, even if it were desirable, would be achieved by abolishing parenthood. While Socrates argued that unity ensues when all property is held commonly, Aristotle objects that social cohesion would actually decline: "Property that is common to the greatest number of owners receives the least attention; men care most for their private possessions, and for what they own in common less, or only so far as it falls to their own individual share for in addition to the other reasons, they think less of it on the ground that someone else is thinking about it, just as in household service a large

---

29 Davis, *Politics of Philosophy*, 15. Emphasis added.
30 Simpson, *A Philosophical Commentary*, 14.

number of domestics sometimes give worse attendance than a smaller number. And it results in each citizen's having a thousand sons, and these do not belong to them as individuals but any child is equally the son of anyone, so that all alike will regard them with indifference" (*Pol.* 1261b).

— at the same time, close bonds would develop in any case, since conspicuous resemblances would lead the guardians to simply suppose that they are related to the children who resemble them: "it would also be impossible to avoid men's supposing certain persons to be their real brothers and sons and fathers and mothers; for they would be bound to form their belief about each other by the resemblances which occur between children and parents" (*Pol.* 1262a). The household, which sequesters women, is designed to control for resemblance's disruptive potential.

— since kinship inhibits violence, its abolishment would lead to more assaults as well as outrages against blood relatives for which the offenders, being ignorant of the relation, could not even perform the proper rites of expiation: "outrage, involuntary and in some cases voluntary homicide, fights, abusive language . . . are bound to occur more frequently when people do not know their relations than when they do, and also, when they do occur, if the offenders know their relationship it is possible for them to have the customary expiations performed, but for those who do not no expiation is possible" (*Pol.* 1262a).

— even worse, it seems, there would be no safeguards against incestuous relationships, and even if the guardians were barred from intercourse, incestuous acts between men and sons or brothers and brothers could not be ruled out: "it is curious that a theorist who makes the sons common property only debars lovers from intercourse and does not prohibit love, nor the other familiarities, which between father and son or brother and brother are most unseemly, since even the fact of love between them is unseemly. And it is also strange that he deprives them of intercourse for no other reason except because the pleasure is too violent; and that he thinks it makes no difference that the parties are in the one case father or son and in the other case brothers of one another" (*Pol.* 1262a). Socrates's cavalier treatment of male-male incest or incestuous feeling seems to scandalize Aristotle more than anything else, demonstrating that kinship, for Aristotle, is most crucially a system to regulate proper relationships between men rather than between genders.

The list of objections goes on for quite a while, with near manic intensity. Aristotle sometimes uses gender-neutral terms in his discussion, but it is clear that the position he is most passionately defending is that of the father, whose position both grounds and stabilizes society as a whole. As an equal citizen among equals and the uncontested head of the household, he is, as it were, both the warp and the weft of the social fabric, incorporating the balance of equality and hierachy that Plato's model threatens.

It is this balance which, for Aristotle, guarantees a modicum of political stability, for the family emerges as the training ground of *philia*, the city's most important cohesive. This takes some explaining: why would an institution defined by the fundamental inequality of its members be the condition of relationships defined by the highest possible degree of equality? In the *Nicomachean Ethics*, generally understood to be the companion to the *Politics*, Aristotle claims that "friendship between relatives itself seems to include a variety of species, but all appear to derive from the affection of parent for child. For parents love their children as part of themselves, whereas children love their parents as the source of their being" (1161b). Love is an effect of physical metonymy, it seems. The same thought appears in the *Politics*, where Aristotle suggests, contra Plato, that

> in the state [as Socrates envisions it] friendship would inevitably become watery in consequence of such association, and the expressions "my father" and "my son" would quite go out. For just as putting a little sugar into a quantity of water makes the mixture imperceptible, so it also must come about that the mutual relationship based on these names must become imperceptible, since in the republic described by Plato there will be the least possible necessity for people to care for one another as father for sons or as son for father or as brother for brother. For there are two things that most cause men to care for and to love each other, the sense of ownership and the sense of preciousness; and neither motive can be present with the citizens of a state so constituted. (1262b)

Father-son relationships are a kind of essence necessary to the most beneficial of all political relationships, friendship, which, in sharp contrast to the asymmetry of paternity, is defined by equality and mutuality. Once the sentiments that develop around the words "my son" or "my father" disappear, Aristotle claims, friendship will become weak and watery—both fatherhood and sonhood emerge as cultural and emotional exercises that condition the soul to relate to others as equals.[31]

---

31 This explains why Aristotle claims that "this community of wives and sons is more serviceable for the Farmer class than for the Guardians" (1262a), for strong friendships are undesirable in the lower classes, rendering them less submissive and more prone to revolt, while "we think that friendship is the greatest of blessings for the state, since it is the best safeguard against revolution, and the unity of the state" (1262b).

How so? In Aristotle, paternity and friendship, while diametrically opposed in many ways, are both forms of relating through another to the self. On the one hand, the *oikos* emerges as a legally lawless space: "Justice between master and slave and between father and child is not the same as absolute and political justice, but only analogous to them. For there is no such thing as injustice in the absolute sense towards what is one's own; and a chattel, or a child till it reaches a certain age and becomes independent, is, as it were, a part of oneself" and, he adds optimistically, "no one chooses to harm himself" (*Nic. Eth.* 1134b). In this sense, fatherhood is indeed not merely prepolitical, but also both prelegal and beyond the law: "Hence there can be no injustice towards them, and therefore nothing just or unjust in the political sense. For these, as we saw, are embodied in law, and exist between persons whose relations are naturally regulated by law, that is, persons who share equally in ruling and being ruled" (ibid.). Fathers ought to have complete power over their sons precisely because they are not fully distinct from each other; paternal control resembles the control reason exercises over desire and the mind exercises over the body.[32] The son is both same and other, *heteros* and *autos*.[33] To the extent that he is other, he is as fully subjected to his father as a slave or as inanimate property, and if a father chooses to hurt him, he can no more be punished than a man who inexplicably chooses to destroy his property. At the same time, the child is a part of his father, so much so that Aristotle will say that the child springs from his progenitor (*goneus*) like a tooth or a hair springs from his body (*Nic. Eth.* 1161b). And to the extent that he is the same, a father will treat him as well as he will treat himself, that is, as well as he would treat his dearest of friends. As Aristotle remarks in his discussion of self-love, a sentiment he defends from the common prejudice against it:

> One should love one's best friend most; but the best friend is he that, when he wishes a person's good, wishes it for that person's own sake, even though nobody will ever know of it. Now this condition

---

[32] "But to resume—it is in a living creature, as we say, that it is first possible to discern the rule both of master and of statesman. The soul (*psuchê*) rules the body (*sôma*) with the sway of a master (*despotikos*), the intelligence (*noos*) rules the appetites (*orexis*) with that of a statesman (*politikos*) or a king (*basilikos*), and in these examples it is manifest that it is natural and expedient for the body to be governed by the soul and for the emotional part to be governed by the intellect, the part possessing reason, whereas for the two parties to be on an equal footing or in the contrary positions is harmful in all cases." *Pol.* 1254b.

[33] *Nic. Eth.* 1161b: "Parents then love their children as themselves (one's offspring being as it were another self—other because separate (*ta gar ex autôn hoion heteroi autoi tôi kechôristhai*)."

> is most fully realized in a man's regard for himself, as indeed are all the other attributes that make up the definition of a friend; for it has been said already that all the feelings that constitute friendship for others are an extension of regard for self.... A man is his own best friend. Therefore he ought to love himself most. (1168b)

Through this set of equations and metonymic substitutions, father-son relationships emerge as the basis of their opposite, but the argument, ingenious as it is, creates a host of problems. It is a commonplace to say that a father sees himself in the son he loves, but the implications, as Aristotle spells them out, are startling enough. What kind of relationship can you have to somebody who is simultaneously your slave and yourself, a separate body and an extension of your own? Someone who is somewhat like your best friend and somewhat like your teeth? Someone you ought to rule in the same way that your mind rules your soul and your soul rules your body, but who, unlike your slave or your tooth, will take your place? If it sounds like a recipe for conflict and for heartbreak, it is:

> a man of very ugly appearance or low birth, or childless and alone in the world, is not our idea of a happy man, and still less so perhaps is one who has children or friends that are worthless, or who has had good ones but lost them by death. (1099b)

It is impossible to be happy without children, *ateknos*, and it is worse to have utterly bad (*pankakos*) children, but the greatest misery is to mourn good children who have died. Both in badness and in death, the child asserts its otherness, its separate, unruly existence. Aristotle's reflections here undercut the promise of succession, which, in theory, will resolve any conflict by deferring and displacing it. The submission of the son is purchased by the promise of the power he will inherit; but neither the bad son nor the dead son fits the paradigm. It is not surprising that the literature that articulates fatherhood is so conspicuously concerned with patricidal children on the one hand and dead children on the other hand—they both expose the fantasma of fatherhood in a way the good son never will. The relationship most indispensable to the city, the very condition of *philia*, is not a *technê*, and being beyond the purview of the law, it cannot be regulated.

As the institution tasked with the cultural transformation of natural inequality into political equality, Aristotelian fatherhood is divided against itself. To be sure, its appeal remains powerful, its promise being nothing less than the alignment of power with body, law, and feeling. Aristotle, however, has watched his tragedies well: the best regime is the most dangerous one, and the perfect city may well be the city that resists the temptation of perfection.

Seven   Hobbes and the End of the Paternal Triad

A chapter on Hobbes may come as a surprise in a book largely devoted to Greek and German material. Hobbes's work, however, constitutes a watershed in the history of paternity, and its importance can hardly be overstated. Allow me to recapitulate: between biblical, ancient Greek, and Roman sources, early modern Europe had inherited a surfeit of theories concerning paternity and its relationship to political power—conflicted within themselves and conflicting with each other. While motherhood, as practice and as metaphor, at this point appears no less historically and culturally circumscribed than fatherhood, its theory had largely anchored itself in the maternal body, in pregnancy, birth, and, to a lesser extent, lactation and breastfeeding. Paternal soma, however, was optional. Motherhood, to be sure, could be transferred (e.g., to adoptive mothers or stepmothers), but by default, the maternal position was habitually and consistently assigned to the birth mother and, symbolically, to the material realm (nature, earth).

Fatherhood, however, precisely because it had been legitimized by heterogeneous strategies, saw each one of them threatened to be undermined by the others. The Theban succession myths, for instance, which will play such a prominent role in modern reformulations of paternity, are structured by two oppositions—bios/nomos and family/state—, distinctions articulated not as complementary but as tragically conflicted. Theban paternity thus emerges as a prime example of Derrida's concept of the *supplément*, a structure whose dynamic can violently shift from the and/or to the either/or. Plato, contemplating kinship systems that would split both the locus of authority and civic loyalty precisely because he considered paternal and political rule to be akin, abolishes fatherhood. Aristotle, in response, grounds fatherhood in *phusis* and in turn abolishes paternity as a model of political rule instead. By contrast, the Old Testament contains a number of highly charged father-son narratives—Abraham/Isaac, Jacob/Esau/Joseph, David/Absalom, the prodigal son—but not a single narrative of questionable or contested fatherhood, and only one very obscure story of patricide. While endless accounts of patrilineal descents point to nothing less than an obsession with paternity as a trope of continuity—"x begets y" is the irreducible point of minimal narrativity in most biblical books—biblical paternity begins with the creatio ex nihilo, rendering the first act of generation an asexual event and, by extension, desexualizing or desomatizing paternity.[1]

As long as motherhood appears as the uncontested or even uncontestable parental relation, fatherhood again and again staked its claims by detour, often through the maternal body. Aristotle began his discussion of human associations by foregrounding the relation between male and female rather than the one between parent and child, and while his biology works hard to give an empirical foundation to the superiority of fathering over mothering, fatherhood in the political realm is ultimately established not via sperm but via marriage.

In monandrous marriage, a rather long-lived cultural ideal probably for that very reason, the tension between paternal bios and paternal nomos is laid to rest, and the sexual and the cultural father are, at least by design, one and the same. While some rituals—such as the ceremonial "picking up" with which a Roman father acknowledged his children—mark the difference between the two, there is a long legal tradition—still widely in effect in Western countries today in various modified forms—that declares a mother's husband to be the father of her children, regardless of biological circumstances. As a consequence, cultures where the desomatized monotheistic model of paternity holds sway have seen the relationship between children born outside of marriage and their biological fathers at times as so highly tenuous that patriarchalists like Sir Robert Filmer could claim that a child born out of wedlock "is not reckoned to have any father at all."[2] A hundred years later, Blackstone's *Commentaries on the Laws of England* (1765–1769) echoes the way in which law does not merely trump genetic relationship but makes it disappear by declaring blood itself a legal construct tied to property: "a bastard ... cannot be heir to any one, neither can he have heirs, but of his own body; for, being *nullius filius*, he is therefore of kin to nobody, and *has no ancestor from whom any inheritable blood can be derived*" (emphasis added).[3]

While these assumptions will linger for a long time to come, the perennial project to control the metaphoric traffic of paternity takes

---

1 Accordingly, the Bible's paternal metaphors rarely use analogies to coitus or birth and instead center on authority, responsibility, and ethics. Thus, Joseph says that God made him "a father to Pharaoh" (Gen. 45:8); Job says he was "a father to the needy" (Job 29.16); Isaiah announces that Eliakim will "become a father to the inhabitants of Jerusalem and to the house of Judah" (Isa. 22:23), etc.
2 Robert Filmer, *Filmer: Patriarcha and Other Writings*, ed. Johann P. Sommerville, Cambridge Texts in the History of Thought (Cambridge: Cambridge University Press, 1991), 192.
3 William Blackstone, *Commentaries on the Laws of England: In Four Books* (Oxford: Clarendon Press, 1775), 459.

a decisive turn in the seventeenth century. Hobbes's commentary on paternal power—Chapter XX of *Leviathan*, "Of dominion paternal and despotical"—is one of the most curious passages in a work hardly lacking in provocations. In 1651, the divine right of kings, deeply indebted to the logic of the paternal triad, still flourished all over Europe. England, however, had not just executed its king but (for a short while) abolished the monarchy altogether—an unprecedented pair of events in Christian Europe. *Leviathan* responds to the civil war with a theory of sovereignty that, seeking to reground monarchic rule, redefines not just the very nature of sovereignty but constructs one of history's most influential accounts of the origin of human society and the nature of human freedom and its loss. It is a central thesis of this book that theories of political power are inextricably interwoven with theories of fatherhood, and that thus each redefinition of legitimate political rule will have to address the role of paternal power—and vice versa. Hobbes is not just no exception to that rule, his writings offer one of its most fascinating instantiations.

With Hobbes, an overburdened concept of fatherhood entered a theoretical crisis of legitimation that would eventually destabilize modern paternity on principle—even though it was meant to do the opposite. Hobbes's writings, beginning with *Elements of Law Natural and Politic* (1640) and *De Cive* (1642) and culminating with *Leviathan* (1651), are a watershed in this regard. They break with all traditional notions of the legitimacy of paternal power more deliberately and more radically than any other canonical texts of early modernity. This is not to say that all of his individual theses on fatherhood are unprecedented, nor is it to imply that *Leviathan* had any immediate effect on the general social consensus on the legitimacy of paternal power. On the contrary, this power appears to emerge from his theories regrounded, and, if anything, strengthened rather than weakened—but only at first. In this regard, Hobbes's father and Hobbes's sovereign share the same ironic fate: one of the most forceful champions of an absolute monarchy is now habitually counted among the founders of the very intellectual tradition that will ground democracy and the rule of law. And a theory in which children are so thoroughly subjected to the power of their guardians that "a Sonne cannot be understood to be at any time in the State of Nature," that is, in a state of unabridged natural rights, may eventually have done more to undermine paternal power than any theory designed to limit its reach.

Obviously, this parallel is not a coincidence. Of all regimes, absolute monarchy has the closest metaphoric and conceptual ties to fatherhood, the more so if it is hereditary. Under the weight and history of that association, whoever argues on behalf of the king will usually argue on behalf of the father (though not vice versa). Hobbes could have allowed the strong cultural investment in fatherhood to support his case for the king, ex- or implicitly. Instead, he chose to thematize paternal power itself, to submit it to the same theoretical curiosity that would prove to be so corrosive.

Hobbes's contemporaries realized immediately that *Leviathan* constituted a threshold with regard to fatherhood—and they reacted strongly. In that work Hobbes's theses on paternal dominion, developed and refined over more than a decade, culminate in equating political and paternal rule to the point where he explicitly states that "in sum, the rights and consequences of both paternal and despotical dominion are the very same with those of a sovereign by institution." But they are the very same now for very different reasons than before, most shockingly, at the time, because they are no longer divinely granted.

The trouble announces itself in the chapter preceding the one on paternal dominion,[4] dedicated to the thorny question of succession, which is, Hobbes argues, most difficult within a monarchy, since "at first sight, it is not manifest who is to appoint the successor; nor many times who it is whom he hath appointed" (*Leviathan*, XIX).[5] Hobbes's theory of (near-) absolute sovereignty entails that "the disposing of the successor is always left to the judgement and will of the present possessor" (178). The sovereign can only be truly sovereign, in short, as long as his will and judgment are not constrained by laws governing his own replacement—including the laws of succession that had long been tied to genealogy. Since such rules would impinge on sovereignty, Hobbes resolutely uncouples succession from inheritance and kinship:

> For the word heir does not of itself imply the children or nearest kindred of a man; but whomsoever a man shall any way declare he would have to succeed him in his estate. If therefore a monarch declare expressly that such a man shall be his heir, either by word or writing, then is that man immediately after the decease of his predecessor invested in the right of being monarch. (178)

The transfer of power—the moment where the prospect of instability looms largest, in other words—depends on "testament and express words," and only where those "are wanting, other natural signs of the will are to be followed: whereof the one is custom. And therefore where

---

4 It is worthwhile noting that *De Cive* takes the opposite route, analyzing, in Chapter IX ("Of the right of Parents over their children and of hereditary Government"), parental authority first, monarchy and succession second.
5 Thomas Hobbes. *Leviathan: Parts I and II*, ed. A. P. Martinich and Brian Battiste (New York: Broadview Press, 2011), 177.

the custom is that the next of kindred absolutely succeedeth, there also the next of kindred hath right to the succession" (178).

Genealogical succession, then, has become a convention—a powerful one and hence the default position, but nonetheless nothing but a convention. This may be the best-known aspect of Hobbes's critique of fatherhood as a significant political category, in line with his general project to de-essentialize political power and refound it in the rational construction of the contract. Hobbes, however, does not merely bracket paternal power but devotes considerable space to its reconfiguration. Paternal, despotical, and sovereign power are "identical" because they equally originate in the hypothetical Hobbesian contract that trades protection for obedience, a contract that has to be neither explicit nor entered into voluntarily to be binding. The metaphysically anchored Christian sovereign triad of god, king, and father is reconfigured into a new triad: that of the sovereign by institution, the despot by conquest (who is not a tyrant), and the father. Those, however, are no longer tied to each other by the dangerous logic of metaphor that posits equivalence as a precarious balance of like and unlike but by a structural logic that applies to all of them equally.

It is neither surprising nor coincidental that Hobbes's analysis of paternal power opens with a scene of violence: "A commonwealth by acquisition," the chapter begins, "is that where the sovereign power is acquired by force; and it is acquired by force when men singly, or many together by plurality of voices, for fear of death, or bonds, do authorise all the actions of that man, or assembly, that hath their lives and liberty in his power" (180). From the beginning, then, the chapter's image of the father is framed by the notions of force, fear, death, and bondage, and its first analogue is neither king nor god, but the despot, that is, the sovereign who acquires sovereignty by force.

In the fourth paragraph, Hobbes finally introduces the paternal distinction: "Dominion is acquired two ways: by generation and by conquest. The right of dominion by generation is that which the parent hath over his children, and is called paternal" (181). The peculiar parallel between conquest and procreation does not merely infantilize the vanquished, it also, somewhat shockingly, appears to render children the equivalent of the spoils of war. The comparison, however, is perfectly logical, implied in the casual substitution of parent by father, of "parental" by "paternal," of dominion by generation, we shall see, is often enough nothing but the effect of dominion by conquest—that is, the conquest of the female by the male. The male part in procreation is, as so often, overshadowed by paternal uncertainty, "for in the condition of mere nature, where there are no matrimonial laws, it cannot be known who is the father unless it be declared by the mother; and therefore the right of dominion over the child dependeth on her will, and is consequently hers" (182). Fatherhood as a *biological* category, then, actually depends on a legal frame—that much is hardly new. But the matter is more complicated and more interesting than this. Maternal power is "natural" only to the extent that birth offers mothers the right of first refusal, as it were.

Hobbes's whole argument rests on the premise that power relations are—or ought to be—rationally determined. Differently put, power relationships are ethical relationships, and for Hobbes, there is no ethical dimension to the act of giving birth. In order to be part of a power relationship, the child needs to become a subject, or rather a subject manqué, so to speak—it needs to enter into a contract it could not have refused, submitting to the dominion of the mother in exchange for its survival.

As the argument progresses, "generation" is no longer synonymous with procreation—in fact, it isn't really generation at all. In a stunningly counterintuitive formulation, Hobbes explains that "the right of dominion by generation . . . is not so derived from the generation, as if therefore the parent had dominion over his child because he begat him, but from the child's consent, either express or by other sufficient arguments declared" (181). What is generated here, then, is not a child but a particular relationship *to* the child, not *zoê*, if one wanted to use Agamben's vocabulary, but a new conflation of *nomos* and *bios*. This redefinition is necessary because children are generated by two parents, but rule, according to one of Hobbes's axiomatic claims, cannot be shared: "For as to the generation, God hath ordained to man a helper, and there be always two that are equally parents: the dominion therefore over the child should belong equally to both, and he be equally subject to both, which is impossible; for no man can obey two masters."[6] If biological parenthood were sufficient to establish dominion, dominion would have to be shared equally; according to Hobbes's theory of sovereignty, this is impossible, and the specter of split sovereignty is so decisively tied to the prospect and reality of civil war that the very idea of shared parental authority is dismissed in the very sentence that introduces it as logically given. In other words, the

---

6 Compare the earlier formulation of the same thesis in *De Cive:* "Those that have hitherto endeavoured to prove the Dominion of a Parent over his children, have brought no other argument than that of generation, as if it were of it selfe evident, that what is begotten by me, is mine; just as if a man should think, that because there is a triangle, it appears presently without any farther discourse, that its angles are equall to two Rights. Besides, since Dominion (that is) supreme Power is indivisible, insomuch as no man can serve two Masters, but two Persons male and female, must concurre in the act of generation, its impossible that Dominion should at all be acquired by generation onely." Hobbes, *De Cive*, ed. Howard Warrender (Oxford: Oxford University Press, 1987), 121.

right of dominion by generation, just postulated as one of only two possibly forms by which power can be acquired, has already become something entirely different.

Again, Hobbes could have solved this problem by taking recourse to powerful and richly elaborated traditions that privilege paternal over maternal power, including any number of immanent, metaphysical, or explicitly theological theories of innate male superiority. Those, however, he explicitly and decisively dismisses as insufficient: "And whereas some have attributed the dominion to the man only, as being of the more excellent sex, they misreckon in it. For there is not always that difference of strength or prudence between the man and the woman as that the right can be determined without war" (181). To be sure, "in Commonwealths this controversy is decided by the civil law: and for the most part, but not always, the sentence is in favour of the father, because for the most part Commonwealths have been erected by the fathers, not by the mothers of families" (181).

In practice, then, we don't have to worry about this much, but in theory, it is once again a question of violence: if men are not "the more excellent sex," dominion can only be established by war[7]—that is to say, by conquest and the contracts it imposes upon the vanquished. Within the state, such conquests are alrady history, leaving behind nothing but historically contingent contracts—"for the most part"—whose validity is no longer self-evident. Paternal dominion is the effect of a "sentence," a speech act backed, like all law, by the monopoly of force that has always already unbalanced the scale. Hobbes's sovereign is, above all, the sovereign of signification, and signification is the core principle of fatherhood. If we were, or had ever been, "in the state of mere nature where there are supposed no laws of matrimony, no laws for the education of children, but the law of nature and the natural inclination of the sexes, one to another, and to their children" (181), then fatherhood would at best be an idiosyncratic affair:

> In this condition of mere nature, either the parents between themselves dispose of the dominion over the child by contract, or do not dispose thereof at all. If they dispose thereof, the right passeth according to the contract. . . . If there be no contract, the dominion is in the mother. For in the condition of mere nature, where there are no matrimonial laws, it cannot be known who is

---

7   *De Cive:* "But what some say, that in this case, the *Father* by reason of the preeminence of sexe, and not the *Mother*, becomes *Lord*, signifies nothing. For both reason shewes the contrary, because the inequality of their naturall forces is not so great, that the man could get the Dominion over the woman without warre." Ibid., 122.

the father unless it be declared by the mother; and therefore the right of dominion over the child dependeth on her will, and is consequently hers. (181–2)

In other words, both paternity as a biological relation and paternity as a legal relation depend on speech. Here, it is the mother's "declaration," which, however, by itself carries no obligation for either her or the father thus declared; parenthood is an act, not a fact, for, as Hobbes explains:

the infant is first in the power of the mother, so as she may either nourish or expose it; if she nourish it, it oweth its life to the mother, and is therefore obliged to obey her rather than any other; and by consequence the dominion over it is hers. But if she expose it, and another find and nourish it, dominion is in him that nourisheth it. For it ought to obey him by whom it is preserved, because preservation of life being the end for which one man becomes subject to another, every man is supposed to promise obedience to him in whose power it is to save or destroy him. (182)

In the state of nature, where there are no obligations but the ones imposed under threat of death, all life is bare life.

In many regards, Hobbes's chapter appears to fit smoothly into all the semiotic systems that map femininity to nature (or "mere" nature) and masculinity to culture or civilization. Hobbes's explicit reference to the perennial and perennially repressed problem of paternal uncertainty locates fatherhood firmly in the realm of the law, and Hobbes does associate the transition from maternal to paternal power with the departure from the state of nature itself—which, as we know, has always already occurred, but which, importantly, is culturally contingent: "women, namely Amazons, have in former times waged war against their adversaries, and disposed of their children at their own wils, and at this day in divers places, women are invested with the principall authority" (*De Cive*, 122).

In the realm of reproduction, Hobbes's distinction between dominion via conquest and dominion via generation collapses into dominion via the conquest of generation. But however familiar Hobbes's moves may appear in that light, his decision to neither theologize nor naturalize or otherwise essentialize the violent history, cultural grounding, and legal institution of paternal power is a radical move, however long it will take to play out. Paternal dominion and political sovereignty no longer share a common reference point in the book of Genesis: they are analogous *only*, no longer mutually dependent or sentimentally cross-charged. Fatherhood has become a purely structural effect: in fact, it is no longer gendered at all, for, as Hobbes establishes with reference to Queens and Amazons, paternal power can be wielded by men and women alike.

Hobbes engages in a radical gamble here. Hitherto, fatherhood had rested on three pillars: first, a Christian monotheism articulated as paternal. Second, a quasi-anthropological argument that postulated the innate superiority of the masculine over the feminine. Third, organic ideologies of blood, sperm, and body that equate sexual generation with both rights and obligation. All of them collapse at the same time, leaving behind nothing but a logic of exchange that seems devoid of comfort or warmth, contributing to Hobbes's reputation as the "Monster of Malmesbury."

Hidden within Hobbes's narrative of the bleakness of unfettered freedom and contractual restraint, however, there is another story, and one we have heard before—a story that will determine the discourse of modern subjectivity like no other. In a brief sentence almost concealed within the relentless logic of power grounded in the specter of death, we suddenly see an infant exposed, and a man who finds it and takes it into his care: "But if she expose it, and another find and nourish it, dominion is in him that nourisheth it" (*Leviathan*, 182). Hobbes has just given us a fleeting glimpse of Oedipus. To be sure, it is prehistorical Oedipus, an Oedipus who could not have fallen into the abyss that tragedy opens up between the father of sperm and the father of care, an Oedipus as fatherless as Sophocles's Oedipus will declare himself to be, and exposed not by his father but by his mother. Nonetheless, it is the vision of the child exposed that is at the heart of Hobbes's theory of paternity. We will encounter this child again—and in yet another gender figuration—in Lessing's *Nathan the Wise*.

But Hobbes's Oedipus is a deeply antitragic figure. After all, Oedipus's mythical fate is set into motion precisely because Oedipus has two fathers, Polybus and Laius, and precisely because within that text, the culture of blood emerges as triumphant over the culture of culture. Perhaps it would be more accurate to say, then, that Hobbes tries to abolish the—or at least *that*—oedipal dilemma, to determine, once and for all, what a father is, to remove all ambivalence, to put a stop to all those oscillations. In doing so, however, Hobbes, the Monster, the eighteenth century's favorite political immoralist, ends in a strange place when he locates the origin of power in the appeal of an infant in need.

So nothing changes, and everything changes. Father and king still have the same powers and for the same reasons,[8] but those

---

8   In some regard, paternal power actually exceeds political power, since the father has the unquestionable right to kill his children, which the monarch does not.

reasons are different now, and fatherhood has become unmoored from everything that had rendered it a self-evident model of legitimacy. Hobbes's reflections on fatherhood, I suggest, will work their effect in a ricochet of de- and re-metaphorization, or, to put it perhaps more accurately, in the contest of competing literalizations. To stay within the ballistic metaphor, Hobbes's shot is directed at all who would dilute the absolute power of the sovereign, but it goes astray when Sir Robert Filmer throws himself into the path of the bullet. In one of the great ironies of reception, the radical royalist Filmer, whose political project is in some regards infinitely close to that of *Leviathan*, objects to Hobbes's monarchy in the name of the patriarchy. These days, Filmer and his articulation of the long-lived theory of the divine right of kings is known almost exclusively as the target of Locke's and Rousseau's parodies, but his response to Hobbes is oddly prescient. In *Patriarcha*, Filmer insists that all power is the power of the father, traded down in direct line from Adam, and through Adam from God himself. Since for him, natural law is always already divine law, Filmer is acutely aware of the subversive implications of Hobbes's radical secularization of paternity:

> I see not . . . how the children of Adam, or of any man else, can be free from subjection to their parents. And this subjection of children being the fountain of all regal authority, by the ordination of God himself; it follows that civil power not only in general is by divine institution, but even the assignment of it specifically to the eldest parents, which quite takes away that new and common distinction which refers only power universal and absolute to God, but power respective in regard of the special form of government to the choice of the people. (*Patriarcha*, 7)

It has not been established whether Filmer had read *Leviathan* when he wrote *Patriarcha*, but Hobbes had already developed his theses on paternity both in *Elements of Law* and in *De Cive*, and in 1652, Filmer published *Observations Concerning the Original of Government upon Mr Hobbes Leviathan* that leave no doubt that he considers Hobbes, fellow absolutist, to be one of his targets. He is particularly incensed by Hobbes's comments on gender. Quoting Hobbes's assertion that "the mother originally hath the government of her children," he replies, in an act of biblical hermeneutics that would strike most readers as perhaps excessively creative:

> But we know that God at the creation gave the sovereignty to the man over the woman, as being the nobler and principal agent of generation. As to the objection that it is not known who is the

father to the son, but by the discovery of the mother, and that he is son to whom the mother will, and therefore he is the mother's, the answer is that it is not at the will of the mother to make whom she please the father, for if the mother be not in possession of a husband, the child is not reckoned to have any father at all. (*Patriarcha*, 192)

There are any number of curiosities here, not least of all the degree to which Filmer and Hobbes agree. Both categorically dismiss the idea of spermal fatherhood as determinative,[9] both identify the father as sovereign over the mother, and both argue in favor of the child's unconditional submission to paternal authority—Hobbes's parental "contract," is, after all, hardly an express consent but an exchange "by other sufficient arguments declared" (*Leviathan*, 182). More importantly, both are deeply beholden to the principle of singular power—one parent, one sovereign, one god. But where Hobbes develops his case for the unitary executive, as it were, on the basis of a static universal structure of sovereignty, Filmer sticks to scripture and inscribes paternity itself genealogically. If paternal rule, along with the expansion of dynastic patriarchies into the state,[10] depends on the subjection of the mother, as Hobbes suggests with rare clarity, Filmer traces it back to the motherless creatio ex-nihilo itself. Parental power doesn't have to devolve into paternal power—with Genesis, absolute paternity is its very origin.

While sacred and profane histories lead to the same place, it is Filmer who understands that the rhetoric of absolutism needs to be anchored metaphysically and affectively if it is to survive. In the last grand clarion call on behalf of the paternal triad, *Patriarcha* marshals every one of its fundamental terms: God, king, nature. Filmer recognizes that the deep threat social contract theory poses to the theopolitical

---

9 I strongly disagree with Carole Pateman's assessment that for Filmer "the procreative power of the father was the origin of political right" (Pateman, 3). It is not Hobbes or the later contract theorists who institute "the sexual contract," as Pateman argues; like Aristotle, patriarchalists such as Filmer fully understood that paternal right rests on conjugal right.

10 See *De Cive*, IX §10: "A *Father*, with his *sonnes* and *servants* growne into a civill Person by vertue of his paternall jurisdiction, is called a FAMILY. This *family*, if through multiplying of *children*, and acquisition of *servants*, it becomes numerous, insomuch as without casting the uncertain dye of warre, it cannot be subdued, will be termed an *Hereditary Kingdome*; which though it differ from an *institutive Monarchy*, being acquired by force in the original, & manner of its constitution; yet being constituted, it hath al the same properties, and the Right of authority is every where the same, insomuch as it is not needfull to speak any thing of them apart." *De Cive*, 126.

order of things had everything to do with the fate of the paternal trope. Identifying fatherhood as a crucial issue of divine royalisms old and new is a noticeably astute move, and it is important to keep in mind that "the Filmerian position," as bizarre as it has come to sound, "very nearly became the official state ideology"[11] by the end of the seventeenth century. His literalist fervor, however, pushed the concept of singularity and continuity to the breaking point, and so his owl flies at semiotic dusk. His account is so rigid that its fantasmatic flavor earns it almost immediate ridicule by Algernon Sidney, then Locke and later Rousseau. *Patriarcha* may well be the clearest exposition of the logic of the paternal triad ever written—but it seems as if its imagery could emerge fully only while slowly fading from view.

Nothing demonstrates the radical novelty of Hobbes's account of fatherhood as clearly as the misunderstandings to which it has given rise, to this day. Roughly speaking, there are two diametrically opposed ways in which his readers get it wrong. Either, they reinscribe into Hobbes's theories the every elements of the paternal triad he had erased, or they assume that Hobbes weakens paternal power. Thus, the conservative writer David Blankenhorn, who considers absent fathers "our most urgent social problem," writes, quoting Philip Abbott and Jean Bethke Elshtain:

> By contrast, in "meer Nature, where there are no Matrimoniall lawes," males simply impregnate females, then move on. All responsibility for children is "in the Mother." This argument leads the contemporary political philosopher Philip Abbott to observe that, "for Hobbes, 'paternity is absent in the state of nature.'" Conversely, as Jean Bethke Elshtain puts it, Hobbes's philosophy clearly suggests that "fatherhood is a defining characteristic of civil society." For Hobbes, in short, the emergence of fatherhood as a social role for men signifies the transition from barbarism to society.[12]

Of course, Hobbes nowhere claims that fathers, in a hypothetical state of nature, "simply impregnate females, then move on"—he is entirely silent on this question, and Blankenhorn's paraphrase is far more indebted to contemporary conservative cultural anxieties than to anything Hobbes wrote. All responsibility is *not* in the mother: in fact, Hobbes's birth

---

11 Gordon Schochet, *The Authoritarian Family and Political Attitudes in Seventeenth-Century England: Patriarchalism in Political Thought* (New Brunswick, NJ: Transaction Publishers, 1988), 193.

12 David Blankenhorn, *Fatherless America: Confronting Our Most Urgent Social Problem* (New York: Basic Books, 1995), 181.

mothers have no responsibility toward their children whatsoever. Neither is it the case that Hobbes identifies fatherhood as a "defining characteristic of civil society"—he identifies it as a historically contingent characteristic of most societies, one contract among others, and one decided in favor of mothers often enough. Paternity isn't "absent" in the state of nature, either: paternity, as far as Hobbes is concerned, is simply the relation of a male who has taken possession of a child or of someone else who is in possession of a child and, in a position to either let it live or let it die, chooses to nurture it. Since no child who depends on nurturance for its survival is ever *in* the state of nature anyway,[13] the question of whether it has a mother or a father is fully contingent, with the birth mother merely being its first potential sovereign, and in no way obligated to remain in that position. While *Leviathan* is clear on all that, *Elements of Law* spells out the implications so drastically as to make Abraham look like a bleeding-heart sentimentalist:

> Children therefore, whether they be brought up and preserved by the father, or by the mother, or by whomsoever, are in most absolute subjection to him or her, that so bringeth them up, or preserveth them. And they may alienate them, that is, assign his or her dominion, by selling or giving them in adoption or servitude to others; or may pawn them for hostages, kill them for rebellion, or sacrifice them for peace, by the law of nature, when he or she, in his or her conscience, think it to be necessary.[14]

Note not only the recurrent "he or she," "his or her," but note, perhaps even more importantly, "or by whomsoever"—neither gender nor biological relationship makes any difference when it comes to defining parental power. Martinich is mostly correct in stating that "mothers have a superior claim to men in the governance of their children, because everyone has the right to their own body and children begin as part of their mothers' bodies," but that claim is not so much "superior" as merely precedent to other claims,[15] and immediately superseded should the mother herself be under the dominion of a man (or, for that matter, another woman).[16]

---

13 *De Cive*, IX §2, states explicitly that only "men of riper yeares are to be accounted equall." *De Cive*, 122.
14 Thomas Hobbes, *The Elements of Law, Natural and Politic: Human Nature and De Corpore Politico*, ed. J. C. A. Raskin (Oxford: Oxford Universirity Press, 1999), 132.
15 Aloysius Martinich, *Hobbes: A Biography* (Cambridge: Cambridge University Press 1999), 157.
16 *De Cive*, IX §§4-5 lists the conditions under which a mother loses her dominion: voluntarily, by exposing the child; if she is taken prisoner; if she is "under what government soever"; if she enters a matrimonial contract that specifies that she submit to her spouse's authority. *De Cive*, 124.

Glen Newey identifies a number of other "writers [for whom] Hobbes remains a mouthpiece for patriarchal orthodoxy," quoting R. W. K. Hinton, Leo Strauss, and Carol Pateman as well as a number of writers who have expressed their doubts on this matter, such as R. A. Chapman or Joanne H. Wright, a list by no means exhaustive on either side.[17] One of the best-known analyses along those lines, of course, is Carol Pateman's *Sexual Contract*. Pateman claims that "Hobbes is a patriarchal theorist but the possibility that is considered by neither conventional political theorists nor feminists is that he is a patriarchalist who rejects paternal right" (54). Of course, they *shouldn't* consider that possibility, because Hobbes does no such thing. For Hobbes, paternal right is absolute: it is simply not the essentialized paternal right of old, grounded in either procreation or divine decree.

An instructive example of the widespread habit of reading Hobbes through the lens of the paternal triad he abolished comes from the eighteenth-century historian Catharine Macaulay, an early feminist critic of both Hobbes and monarchy:

> That the universe is governed by one God we will not dispute; and will also add, that God has an undoubted right to govern what he has himself created, and that it is beneficial to the creature to be governed by the Father of all things; but that this should be an argument for a man to govern what he has not created, and with whom a nation can have no such paternal connexion is a paradox which Mr. Hobbes has left unsolved. . . . [I]f Mr. Hobbes could prove that paternal power instituted by God was monarchical, he cannot from this conclude that the monarchical government is preferable to all others, without falling into his usual absurdities, viz. that a man ought to have a right of governing creatures whom he has not generated, because God has given him the right of governing creatures whom he has generated.[18]

---

17 Glen Newey, "Not a Woman-Hater: Hobbes' Critique of Patriarchy," in *The Politics of Gender: A Survey* (London: Routledge, 2010), 11; Hinton, "Husbands, Fathers, and Conquerors I," *Political Studies* 15 (1967): 291–300; Strauss, *The Political Philosophy of Hobbes: Its Basis and Its Genesis*, trans. E. Sinclair (Chicago: University Chicago of Press, 1952); Chapman, "Leviathan Writ Small: Thomas Hobbes on the Family," *American Political Science Review* 69, no. 1 (1975): 76–90; Wright, "Going Against the Grain: Hobbes's Case for Original Maternal Dominion," *Journal of Women's History* 14 (2002): 123–55.
18 Catharine Macaulay, "Loose remarks on certain positions found in Mr. Hobbes's philosophical rudiments of government and society with a short sketch of a democratical form of government in a letter to Signior Paoli (London: W. Johnson in Ludgate-Street. T. Davies in Russell-Street Covent-Garden.

Her critique of the paternal triad is astute—she identifies the instability of the metaphoric operation in which the difference can at any point supersede sameness, here because the monarch differs from both God and father because he has not "generated" his subjects. Hobbes, of course, neither derived political power from divine power (though he did point to the monarchical nature of divine rule) nor did he base paternal power on generation. It is a demonstration of the tremendous reach of the triad that even one of its fiercest critics cannot conceive of its absence in a justification of monarchies.

Hobbes, however, has not so much refuted or dismissed all the elements that have kept the institution of fatherhood simultaneously unstable and resilient as he has unlinked and demetaphorized them. There is still a monarchic deity (at least, I side with those who do not read Hobbes as an atheist), but divine monarchy does not confer legitimacy on human monarchs. There is no new theory of procreation here, but procreation no longer confers any ethical obligations toward nor any rights over the procreated. The king is no longer the father of his subjects—he merely has the same rights over them because he renders them the same services a father renders his children. And he is no longer a "he," or even a natural person. As Newey points out,

> the theory of "absolute" sovereignty that Hobbes advanced in *Leviathan* is gender-neutral, for more than one reason. It is gender-neutral because the entity that wields sovereignty in the theory need not be a natural person at all: it may be a committee or other corporate body, and it is in the nature of such bodies to be genderless. In addition, even given that . . . Hobbes makes explicit his preference for a polity in which the sovereign *is* a natural person rather than a corporate body, at no point does Hobbes make any sugestion that this person must or should be a male. . . . The conclusion follows, that power for Hobbes is not gendered. It is not simply that Hobbes fails to identify political or domestic power as essentially masculine: he goes to some lengths in all his three major political works to deny this. (12)

In consequence, but far more shockingly, "paternal dominion" is no longer gendered, either. To the extent that "father" names a power relation, fathers are now accidentally male, not by any innate necessity.

E. and C. Dilly in the Poultry. J. Almon in Piccadilly. Robinson and Roberts in Pater-Noster Row. And T. Cadell in the Strand, 1769), quoted in Wendy Gunther-Canada, "Catharine Macaulay on the Paradox of Paternal Authority in Hobbesian Politics," *Hypatia* 21, no. 2 (Spring 2006): 150–73.

It is easy to see why Hobbes's contemporaries, and not only they, would be deeply troubled by this tabula rasa of paternity. Elements of his critique of fatherhood will prove extraordinarily fruitful—to the extent that they are adopted, but also to the extent that they are vigorously refuted. I imagine it would be possible to read the history of polical theory for the following hundred years as one sustained exercise to restore to either fatherhood or political power or to both (either separately or in conjunction) their affective, metaphysical, and gendered foundations. If such a history were to be written, it would include passages like the ones that follow below. This little collection is not meant to demonstrate a linear progression toward a consensus on fatherhood—no such consensus emerges—, nor is it meant to suggest that Hobbes's theses on fatherhood work their way through political theory in a determinate fashion. On the contrary, it is safe to say that Hobbes's view of paternity never took hold, certainly not in unadulterated form, but that he left to his successors the task of reinventing fatherhood as a category of benign, legitimate rule in the vacuum of its secularization.

Locke inherits from Hobbes the theory that paternal power is not innately superior to maternal power but turns the argument against Hobbes by refusing the latter's assertion that sovereignty must be indivisible. In an early linguistic turn of sorts, he insists that "it may not be amiss to offer new [words and names], when the old are apt to lead men into mistakes, as this of *paternal power* probably has done." Disagreeing with both Hobbes and Filmer, he posits that motherhood and fatherhood have equal claims to parental power and concludes:

> it will but very ill serve the turn of those men, who contend so much for the absolute power and authority of the *fatherhood*, as they call it, that the mother should have any share in it; and it would have but ill supported the *monarchy* they contend for, when by the very name it appeared, that that fundamental authority, from whence they would derive their government of a single person only, was not placed in one, but two persons jointly.[19]

Shaftesbury resurrects the *zoon politikon* against Hobbes's rabid anti-Aristotelianism and simply *posits* parental affection as the correlate of the naturalness of sexual desire, a claim that has little to recommend itself theoretically but has resonated powerfully:

> In short, if generation be natural, if natural affection and the care and nurture of the offspring be natural, things standing as they

---

19 John Locke, *Two Treatises on Government* (Oxford, 1821), 230.

do with man and the creature being of that form and constitution he now is, it follows that society must be also natural to him and that out of society and community he never did, nor ever can, subsist.[20]

Rousseau, contra Hobbes, resurrects the traditional view that "the most ancient of all societies, and the only one that is natural, is the [patriarchal] family," but contends that "even so the children remain attached to the father only so long as they need him for their preservation," temporalizing both power and obligation.[21]

Kant's essay "On the common saying: 'This may be true in theory, but it does not apply in practice'" (1793) contains a chapter, "On the relationship of theory to practice in political right," that is subtitled, in brackets, "(Against Hobbes)." At first glance, it appears to be true that "Kant leaves his Hobbes-criticism implicit," as Timo Airaksinen and Arto Siitonen claim.[22] But Kant bases his case on his rejection of the Hobbesian claim that sovereign power and paternal power are one and the same, resurrecting it as a metaphorical association only to dismantle it on metaphorical grounds and then suggesting a metaphorical solution (this is one of many passages that should lay to rest the perennial misunderstanding of Kant as a foe of tropes):

> A government might be established on the principle of benevolence towards the people, *like* that of a father towards his children. Under such a paternal government, the subjects, *as* immature children who cannot distinguish what is truly useful or harmful to themselves, would be obliged to behave purely passively and to rely upon the judgment of the head of state as to how they ought to be happy, and upon his kindness in willing their happiness at all. Such a government is the greatest conceivable despotism, i. e., a constitution which suspends the entire freedom of its subjects, who thenceforth have no rights whatsoever. The only conceivable government for men who are capable of possessing rights, even if the ruler is benevolent, is not a paternal but a patriotic government. A patriotic attitude is one where everyone in the state, not excepting its head, regards the commonwealth *as*

---

20 Anthony Ashley Cooper, Third Earl of Shaftesbury, *Characteristics of Men, Manners, Opinions, Time,* ed. Lawrence E. Klein (Cambridge: Cambridge University Press, 1999), 283.
21 Jean Jacques Rousseau, *Social Contract & Discourses*, trans. and intro. G. D. H. Cole (New York: E. P. Dutton & Co., 1913), 6.
22 "Kant on Hobbes, Peace, and Obedience," *History of European Ideas* 30 (2004): 315.

a maternal womb, or the land *as* the paternal ground from which he himself sprang and which he must leave to his descendants as a treasured pledge. (Emphases added)[23]

Note that Kant appears to suggest that maternal or paternal tropes will do equally well as long as they remain tied to the commons rather than to government.

The most drastic solution to the problem of fatherhood is also the most short-lived: By 1793, a draft of the new *Code Civil* declares that "The imperious voice of reason has made itself heard; it says, no more paternal power."[24] The sentence is missing from the code's final version.

---

23 Immanuel Kant, "On the common saying: 'This may be true in theory, but it does not apply in practice'," *Political Writings* (Cambridge: Cambridge University Press, 1991), 74.
24 Quoted in Emile Masson, *La puissance paternelle et la famille sous la Révolution* (Paris, 1910), 227.

Section IV
The Rise of the Son

Eight Lessing: Paternal Abdication

"I Will Be King No More"
G. E. Lessing, *Philotas*

On September 27, 2008, John S. D. Eisenhower, "the only living presidential son to serve in combat while his father was in office," relates a conversation he had with his father in 1952, discussing his assignation to an infantry unit fighting in Korea. Young Eisenhower explains his reason for refusing alternative assignments and continues:
"My father, as a professional officer himself, understood and accepted it. However, he had a firm condition: under no circumstances must I ever be captured. He would accept the risk of my being killed or wounded, but if the Chinese Communists or North Koreans ever took me prisoner, and threatened blackmail, he could be forced to resign the presidency. I agreed to that condition wholeheartedly. I would take my life before being captured."[1] John Eisenhower concludes in retrospect that he had been "unfair and selfish and that my father was being far too conciliatory in giving me such permission," and he advocates that the children of high government officials should stay out of combat altogether, a solution that would spare at least *those* fathers a potentially wrenching test of their loyalties or, worse, apparently, force them to choose fatherhood over office and resign. Eisenhower gives no indication that he is aware of having reenacted an ancient mythical conflict, but we can safely assume that G. E. Lessing, who marshals Greek and Roman mythemes with frequency and enthusiasm, was deeply familiar with it when he wrote the strange little tragedy *Philotas* (1759).

The plot is simple: Philotas, a young prince who has worn the *toga virilis* for only seven days, begs his wounded father, the king, for permission to enter the ongoing war with Aridaeus, his father's former friend. On his first battle, Philotas is wounded and captured by Aridaeus's army. The action takes place in Aridaeus's camp; the dramatis personae include Aridaeus, his general Strato, and the soldier Parmenio, a member of the army of Philotas's father. Philotas,

---

[1] John S. D. Eisenhower, "Presidential Children Don't Belong in Battle," *New York Times*, Op-Ed, September 28, 2008, http://www.nytimes.com/2008/09/28/opinion/28eisenhower.html

humiliated, fears that his capture will force his father to surrender. As coincidence will have it, however, Aridaeus's son Polytimet is captured as well, and the stage appears set for a simple exchange of prisoners. Instead, Philotas decides to kill himself in his father's (presumed) political interest. In response, King Aridaeus indicates he will make any concession to have his own son returned and announces that he will abdicate his throne once Polytimet is back safely. The play closes with King Aridaeus addressing the weeping Strato over Philotas's body:

> Do cry for him! —Me too! —Come! I need to have my son back. And don't interfere (*rede mir nicht ein*) if I buy him too dearly! — In vain we have spilled rivers of blood; in vain conquered lands. There he strides away with our prey, the greater victor. —Come! Get me my son! And once I have him, I will be King no more. Do you people believe that one doesn't get fed up?[2]

Philotas recuperates Laius's tragic dilemma—personal vs. political fatherhood, the survival of the state vs. the survival of the son—, but he introduces into it a new logic I'm tempted to call filisuicide: the son sacrificing himself in the name of the father and in the interest of the state, but, we are led to presume, in violation of his father's actual desire.

One of *Philotas*'s most noticeable features is the absence of any female figures. The female exclusively figures metaphorically, and predominantly in Philotas's casually misogynist rants: he complains about the luxury of the tent in which he is held and suspects it of belonging to the king's concubines (*Beischläferinnen*). He requests that the king encounter him "as a soldier, not as a woman."[3] He makes Parmenio, his father's soldier, swear an oath according to which Parmenio's son "would become the mockery of women"[4] should he

---

2   "Beweine ihn nur!—Auch ich!--Komm! Ich muß meinen Sohn wieder haben! Aber rede mir nicht ein, wenn ich ihn zu teuer erkaufe!—Umsonst haben wir Ströme Bluts vergossen; umsonst Länder erobert. Da zieht er mit unserer Beute davon, der größere Sieger!—Komm! Schaffe mir meinen Sohn! Und wenn ich ihn habe, will ich nicht mehr König sein. Glaubt ihr Menschen, daß man es nicht satt wird?—(Gehen ab.)" Scene 8.

3   "Aber höre, wenn du der bist, dessen Miene du trägst—bist du ein alter ehrlicher Kriegsmann, so nimm dich meiner an, und bitte den König, daß er mir als einem Soldaten, und nicht als einem Weibe begegnen lasse." Scene 2.

4   "Wenn du dein Wort nicht hältst, so möge dein Sohn ein Feiger, ein Nichtswürdiger werden; er möge, wenn er zwischen Tod und Schande zu wählen hat, die Schande wählen; er möge neunzig Jahre ein Spott der Weiber leben, und noch im neunzigsten Jahre ungern sterben." Scene 5.

break his word. When Aridaeus tells him that he is listening "with astonishment," Philotas responds, dismissively, "Oh, you could listen to a woman with astonishment as well."[5] He talks about "effeminate" princes, and when Parmenio compares Philotas's wound to the love bites of an "ardent girl," Philotas responds, "what do I know about these things."[6]

This discourse of effeminacy, which comes so easily to Philotas, is not echoed by the adult men, the king, the general, and the soldier, with one notable exception. Aridaeus, shocked at Philotas's suicide, flies into a brief rage: "But take this, take this one tormenting thought with you: as a truly inexperienced boy you believed that all fathers are of the same kind, of the weak, womanly kind to which your father belongs. They are not! I am not! What do I care about my son?"[7] Aridaeus's filicidal flash, however, subsides quickly, and he orders his general to make any politcal concession necessary to regain Polytimet.

Misogyny, then, emerges as an integral part of the filisuicidal structure Philotas has internalized. At the same time, the father, as is typical for many of Lessing's plays, usurps the maternal position: "If I knew that the young madcap did not at all moments long for his father, and did not long for his father the way a lamb longs for his mother: in that case I would just as well not have fathered him,"[8] Parmenio says, thinking about his own son. In other words, the strictly dyadic structure of this family, if family we want to call it, bars Philotas from all possibility of oedipal revolt, and Philotas is hostage to a notion of fatherhood that is simultaneously excessive and lacking. Even his suicidal liberation is framed in terms of this dyad: when he kills himself, he declares, "my father's son is free."[9]

This point is born out by Lessing's dramatis personae, which does not list Philotas's father, one of the strongest dramatic presences in absence I can think of. Unlisted, he remains unnamed as well: throughout the play, he is simply "my father." Second, three of the characters are listed

---

5 "Ach!—Auch ein Weib kann man mit Erstaunen hören!" Scene 7.
6 "Parmenio. Ein kleines liebes Andenken. Dergleichen uns ein inbrünstiges Mädchen in die Lippe beißt. Nicht wahr, Prinz?—Philotas. Was weiß ich davon?" Scene 5.
7 "Stirb nur! stirb! Aber nimm das mit, nimm den quälenden Gedanken mit: Als ein wahrer unerfahrner Knabe hast du geglaubt, daß die Väter alle von einer Art, alle von der weichlichen, weiblichen Art deines Vaters sind.—Sie sind es nicht alle! Ich bin es nicht! Was liegt mir an meinem Sohne?" Scene 8.
8 "Aber wüßte ich, daß sich der junge Wildfang nicht in allen Augenblicken, die ihm der Dienst frei läßt, nach seinem Vater sehnte, und sich nicht so nach ihm sehnte, wie sich ein Lamm nach seiner Mutter sehnet: so möchte ich ihn gleich—siehst du!—nicht erzeugt haben." Scene 5.
9 "Dein Sohn, König, ist gefangen; und der Sohn meines Vaters ist frei." Scene 8.

alongside their occupations: Aridaeus, King; Parmenio, Soldier; Strato, General. Philotas himself, however, appears neither as prince nor as soldier but as *captured* or *caught* (*gefangen*). Captured literally, he is also caught in a lethal mode of speech, thought, and feeling marked in equal parts by a code of hypermasculinity and childlike dependency on the image of the father who remains nameless perhaps precisely because he is a filial fantasm.

From *Miss Sara Sampson* to *Philotas, Emilia Galotti,* and *Nathan der Weise* (*Nathan the Wise*),[10] Lessing, Germany's premier dramatist of paternity, will be obsessed with rearticulating the status of the father within monotheism's intellectual endgame. Increasingly indebted to Spinoza, whose deanthropologization of the divine was also a determined depaternalization, Lessing seeks to reground paternal power as moral authority, uncoupled from discourses of either nature or divinity. In this last regard, he is a Hobbesian, but like most eighteenth-century critics of Hobbes, foremost among them Shaftesbury, he reacts to the denaturalization and detheologization of power by a remoralization of authority.

Philotas has all the hallmarks of programmatic literature, beginning with its relentless dualities—two kings, two sons, two soldiers, two captures—and dualisms—war/ peace, friendship/enmity, fatherhood/ sonhood, fatherhood/ kingship, state/family, feeling/calculation, and so on. In contrast to Lessing's other plays, and in this regard resembling Athenian tragedy more closely than most eighteenth-century tragic production, *Philotas* has no apparent villains. Everybody's intentions are honorable, and Philotas himself is the ultimate object of male-male social desire: charming, beautiful, eloquent, and endearingly tempestuous, he qualifies for instant adoption by the numerous paternal figures that surround him.[11] In the absence of Philotas's father, fatherliness itself abounds. The structural symmetry of the setup is violently shattered when Philotas removes himself from the simple trade in sons to which the fathers are committed.

From the beginning, the play stages the failure of the exchange as an effect of the tension between familial fatherhood and the symbolic paternity of kingship. Before he learns of Polytimet's capture, Philotas laments: "What I held to be my greatest happiness, the tender love with which my father loves me, turns into my greatest unhappiness. I fear,

---

10 *Gotthold Ephraim Lessing, Gesammelte Werke in zwei Bänden* (Munich: Hanser, 1959).
11 I confess myself baffled by Susan Gustafson's repeated claim that Philotas "draws no more sympathy in the play than his father" or that he is "unsympathetic to the audience." Susan Gustafson, "Abject Fathers and Suicidal Sons: Lessing's *Philotas* and Kristeva's *Black Sun*," *Lessing Yearbook* 24 (1997), 7.

I fear; he loves me more than he loves his empire."[12] Philotas speaks the language of rigid polarities: greatest happiness or greatest unhappiness, tenderly beloved or worst enemy. The ease with which the two poles reverse goes hand in hand with the system of equivalences the play upholds both in its structure and in its discourse. Thus, Parmenio is, in Philotas's words, "my father's Strato," and Aridaeus sums up the situation as follows: "Thus fate willed it! From equal scale pans it took equal weights, at the same time, and the scales remained equal still."[13]

The tension between equivalence and polarity comes to a head in the figure of the father-king: "Yes, Prince," Aridaeus responds to Philotas's impassioned speech about "wasting the blood" of his future subjects, "what is a king if he is no father! What is a hero without human kindness (*Menschenliebe*)?"[14] This is the language of the *Landesvater*, who, we assume, spills "rivers of blood" only with the kindest intentions: filicide is, after all, one of the mythical constants of paternity, both familial and symbolic. Accordingly, the happy congruence of paternity and kingship comes apart in Philotas's anguished vision: "When I die of shame and slink down to the shadows unlamented, how dark and proud will be the souls of the passing heroes who had to buy with their lives the king's advantages which as a father he forsook for an unworthy son."[15]

As we saw in Chapter 2, the post-Freudian reception of the Oedipal myth had either ignored King Laius or presented him as a sinister figure, defined not by the conflicting duties and inclinations that fatherhood bestows, but rather by the unadulterated desire to see his child dead. Lessing's texts, by contrast, are so fascinating precisely because they teeter on the cusp of patriarchal and filiarchal logics. Before Aridaeus instructs Strato to get his son back at any price, he impersonates, for a brief moment, the quintessential "bad father" John Munder Ross suspects Laius to be when he considers sacrificing Polytimet. Aridaeus, however, breaks down in this middle of his speech in an incoherent ejection marked once again by inversion and equivalence. "Strato, I am now orphaned, I poor man! —You have a son; be he mine!—for a son

---

12 "Was ich für mein größtes Glück hielt, die zärtliche Liebe, mit der mich mein Vater liebt, wird mein größtes Unglück. Ich fürchte, ich fürchte; er liebt mich mehr, als er sein Reich liebt!" Scene 2.
13 "So wollt' es das Schicksal! Aus gleichen Wagschalen nahm es auf einmal gleiche Gewichte, und die Schalen blieben noch gleich." Scene 3.
14 "Ja, Prinz; was ist ein König, wenn er kein Vater ist! Was ist ein Held ohne Menschenliebe!" Scene 7.
15 "Wann ich denn vor Scham sterbe und unbedauert hinab zu den Schatten schleiche, wie finster und stolz werden die Seelen der Helden bei mir vorbeiziehen, die dem Könige die Vorteile mit ihrem Leben erkaufen mußten, deren er sich als Vater für einen unwürdigen Sohn begibt." Scene 2.

one must have—fortunate Strato!" One must have a son in order to be a father, but one must sacrifice one's son(s) in order to be a *Landesvater*.[16]

When the dying Philotas reminds him that his own son is actually still alive, Aridaeus responds: "He still lives?—Then I must have him back. You just die! I will have him back anyway. And in exchange for you! Or I will inflict so much dishonor, so much disgrace onto your dead body!"[17] Again, Philotas interrupts the King: "The dead body!—If you want to take your revenge, King, so bring it back to life!" and Aridaeus relents: "Ach! Wo gerat ich hin!" The idiom is difficult to translate—we might render it as "Oh, where am I going with this," but the German, *hingeraten,* suggests an involuntary movement of speech, a discourse that has taken hold of Aridaeus and has deposited him at an unfamiliar place. If so, the veiled reference to the treatment of Hector's body would imply that Aridaeus's speech has now twice been taken over by two ancient discourses: like Philotas, he performs classical reception as interruption.

Read that way, the play, in good Enlightenment manner, stages the emergence of a new reason to take the place of the old stories, and Aridaeus's rapid reversal would allow us to observe the critical turn in action: the political model organized around filicide and cruelty gives way to one characterized by *Menschenliebe*, love of humanity. The bad father who demands the son's death in the service of the state becomes the good father who, abdicating political power—"I will be king no more"—, protects him at all costs: Polytimet means "the dearly bought one."

Such tragic optimism, however, is undercut by the fact that the play can only imagine decisions *as* paternal decisions, for better or for worse. After all, all actors' speech affirms the very logic under critique: everybody implicitly or explicitly accepts Philotas's assertion that acting in the interest of the son means to act against the interest of the state, and the play's multiple substitute fathers not only hasten to admire and enable young Philotas's heroic perorations, but expect him, in classic tragic irony, to surpass his father once he accedes to the throne. Philotas, in sum, is just a bit too lovable, and while any reading that sees the play as patriotically endorsing Philotas's sacrifice strikes me as severely off the mark, there is indeed a dark attraction to it that pervades the tragedy.

The affirmative readings, however, that celebrate *Philotas* as a play that replaces patriarchal logics with Enlightenment *Menschenliebe* have

---

16 "Strato, ich bin nun verwaiset, ich armer Mann!—Du hast einen Sohn; er sei der meinige!—Denn einen Sohn muß man doch haben." Scene 8.

17 "Lebt er noch?—So muß ich ihn wieder haben. Stirb du nur! Ich will ihn doch wieder haben! Und für dich!—Oder ich will deinem toten Körper so viel Unehre, so viel Schmach erzeigen lassen!—Ich will ihn—" Scene 8.

to repress what here emerges as the *actual* locus of split paternity: the discourse of the son. While Aridaeus quickly disavows the language that threatens to take hold of him—"Ach, wo gerat ich hin!"—, Philotas insists on it. He is the one who introduces the image of the father-king in conflict, and unlike the tragedy's embodied father figures, he never abandons it. In his first speech, he declares that "my earliest childhood has never dreamed of anything but weapons and camps and battles and storms," another curious phrase that suggests that we are spoken (or dreamt) as much as we speak (or dream). The recollection is preceded by his first words, and the first words of the play as a whole: "So I am truly caught?—Caught!" ("So bin ich wirklich gefangen?—Gefangen!") and he imagines, for a brief moment, that his capture is as much of a dream as his early childhood battles. But we may also read the language of the dreams of war as that which has captured him and will not let go.

The language of thoughts unbidden certainly makes a powerful reappearance later in the play. After articulating, at great length, the untenable situation into which he believes he has placed his father, Philotas says:

> And now—which thought was it I just thought? No; which a god thought within me—I must follow it (*ihm nachhaengen*)! Let yourself be bound, fleeting thought!—Now I'm thinking it again! How widely it spreads, and yet wider; and now it radiates through my entire soul![18]

He has not caught the thought, it appears, but rather the thought has caught him. Philotas, who suspects that his father may love him more than he loves his empire, outflanks such suspect paternal desire in the name of a thought that "a god" thinks within him. Such is the beauty of the paternal triad: its positions are not only highly mobile, they are indeed interchangeable, and if the father-king proves inadequate to the demands his political incarnation imposes on him, a higher instance can think differently. In such cases, *Philotas* suggests, agency (if we may still call it that) reverts to the son who acts in the name of symbolic paternity. "The son," Philotas says to Parmenio, stalling the exchange, "is done with you, but not the prince. That one must feel; this one must think. How gladly the son would be around his beloved father, right now, sooner than possible; but the prince—the prince cannot."

---

18 "Und nun—welcher Gedanke war es, den ich itzt dachte? Nein; den ein Gott in mir dachte—Ich muß ihm nachhängen! Laß dich fesseln, flüchtiger Gedanke!—Itzt denke ich ihn wieder! Wie weit er sich verbreitet, und immer weiter; und nun durchstrahlt er meine ganze Seele!" Scene 4.

The German syntax, impossible to reproduce in translation, opens up a vast distance between son and beloved father: "Wie gern wollte der Sohn gleich itzt, wie gern wollte er noch eher, als möglich, wieder um seinen Vater, um seinen geliebten Vater sein; aber der Prinz—der Prinz kann nicht" (scene 5). For the first time, as far as I know, it is no longer paternity that is split between familial and symbolic, father and king, but filiality.

While the father, then, imagines that the son longs for him like the lamb longs for its mother, the son's own desires emerge as more complex. They call for a father both tender and terrible, and if the father refuses to act in the name of the law, the son will shoulder the paternal burden: "Should I not judge myself more strictly than they and my father judge me?"[19] Philotas asks. Against its overt endorsement of a new and newly benign fatherhood, then, the play produces a subtext that heralds the father of modernity, who rejects the ancient filicidal demands only to be rejected in turn by the children who will enforce them against the father's "womanish" weakness. The patriarchy is at its most effective, in other words, if fathers no longer need to sacrifice their children because the children sacrifice themselves to an idea of paternity that no longer requires name, embodiment, or, ultimately, fathers.

Lessing will return to this variable structure several times, searching for a paternal position the Enlightenment can no longer support— the cultural investment in the image of the good father comes up hard against the philosophical-political investment in the autonomous individual—or rather, the *male* autonomous individual. Hence, *Philotas* has to impose paternal power upon himself, and Lessing turns to daughters.

Given the extensive scholarship on Lessing and fatherhood,[20] I will keep my comments brief and stress some aspects I believe have

---

19 "Soll ich mich nicht strenger richten, als sie und mein Vater mich richten?" Scene 4.
20 Of particular interest are Judith Frömmer, *Vaterfiktionen: Empfindsamkeit und Patriarchat im Zeitalter der Aufklärung* (Munich: Fink, 2008); Susan E. Gustafson, *Absent Mothers and Orphaned Fathers: Narcissism and Abjection in Lessing's Aesthetic and Dramatic Production* (Detroit, MI: Wayne State University Press, 1995); Peter Horst Neumann, *Der Preis der Mündigkeit: Über Lessings Dramen* (Stuttgart: Klett-Cotta, 1977); Claudia Nitschke, *Der öffentliche Vater: Konzeptionen paternaler Souveränität in der deutschen Literatur (1755–1921)* (Berlin: Walter de Gruyter, 2012); Brigitte Prutti, *Bild und Körper: Weibliche Präsenz und Geschlechterbeziehungen in Lessings Dramen* (Würzburg: Königshausen und Neumann, 1996); Helmut J. Schneider, "Lebenstatsachen: Geburt und Adoption bei Lessing und Kleist," *Kleist-Jahrbuch* (2002): 21–41. This is by no means an exhaustive list of relevant literature, but it represents a reasonably representative range of interpretations.

been neglected. To be sure, it has hardly escaped critics' attention that Lessing's fathers, with the exception of *Philotas*'s nameless king, are fathers of daughters and that their mothers are largely absent.[21] Susan Gustafson's reading of the "absent mothers, orphaned fathers" in Lessing's work remains one of the most coherent and complete explorations of Lessing's somewhat startling family configurations, but I suspect that psychoanalytic readings such as hers are driven by twentieth-century investments in the tragic family, that is to say by Freudian and post-Freudian models that can conceive of fatherhood only as a position within a necessarily and intrinsically triadic structure of father-mother-child, or Koschorke's "Holy Family."[22] Its most prominent manifestation would of course be the oedipal setup that introduces an element of sexual tension and insists on its centrality. I wonder, though, whether triadic kinship is not really a preoccupation of the nineteenth century and onward,[23] and whether, in particular, the Freudian family and the complexity of the maternal position within it are of relatively minor interest to much of eighteenth-century thought.

Friedrich Kittler famously argued that modernity from the Enlightenment on is dedicated to the production of the nuclear family

---

21 For a range of relevant commentary, see Gail K. Hart, "A Family Without Women: The Triumph of the Sentimental Father in Lessing's *Sara Sampson* and Klinger's *Sturm und Drang*," *Lessing Yearbook* 22 (1990): 113–32; Denis Jonnes, "Solche Väter: The Sentimental Family Paradigm in Lessing's Drama," *Lessing Yearbook* 12 (1981): 157–74; Friedrich A. Kittler, "Erziehung ist Offenbarung: Zur Struktur der Familie in Lessings Dramen," *Jahrbuch der deutschen Schiller-Gesellschaft* 21 (1977): 111–37; Manfred K. Kremer, "Does Emilia Use Force against Her Father? Reflections on Lessing's *Emilia Galotti*," *Lessing and the Enlightenment*, ed. Alexej Ugrinski (New York: Greekwood, 1986), 113–19; Ariane Neuhaus-Koch, *G. E. Lessing: Die Sozialstrukturen in seinen Dramen* (Bonn: Bouvier, 1977), 52f; Heidi Schlipphacke, "The Dialectics of Female Desire in G. E. Lessing's *Emilia Galotti*," *Lessing Yearbook* 33 (2001): 55–78; Inge Stephan, "'So ist die Tugend ein Gespenst': Frauenbild und Tugendbegriff im bürgerlichen Trauerspiel bei Lessing und Schiller," *Lessing Yearbook* 17 (1985): 1–20; Ingrid Walsøe-Engel, *Fathers and Daughters: Patterns of Seduction in Tragedies by Gryphius, Lessing, Hebbel and Kroetz* (Columbia, SC: Camden House, 1993); Karin Wurst, *Familiale Liebe ist die 'Wahre Gewalt': Die Repräsentation der Familie in G. E. Lessings dramatischem Werke* (Amsterdam: Rodopi, 1988).

22 Albrecht Koschorke, *Die Heilige Familie und ihre Folgen* (Frankfurt am Main: S. Fischer, 2000).

23 It is important to note, of course, that the nuclear family as a form of kinship organization precedes both the eighteenth and the nineteenth century, and that some scholars have argued for its remarkable stability. See Peter Laslett, *The World We Have Lost* (London: Methuen, 1965); ed. Peter Laslett and Richard Wall, *Household and Family in Past Time* (Cambridge: Cambridge University Press, 1972); Alan Macfarlane, *Marriage and Love in England: Modes of Reproduction 1300-1840* (Oxford: Blackwell, 1986).

as the dominant form of kinship, with the central position within the family shifting from the father to the mother:

"The lengthy process of reshaping the population of central Europe into modern nuclear families was directed by paternal figures only during its first phase in Germany, up to Lessing's time . . . In a second phase, which coincided with the Age of Goethe . . . mothers stepped into the position previously held by fathers."[24] I am not at all convinced that the eighteenth century's preoccupation with fathers and fatherhood is primarily directed toward the nuclear family, however, and Lessing would surely the worst possible example: *Philotas* has no female characters at all, *Miss Sara Sampson* and all the children of *Nathan the Wise* are motherless, and Emilia Galotti's mother, while certainly a plot catalyst at the tragedy's outset, becomes entirely irrelevant as the play progresses toward its climax.[25] If anything, Lessing's dramatic production reveals that the actual focus of eighteenth-century investigations into family structures is the fitful and troubled rewriting of paternity in the wake of Hobbes, Locke, Rousseau, and Spinoza, whose work—if in sometimes drastically divergent ways—combined to undermine the long reign of fatherhood as political metaphor, leaving a vacuum in the place where affect, law, and body had converged in a figure both violent and tender. The possibility of such convergence had long been so utterly crucial to the very idea of sociopolitical community, and it will prove so difficult to re-figure, that the reinvention of the father emerges as a central project. The time for reactionary theological projects such as Filmer's *Patriarcha* had passed—after all, long before Hegel and Nietzsche, Lessing's *Die Erziehung des Menschengeschlechts* (*The Education of Humanity*, 1780) suggests that God's historical task is his own abolition as moral instance.

Lessing could not imagine a world without fathers, but he certainly did understand that new fathers were needed, that fatherhood needed a different foundation. To be sure, he did not challenge monarchical power directly—neither in the political nor the familial realm. But Lessing's fathers can no longer take their authority for granted, it no longer accrues to them automatically—instead, fatherhood becomes an ethical position, grounded in and reinforced by affect, that is configured as being beyond the law—in fact, in both *Emilia Galotti* and

---

24 Friedrich A. Kittler, *Discourse Networks 1800/1900*, trans. Michael Metteer with Chris Cullens (Stanford, CA: Stanford University Press, 1990), 27.

25 I agree with Gustafson, *Absent Mothers*, that the erasure of motherhood is a significant and constitutive element of Lessing's construction of paternity, but this erasure, as I have shown in previous chapters, is common to the history of fatherhood, and not particular to Lessing.

Nathan the Wise, paternal power asserts itself explicitly as *illegal,* albeit in very different ways.

Why are Lessing's fathers fathers of daughters? At first glance, the father-daughter relationship has often (though by no means always) served to illustrate the gentle side of fatherhood—compare, say, Oedipus's relationship to Eteocles and Polyneices to his relationship to Antigone and Ismene. For Lessing, writing in the age of sentimentality, the greater emotional intimacy of the father-daughter dyad must have been part of its appeal—it is difficult to imagine Sara Sampson's father addressing his sorrow to a dying son in quite the same terms. As Gustafson suggests, "The father *wants* to locate his own ideal image within the confines of his relationship to his daughter" (14), and Lessing's ideal father is tender and protective. I suspect, though, that Lessing's daughters are, more importantly, a tacit acknowledgment that the father-son relationship can no longer serve to model natural authority. Under conditions of emerging political modernity, the stress is on the sons' autonomy, which the father-son plots of old cannot accommodate, while it is still easy to speak and think of daughters as their fathers' property; when Daja asks Nathan whether "you call everything you own yours with as much right [as you call Recha yours]," Nathan replies:

> Nothing with greater right! All what
> I own otherwise, nature and luck have
> Apportioned me. This property alone
> I owe to virtue.[26]

We find ourselves at the dawn of the filiarchy. Lessing relegates the politicized father-son dyad of *Philotas* to a fictional classical past in which its central paradox—filicide as both the climax and the abolition of paternity—forces the abdication of the father-king who has already left the stage (though he does need to leave his double behind). *Emilia Galotti,* closely related to *Philotas* in many ways, may well be the less radical yet the more symptomatic play—it is certainly more complex and more psychologically nuanced than the almost mathematically constructed *Philotas*. Again, though, we encounter a case of filisuicide, even if this one requires the father's active participation. When Odoardo Galotti's daughter, abducted by the ruling Prince Hettore's advisor Marinelli for political reasons disguised as erotic ones, reveals her fear that she will succumb to the seductions of the Prince and his court, Odoardo himself kills

---

26 "Nichts mit größerm! Alles, was/ Ich sonst besitze, hat Natur und Glück/ Mir zugeteilt. Dies Eigentum allein/ Dank ich der Tugend." *Nathan der Weise,* Act I, scene 1.

her—but only at her injunction. Once again, it is the child who demands her own death in the name of ancient—specifically Roman—fatherhood. If in *Philotas*, everybody wants to be father to the prince, in *Emilia Galotti*, everybody wants to be child to Odoardo. Appiani, the Countess Orsina, and finally Hettore Gonzaga himself succumb to his appeal: "O Galotti, if you wanted to be my friend, my guide, my father!" This is the benign version of fatherhood, casting Odoardo as the figure of virtue, wisdom, and bourgeois integrity. Emilia herself, however, faced with the threat of her desire that would remove her from her father's ethical sphere, insists that the essential gesture of true fatherhood is filicide. Evoking the Roman legend of Virginia, she shames Odoardo into violence:

> (*in a tone of bitterness, while she plucks the rose apart*): Long ago, there was indeed a father who, in order so save his daughter from shame, sunk the first steel at hand into her heart—gave her life for the second time. But all those deeds are of long ago. There are none such fathers anymore."[27]

When Virginius killed Virginia in order to remove her from the power of Appius Claudius, who sought to make her his mistress, he initiated a revolt that overthrew the decemvirs and restored the republic. German Studies has long debated whether *Emilia Galotti*'s variation on the Virginia motif ought to be read as an antifeudal political statement. Richard T. Gray argues that

> [w]hen Odoardo fails to use the dagger on the Prince, the seducer and commodifier of (female) subjects for whom it is intended, turning it instead against his own daughter, the object of the Prince's seduction and commodification, he implicitly throws his support behind the forces of alienation and mastery. Odoardo refused to strike a blow against the principles that the Prince and Marinelli represent; indeed, he himself becomes their accomplice insofar as he commits the ultimate act of violence against Emilia's subjectivity.[28]

---

27 "(In einem bitteren Tone, während daß sie die Rose zerpflückt.) Ehedem wohl gab es einen Vater, der seine Tochter von der Schande zu retten, ihr den ersten, den besten Stahl in das Herz senkte—ihr zum zweiten Male das Leben gab. Aber alle solche Taten sind von ehedem! Solcher Väter gibt es keinen mehr!" *Emilia Galotti*, Act V, scene 7.

28 Richard T. Gray, *Stations of the Divided Subject: Contestation and Ideological Legitimation in German Bourgeois Literature, 1770–1914* (Stanford, CA: Stanford University Press, 1995), 95. For a—to me—far more plausible reading, see Wolfgang Wittkowski, "Bürgerfreiheit oder –feigheit? Die Metapher des 'langen Weges' als Schlüssel zum Koordinatensystem in Lessings politischem Trauerspiel *Emilia Galotti*," *Lessing Yearbook* 27 (1985): 65–87.

It is rather difficult to argue from a contemporary perspective that a young woman who would rather die than be seduced is acting rationally and autonomously. We might do well to consider, however, that nothing in the play's text gives us license to understand Emilia's torment as anything but genuine. In Gray's reading, which erases Emilia's subjectivity in the very act of lamenting its destruction,[29] she oddly does not appear to act at all. This is all the more surprising as she is given the most intriguing line of the play, "What they call violence is nothing: seduction is the true violence."[30] If we take her at her word, then Odoardo's act of murder, surely the kind of thing "they call violence," is "nothing." The "true violence"—or power—resides in Emilia's capacity to seduce her father into killing her, forcing him to embody an ancient model of paternity against his will. As Schlipphacke points out, Odoardo's lack of conviction and authority prior to his final meeting with Emilia can be read, ironically, as his wish to escape his confining role of patriarch."[31]

In this—admittedly uncomfortable—reading, Lessing invokes in Odoardo the father as the master over life and death in the same way in which Sophocles invoked in Oedipus the father-as-king—to mark his demise in a dramatic and bloody climax. Odoardo Galotti is the figure of a turning—in this sense, he has no antagonist, because he is split within himself, both old father and new father. The tragedy's ambivalent ending, which neither endorses nor condemns Odoardo's act but rather inscribes it into a deeply unstable configuration of law and legitimacy, points to a dialectic of paternity that will take another two hundred years to unfold. In this light, it is precisely in *not* killing the Prince that the deeply political reconfiguration of an overtly private relationship reveals itself. Standing next to his dead daughter, Odoardo addresses the Prince:

> Well there, Prince! Do you still like her? Does she still incite your lust? Now, lying in her blood, which screams for revenge against you? (*after a pause*) But you are waiting to see where this is going? You expect, perhaps, that I will turn the steel against myself in order to conclude my deed like a stale tragedy? You are mistaken. Here! (*throwing the dagger at the Prince's feet*) Here it lies, the bloody witness to my crime! I am leaving to turn myself in,

---

29 Gray is hardly alone in ignoring Emilia's agency; for a superb critique of these omissions, see Schlipphacke, "The Dialectics of Female Desire."
30 "Was Gewalt heißt, ist nichts: Verführung ist die wahre Gewalt." *Emilia Galotti*, Act V, scene 7.
31 Schlipphacke, "The Dialectics of Female Desire," 62.

to jail. I am leaving and will await you there as judge—And then there—I will await you in front of the judge of us all! [32]

This is a brilliant move: the father remains the figure of the law by evoking it himself before submitting to it—again, Odoardo resembles Oedipus, who had condemned himself to exile. Odoardo's sophisticated challenge reveals that power has been split into many pieces. Marinelli, whose name is a thinly disguised reference to Machiavelli, the eighteenth-century name for a de-moralized politics who in the Prince's self-exculpating final words becomes "the devil," is the figure of political power as corruption. The Prince—another reference to Machiavelli, but just as importantly a filiarchal rather than a patriarchal title—is nominally sovereign and hence the source of a law he will either have to betray or turn against himself. Odoardo has become both a lawbreaker and the law's champion, occupying the split paternal position as both violence and as the figure of justice. Refusing to reenact "a stale tragedy," *Emilia Galotti* does not kill the tyrant but rather leaves him to self-destruct. The contradictions can only be contained by invoking the divine father, "the judge of us all," who will guarantee that paternity will remain to exert its symbolic force as Law at a time where familial and political fathers alike have been deeply compromised.

Nathan the Wise (1778), set in Jerusalem during the Third Crusade, exemplifies the depth of Lessing's dilemma—and perhaps nowhere as much as in its convolutions that constitute such a clear departure from the structure of the earlier plays. For all the challenges outlined above, tragic fathers remain easy to construe. By contrast, *Nathan* can barely sustain the tremendous effort involved in imagining successful fatherhood. It is the only one of Lessing's play that explicitly investigates the paternal triad, in an entanglement of fatherhood, politics, and religion that achieves its precarious coherence at the cost of a sheer flabbergasting accumulation of random coincidence.

Nathan, a wealthy Jewish merchant, learns that his daughter Recha has been saved from fire by a Knight Templar, Conrad von Stauffen, who in turn had been pardoned by the Muslim leader Saladin because the captive reminded him of his favorite brother, Assad. Feeling

---

32 "Nun da, Prinz! Gefällt sie Ihnen noch? Reizt sie noch Ihre Lüste? Noch, in diesem Blute, das wider Sie um Rache schreiet? (Nach einer Pause.) Aber Sie erwarten, wo das alles hinaus soll? Sie erwarten vielleicht, daß ich den Stahl wider mich selbst kehren werde, um meine Tat wie eine schale Tragödie zu beschließen? Sie irren sich. Hier! (Indem er ihm den Dolch vor die Füße wirft.) Hier liegt er, der blutige Zeuge meines Verbrechens! Ich gehe und liefere mich selbst in das Gefängnis. Ich gehe und erwarte Sie als Richter—Und dann dort—erwarte ich Sie vor dem Richter unser aller!" *Emilia Galotti,* Act V, scene 8.

indebted to Saladin, Nathan agrees to lend him urgently needed money, a deal brokered by the Derwish Al-Hafi. In the meantime, the Templar, impressed enough by Nathan's grace to overcome his anti-Semitism, falls in love with Recha, who is already enraptured by him, though apparently not erotically. When Nathan arrives at Saladin's palace, the Sultan does not ask him for money but instead demands to know which of the monotheistic religions is superior. Nathan responds with the famous parable of the ring—the story of a man whose family had passed down, from father to best-beloved son, a ring bequesting God's favor to its wearer. Unable to decide between his three equally cherished sons, the man orders copies of the ring that are so well made that nobody can tell the difference between them, and since none of the sons appears clearly favored by divine power, it is determined that the true ring has been destroyed.

Nathan, now favorably impressed with Saladin and his sister Sittah, offers to lend him the money Saladin never asked for, explains his motivation, and moves Saladin to invite the Knight Templar to his house. Upon returning from the palace, Nathan encounters Conrad, who confesses his love for Recha. In the course of the conversation, it transpires that the Knight Templar is the bastard son of Nathan's old friend by the same name, information that troubles Nathan, who leaves abruptly. When Daya, Recha's hired companion, tells Conrad that Recha is not Nathan's biological daughter and was born a Christian, the Knight, in religious confusion, seeks the advice of Jerusalem's Christian Patriarch, the only villain in the play, presenting the story as a hypothetical one, and is told that a Jew who had raised a Christian girl in his faith had to die by fire. Deeply troubled in turn, Conrad accepts Saladin's invitation to visit while the Patriarch seeks to uncover the details behind Conrad's story. Numerous further complications ensue before we learn that Conrad is in fact both Recha's brother and Saladin's nephew, and the curtain falls on "silent repetition of embraces all around."

Nathan the Wise has generally and plausibly been read as Lessing's humanist polemic on behalf of religious tolerance, honoring his friend Moses Mendelssohn, combating the widespread anti-Semitism of his time, and engaging in vigorous attacks on Christian clergy, with whom Lessing loved to cross swords. It it surely all that, but it is also one of the clearest documentation of an Enlightenment crisis of paternity that seeks to save the figure of the father at a time where its support system has crumbled.

It is impossible to extract a definitive reading of paternity from *Nathan*—on the one hand, the play appears to place fatherhood squarely in the realm of affect, as opposed to either *nomos* or *bios*:

I'd like to remain Recha's father
oh so dearly!—But can't I remain it
even if I cease to be called it?—To her,
to her herself I will be called it evermore
when she realizes how much I'd like to be it.[33]

Once again, it is the child who gets to define fatherhood, to render "it" itself, to give it its name. Paternal "blood . . . at best provides the first right to acquire the name."[34] The name of (the) father emerges out of the naming of the father, and this may well be another reason why Lessing's mothers, traditionally the ones to designate or mediate paternity, need to be eliminated. But fatherhood's removal from genetic kinship is embedded in a plot that relies on nothing but bloodlines (one more piece of evidence suggesting that we are not dealing with the redefinition of kinship or the family here but with establishing fatherhood as a separate category). Legal, biological, and affective fatherhood all retain their legitimacy, but they can no longer be integrated into a single figure. They coexist without clear hierarchy, akin to the three rings who can no longer be distinguished. It is Saladin who marks this tripling of paternity and, for the briefest of moments, suggests that it might be abolished altogether:

Do you know what? As soon as two fathers
Fight over you: —leave them both; take
The third one!—Then take me as your father!
I want to be a good father,
Quite a good father!—but stop! I have
An even better idea.—What need have you
Of fathers at all?[35]

Indeed—the child who can name her own father might choose not to name anyone at all, though Recha, of course, wouldn't dream of

---

33 Ich bliebe Rechas Vater/Doch gar zu gern!—Zwar kann ichs denn nicht bleiben,/Auch wenn ich aufhör', es zu heißen?—Ihr,/Ihr selbst werd' ichs doch immer auch noch heißen, /Wenn sie erkennt, wie gern ichs wäre." *Nathan der Weise,* Act IV, scene 7.
34 "Ja wohl: das Blut, das Blut allein/Macht lange noch den Vater nicht! macht kaum /Den Vater eines Thieres! Giebt zum Höchsten/Das erste Recht, sich diesen Namen zu/Erwerben!" *Nathan der Weise,* Act V, scene 7.
35 Und weißt du was? Sobald der Väter zwey/Sich um dich streiten:—aß sie beyde; nimm/Den dritten!—Nimm dann mich zu deinem Vater!/Ich will ein guter Vater,/Recht guter Vater seyn!—Doch halt! mir fällt/Noch viel was Bessers bey.—Was brauchst du denn/Der Väter überhaupt?" *Nathan der Weise,* Act V, scene 7.

un-fathering Nathan—Lessing may have nagging doubts about the constitution of fatherhood, but he is not ready to abolish it. In that sense, Nathan's resurgence as Recha's one and only father is never truly in doubt—Recha was too dearly bought, the replacement for no fewer than seven sons who died in the traumatic pogrom, marking, in passing but no less shockingly, the tremendous cost of the shift Lessing's drama works through.[36] Removing "blood" from fatherhood is, it seems, a bloody affair.

His paternal triumph, thus, comes at a steep price when Nathan centers a group portrait in which everybody but him is related to everybody else, and the image of the purely ethical fatherhood the play's protagonist appears to embody sets him apart from the family he has brought together. Lessing's plays present paternity teetering on the brink of abdication. Overtly patriarchal in structure and aesthetic, they mark the transition to a filiarchy where—and this is the deepest of Lessing's many ironies—the children exert their power by forcing their fathers into a paternal position that can no longer be inhabited. Paternal subjectivity comes into full view one last time—as a position of power conjured from ancient tales by those over whom it is wielded.

---

36 The topos of "seven sons" belongs to international folklore, and we might wonder whether the trade—"auf Sieben/Doch nun schon Eines wieder!"—also signals a conscious departure from the mythical past. *Nathan, der Weise,* Act IV, scene 7.

Nine Kleist and the Resurrections of the Father

English has no equivalent to the German *zeugen*, a word that means, simultaneously, to beget and to bear witness. Its strong polysemy reinforces the need to establish paternity through an act of signification or an oath; the word intertwines biology and document, that which is supposed to be the most natural and that which is supposed to be the most cultural, semen and the courts, the private act of coupling and the public act of naming. The previous chapter analyzed the unraveling of the affirmative project in which all those elements could still be aligned. The briefest perusal of Heinrich von Kleist's dramas and prose shows how deeply involved he is in paternity's many dilemmas, and how much of them he borrows from Lessing, only to drive into full view the ironies Lessing left implicit.

Kleist's intense engagement with the question of (patriarchal) law is so well documented that it can be taken for granted. Less, however, has been written on the central theme of the bios/nomos split in his writings on fatherhood, despite the conspicuous place the theme holds in so many of his works.[1] Paternal uncertainty plays an important role in *Amphitryon, Das Käthchen von Heilbronn* (1807), *Der Findling* (1811), and *Die Marquise von O....* (1807), and, perhaps, in *Das Erdbeben in Chili* (1807).[2] Adoptive vs. sexual fatherhood is deeply significant in

---

1 This is not to say that this essay is not indebted in many regards to previous relevant work on the theme. For a selection of different analyses and viewpoints, see Thomas Dutoit, "Rape, Crypt and Fantasm: Kleist's Marquise of O ...," *Mosaic* 27, no. 3 (1994): 45–64; Marjorie Gelus, "Patriarchy's Fragile Boundaries under Siege: Three Stories of Heinrich von Kleist," *Women in German Yearbook* 10 (1995): 59–82; Dagmar Lorenz, "Väter und Mütter in der Sozialstruktur von Kleists 'Erdbeben in Chili.'" *Études Germaniques* 33 (1978): 270–81; Anthony Stephens, "Kleists Familienmodelle," *Kleist-Jahrbuch* 1988–9: 222–41; and David Wellbery, "Semiotische Anmerkungen zu Kleists *Das Erdbeben in Chili*," in *Positionen der Literaturwissenschaft: Acht Modellanalysen am Beispiel von Kleists 'Das Erdbeben in Chili,'* ed. D. E. Wellbery (Munich: Beck, 1985), 69–87.
2 Various scholars have suggested that Fernando may be the father of Josephe's child; see Gelus, "Patriarchal Boundaries," 63, and the references cited there. Such hermeneutic hunts for paternity are quite common in Kleist scholarship, representing a curious antiliterary desire for "what really happened," as if, in Kleist, the question of "who is the father?" weren't entirely secondary to the question of *"what* is a father?"

Amphitryon (1807), *Das Erdbeben in Chili*, and *Der Findling*. Filicide, the violent bodily climax of paternal power that Freud has hidden from our view in the three-card monte of the Oedipus complex, occurs in the climactic final scenes of *Das Erdbeben in Chili, Der Findling*, and, twice, in *Die Familie Schroffenstein* (1803).

In his pursuit of double or triple paternity, Kleist can and does draw on religious and secular myth, on ancient and on modern history, and his narratives involve classical narrative and cultural patterns as well as the literary, political, and philosophical texts of his time.[3] His strategy is not simply one of eclecticism. Rather, as I will argue, his writing demonstrates the extent to which the reconceptualization of fatherhood took recourse to ancient mythical, philosophical, and political models at a time when Germany still dreamed of being or becoming the next Athens.

Much of legal theory of the time is characterized by attempts to conceptualize the family as a space protected both by and from the law—not quite a lawless realm, to be sure, but a privileged realm that, while first constituted legally, then emerges as in some regards beyond the law of the very state whose stability the family is meant to ground as its basic and constitutive element. One of the most sophisticated accounts of that logic is to be found in Hegel's famous reading of *Antigone* in the *Phenomenology of Spirit*. Even though Hegel postulates the triumph of human law (which operates in the service of the state) over divine law (which operates in the service of the individual family member), he also defines the family as a realm that operates apart from and in some regards in opposition to the state.

It may well be that this distinction, which pervades the legal debates of the late eighteenth and early nineteenth centuries in various permutations, reflects a compromise with the widespread resistance to the introduction of a universal state law that would abolish both regional legal particularities and class privileges. It is certain, in any case, that Kleist's novellas are deeply involved in both processes. Most prominently, *Michael Kohlhaas* stages the struggle between the desire for universally binding law and the cathexis to the presumably more "organic" legal practices of the regions.[4] While many of his other texts

---

3   In addition to the texts mentioned, as Terry Castle kindly pointed out to me, Kleist evokes various "ur-names," plot twists, motifs, and settings of English literature, stemming both from Elizabethan and Jacobean revenge tragedy and, intriguingly, the English Gothic novel of the 1790s, especially Horace Walpole's *The Castle of Otranto* and M. G. Lewis's *The Monk*. These allusions demonstrate on the intertextual level what appears to me obvious on the conceptual level— that is, that the importance of English thought to Kleist's oeuvre cannot be reduced to Shakespeare's pervasive presence on the German literary scene.

4   Kleist writes *Kohlhaas* in the tense climate surrounding the institution of the *Allgemeines Preussisches Landrecht*. The standard study on the process is

take as their point of departure the distinction between a public, male-gendered realm of positive law and documents and a putative private, female realm of an ethics of feeling based on individual relations. The motif is prominent in Kleist's well-known letter to Wilhelmine von Zenge, dating from May 1800:

> the man is not just his wife's husband (*der Mann seiner Frau*), but also a citizen of the state, whereas the women is nothing but her husband's wife; the man does not merely have obligations towards his wife, but also obligations towards his fatherland, whereas the woman has no other obligations than obligations towards her husband; consequently, the happiness of the woman is an important and indispensable, but not a man's *only* object, wheras the man's happiness is the *sole* object of the woman; hence, man cannot work for his wife *with all his strength*, whereas woman works for her husband *with her entire soul*.[5]

Since the woman's happiness depends entirely on her husband's happiness, the latter is the sole object of marriage; conversely, however, marriage is also its only source: "he receives the entire sum of his domestic, that is to say *all* of his happiness from her." If not the family, but marriage is the only source of male happiness, if all happiness is domestic dyadic happiness, then it is continuously threatened by all interference from the state, the fatherland, the public realm; the man's happiness not only depends on the distinction between public and private, it is also entirely dependent on woman's recognition of him *as* private individual.

It is striking that Kleist's letter does not mention children, whose happiness is traditionally as much the focus of woman's "entire soul" as her husband's well-being. The precarious idyll he sketches here is strictly dyadic, because fatherhood does not allow for the public-private distinction that emerges here; on the contrary, paternity always implies both a public and a private dimension; it belongs both to the law and to marital intimacy, a product both of the body and the

---

still Reinhart Koselleck, *Preussen zwischen Reform und Revolution; Allgemeines Landrecht, Verwaltung und soziale Bewegung von 1791 bis 1848* (Stuttgart: Klett, 1967). An excellent synopsis of historical changes in the meaning of the word "family" is to be found in Dieter Schwab's entry on "Familie" in *Geschichtliche Grundbegriffe. Historisches Lexikon zur politisch-sozialen Sprache in Deutschland*, eds Otto Brunner et al., vol. 2 (Stuttgart: Klett-Cotta, 1975), 253–301. See also Eva-Maria Anker-Mader, *Kleists Familienmodelle: Im Spannungsfeld zwischen Krise und Persistenz* (Munich: Wilhelm Fink, 1991), 13–16 and 25–38.

5 Heinrich von Kleist, *Werke und Briefe in vier Bänden*, vol. 4 (Frankfurt am Main: Insel, 1986), 55–6.

document—and either one can both support or subvert the other. Three of Kleist's novellas stage these mutual subversions: *The Marquise of O...*, *The Earthquake in Chile*, and *The Foundling*.

These texts are famously dense and demanding, generating and resisting interpretation to a degree that is often reserved for lyrical poetry. Despite the many divergent readings they have engendered, however, over the last decades a consensus has emerged that locates Kleist in the tension of Enlightenment and post-Enlightenment, precariously balanced between Kant and Nietzsche, exquisitely and desperately attuned to the catastrophe of secularization that has already begun to think, if not fully to articulate, the death of God. While it is certainly no longer true that "the family in Kleist is a strangely neglected phenomenon,"[6] scholarly work concerned with the family tends to focus on gender, and much of it fails to connect the familial crises that pervade Kleist's work as intimately connected to Kleist's own metaphysical crises as well as to the larger philosophical issues at stake at the time.[7] The following three readings aim to show how deeply his stories involve the larger questions animating this book.

The Marquise of O...
During a battle for her father's fort, a group of soldiers threaten to rape the Marquise von O..., a widow, who faints during the ordeal; she is saved by a young Russian officer, the Count of F.... Soon thereafter, she finds herself pregnant without any recollection of sexual congress—in a brilliant inversion of the principle of paternal uncertainty, it is the father who holds the knowledge of his paternity, the mother who has no access to it. Her father disavows her. In a scandalous move, the Marquise advertises for the father in a newspaper; at the appointed hour, the Count of F.... appears and admits to having raped the Marquise while she was unconscious. They marry, but the Marquise insists on separate households until they reconcile a year later.

Two of the *Marquise*'s scenes of fatherhood are of special interest, and both have been commented on widely. The first is the rape and insemination of the Marquise's unconscious body during the battle for her father's fort, marked—or perhaps disdescribed would be a better term—by nothing more than a grammatically unmotivated dash in a

---

6   Walter Müller-Seidel, "Der rätselhafte Kleist und seine Dichtung," *Die Gegenwärtigkeit Kleists: Reden zum Gedenkjahr 1977*, ed. Wieland Schmidt (Berlin: Erich Schmidt Verlag, 1980), 18.

7   Of course, there are exceptions to this rule, as attested by some of the literature cited in this essay. See also Joachim Bohnert, "Kleists Fichte ('Amphitryon')," *Resonanzen: Festschrift für Hans Joachim Kreutzer zum 65. Geburtstag* (Würzburg: Königshausen & Neumann, 2000), 241–54.

sentence toward the beginning of the story. The second scene is the reconciliation between the Marquise and her father, who had banned her after learning of her pregnancy and readmits her after her mother has convinced him of her innocence. The passage remains, to my taste, one of the most disturbing scenes in German literature. This is what the mother, having left after bringing about the reconciliation, sees upon her return, first through the keyhole, then through the open door, then from close up:

> the daughter still, her neck bent back, eyes firmly closed, lying in the father's arms; while the latter, sitting on the armchair, pressed long, hot, and thirsty kisses on her mouth, the great eye full of shiny tears: just like one in love! The daughter did not speak, he did not speak; his face bent over her he sat, like over the girl of his first love, and he arranged her mouth and kissed her. The mother felt as if one blessed; unseen, as she stood behind his chair, she hesitated to disturb the pleasure (*Lust*) of the heavenly reconciliation that had come to her house. Finally, she approached the father and, just as he, with fingers and lips, was busy again over his daughter's mouth in inexpressible pleasure (again, *Lust*), bending around the chair, looked at him from aside.[8]

The Marquise, it seems, is once again unconscious—in any case, she acts as if she were: she is lying still, not speaking, not moving, entirely the object of her father's mouth and fingers (and it is the fingers which make the scene so obscene, I think, perhaps precisely because they are so erotic as to almost spoil eroticism itself for the reader). She is so passive that her very mouth needs to be arranged for the kiss—*er legte ihr den Mund zurecht*, a formulation that invokes and conceals *Recht*—the word for both right and the law, fitting since this is a scene of

---

8   "die Tocher still, mit zurückgebeugtem Nacken, die Augen fest geschlossen, in des Vaters Armen liegend; indessen dieser, auf dem Lehnstuhl sitzend, lange, heiße und lechzende Küsse, das große Auge voll glänzender Tränen, auf ihren Mund drückte; gerade wie ein Verliebter! Die Tochter sprach nicht, er sprach nicht; mit über sie gebeugtem Antlitz saß er, wie über das Mädchen seiner ersten Liebe, und legte ihr den Mund zurecht und küßte sie. Die Mutter fühlte sich, wie eine Selige; ungesehen, wie sie hinter seinem Stuhle stand, säumte sie, die Lust der himmelfrohen Versöhnung, die ihrem Hause wieder geworden war, zu stören. Sie nahte sich dem Vater endlich, und sah ihn, da er eben wieder mit Fingern und Lippen in unsäglicher Lust über den Mund seiner Tochter beschäftigt war, sich um den Stuhl herumbeugend, von der Seite an." Heinrich von Kleist, *Erzählungen*, vol. 4 of *Gesamtausgabe* (Munich: Deutscher Taschenbuch Verlag, 1964), 125–6. All translations are my own. Further quotations from this volume indicated by page numbers in parentheses.

repossession. Weeping and ostensibly weak, the father asserts his right to his daughter in a way that brings to the foreground all the sexual tension that the well-known father-daughter scenes of *Empfindsamkeit* (sentimentalism) had only implied or concealed under that torrent of words that is here cut off.[9]

Previously, the structure of paternity had been severed twice—biologically, in a pregnancy apparently without a father, and legally, in the separation of father and daughter accompanied by "papers concerning her property."[10] Conversely, the first reconciliation—between the Marquise and her father—is intensely physical, stressed to be wordless, and all but repeats the first disruption that had been conspicuously concealed in the dash. Thus, Kleist belatedly fulfills the narrative contract he had suspended in withholding any representation of the rape—fulfills or perhaps over fulfills, giving his audience more than it had bargained for in exposing the voyeurism of reading with a rare relentlessness.

The second reconciliation—between the Marquise and the Count of F...—is accompanied by a contract in which the Count renounces all the rights and assumes all of the responsibilities of a husband—a piece of writing that institutes him legally as the child's father but bars him physically from both wife and son. In the second disruption, the Marquise moved out of her father's house; in the second reconciliation, it is the Count who is not admitted to the father's house in which his wife still lives. The chiasmic tension between document and body, which is also a tension between two models of fatherhood, is finally resolved in yet another set of doublings when the Count, after a year in the doghouse, is allowed to court his wife the Marquise again, to marry

---

9   Weiss points out the extent to which "the bizarre behavior of the father" can also "be read as a parody of the innumerable sentimental scenes of reunion in the popular fiction and domestic drama of Kleist's day." Hermann Weiss, "Precarious Idylls: The Relationship between Father and Daughter in Heinrich von Kleist's Die Marquise von O ...," *Modern Language Notes* 91 (1976): 538, 541. Krüger-Fürhoff, in an intriguing reflection on the German term *Vaterliebe*, suggests that "Kleist's novella uses and parodies theatrical *topoi* from bourgeois theater and *tableaux vivants* in order to represent incest as an aesthetic event." Irmela Marei Krüger-Fürhoff, "Epistemological Asymmetries and Erotic Stagings: Father-Daughter Incest in Heinrich von Kleist's *The Marquise of O...*," *Women in German Yearbook* 12 (1996): 72. In addition, Newman has reflected on the numerous ways in which Kleist's *Findling* repeats and reconfigures motifs from earlier bourgeois drama. Gail Newman, "Family Violence in Heinrich von Kleist's *Der Findling*," *Colloquia Germanica: Internationale Zeitschrift fur Germanistik* 29 no. 4 (1996): 287–302.

10 "über ihr Vermögen lautenden Papiere" (Kleist, 113).

her a second time, to move to the house that came to her out of her first marriage, and to produce "a whole line of young Russians" with her.[11]

One might be tempted to read the events as a straightforward manifestation of the typical triad of late Enlightenment—transition from one state of order to the next through an interlude of violent disruption and uncertainty, characterized by an interim loss of consciousness and reason. In this sense, the *Marquise* would transpose to the novella the structure of ancient tragedy, as it was widely understood at the turn of the eighteenth century. Reconciliation would be, in this case, the reconvergence of the natural and the legal father who is rewarded by the woman of his dreams, lifelong happiness, and abundant progeny of the right gender and nationality (male Russians). There are at least two problems, however, with such a reading, one on the level of plot, one on the level of narration. The story suggests that there are at least two other contenders for the Marquise's impregnation—her father and Leopardo, the hunter;[12] moreover, relatedly and perhaps more importantly, the irony, ambiguity, and not least the violence pervading the story are so conspicuous that the happy end resembles a farce, and we would mistrust it even if it were not for Kleist's other narratives of interrupted fathering.[13]

The Earthquake in Chile

The novella begins with a catastrophic earthquake, modeled on the historic one that nearly destroyed Santiago in 1647. It saves Josephe Asteron, the unmarried young mother of Philipp, from her impending execution, and brings down the jail in which the father of the illegitimate child, Josephe's former tutor Jeronimo Rugera, had been incarcerated. The three meet again in a valley outside the city where, for a while, the dire circumstances have created a classless utopian society characterized by generosity, love, respect, and mutual support. Josephe and Jeronimo befriend another young family, Don Fernando, his wife Donna Elisabeth, their son Juan, and Fernando's sister-in-law Donna

---

11 "eine ganze Reihe von jungen Russen" (ibid., 130).
12 As Krüger-Fürhoff suggests, a "malicious reading might argue that the text proves the count's paternity as little as the father's continence." "Epistemological Asymmetries," 77.
13 In her essay on rape and the law in the *Marquise*, Christine Künzel in my opinion correctly writes of the "Irritation, die das 'herbeigezwungene Happy End auslöst," the puzzlement and irritation which the forced happy end produce, and suggests that Kleist's text may very well be a parody of justice. Künzel, "Heinrich von Kleists *Die Marquise von O ...*: Anmerkungen zur Repräsentation von Vergewaltigung, Recht und Gerechtigkeit in Literatur und Literaturwissenschaft," *Figurationen* 1, no. 1 (2000): 178. See also Anker-Mader, *Kleists Familienmodelle*, 99.

Constanze. Six of them—Elisabeth is hurt and stays in the valley—walk into the city to participate in a Dominican mass where the survivors are called to plead with God to spare Chile from further harm. During the service, the Canon blames the earthquake on the transgressions of the citizens, and he explicitly invokes the case of Josephe and Jeronimo. Someone recognizes them, and a riot full of violence and confused identities breaks lose. Josephe, Jeronimo, Juan, and Constanze are killed in a scene of rare brutality; the story closes when Fernando and Elizabeth adopt Philipp.

The story's title sign, the earthquake, has been read as the violent tremor of consciousness, of representation, of meaning, of perception, of civilization, of religion, and it may be the German post-Enlightenment texts par excellence, not only because it is habitually read as the literary correlate of Kleist's famous *Kant-Krise*. Reading the earthquake as a violent reconfiguration of fatherhood is not merely to add another layer to these figurations. Rather, I contend that due to its uneasy, unstable, but exceptionally strong connection to tradition and creation, writing and replicating, identity and difference, body and institution, fatherhood emerges the master metaphor for order—the harmony of nature under the aegis of culture—and hence evokes that which threatens it, namely sociopolitical, intellectual, and natural revolution, which all equate to patricide in the semiotic system of oppositions that organizes patriarchy in general and even (or rather especially) the most enlightened monarchy in particular. In the Kleistian context, fatherhood is always already Laiusian rather than Oedipal, and hence proceeds under the sign of filicide—attempted or real, fantasized or enacted.

Here are the natural and symbolic fathers whom *The Earthquake in Chile* presents or evokes, in the order of appearance: Don Asteron, Josephe's father; Jeronimo the tutor, father of Josephe's illegitimate child Philipp; the Bishop who orders Josephe's trial; the Viceroy who commutes her sentence from death by fire to death by hanging; Don Fernando, father of Juan, whose skull is shattered on the church pillar in the story's penultimate scene; the Canon, who takes the place of the Bishop and whose sermon instigates the violence; Don Ormez, commander of the city and Don Fernando's father, whose authority is evoked in the church scene preceding the murders; Jeronimo's father, who makes his first and last appearance during the murders only to first name and then kill his son. Of all these fathers, two are known to survive; Asteron's house, the seat of familial patriarchy, is covered by a lake from which reddish steam rises. Josephe encounters "the corpse of the Bishop" (*Leiche des Erzbischofs*, 135) that has been pulled out of the debris of the cathedral; the Viceroy's palace is simply "sunk" (*versunken*, 135) and he is presumed or at least announced dead by the crowd. Jeronimo—who, like Fernando, appears as both father and son—is killed by *his* father. Among the material casualties are, in addition, the jail and the courthouse, realms of the law and its execution.

If that weren't enough, the extent to which the theme of fatherhood— as biological, social, and symbolic paternity—and its dissolution and tenuous reconstitution pervade the text becomes manifest in the church and murder scene. The crowd has just begun to focus on the group around Don Fernando. Josephe is carrying Fernando's son Juan; Jeronimo carries Philipp; Josephe is paired with Don Fernando; Donna Constanze, Fernando's sister-in-law, with Jeronimo. I quote with interspersed comments:

"'Are you mad?' cried the young man. . . : 'I am Don Fernando Ormez, son of the commander of the city, whom you all know.'" This is the first appeal to parental authority—up until then, Don Fernando had no patronym, and his relationship to secular power is mentioned here for the first time. "Don Fernando Ormez? asked a shoe cobbler who had worked for Josephe and knew her at least as well as he knew her small feet. Who is the father to this child? he turned to Asteron's daughter in impertinent defiance." Notice that both Don Fernando and Josephe are now characterized in their relationship to their fathers, and the question that sets the violence in motion is a question about paternity—that is, identity at a remove. "Don Fernando paled. . . : Josephe cried, *von entsetzlichen Verhältnissen gedrängt*,"—that is, driven by terrible circumstances, but also, since *entsetzlich* echoes and inverts *gesetzlich*, pushed by relations in which the law is suspended—"this is not my child, Master Pedrillo . . . : this young lord is Don Fernando Ormez, son of the commander of the city whom you all know!" The appeal to paternal-patriarchal authority is repeated in near identical words, but will prove to be in vain. "Now it so happened that in this same moment"—*es traf sich . . . in demselben Augenblicke*, the famous Kleistian contingent convergence that occurs obsessively throughout the text, undermining all teleological readings—"that little Juan, terrified by the tumult, strove away from Josephe's breast into the arms of Don Fernando." Kleist, in a quasi-Hobbesian move, introduces the image of the father as the one who protects rather than the one who generates. "Thereupon: He *is* the father! cried one voice; and: he *is* Jeronimo Rugera! another one, and: they *are* the blasphemous ones (*die gotteslästerlichen Menschen*)! a third one; and stone them! stone them! the whole Christianity assembled in the temple of Jesus"—that is, in the temple of the quintessential son.[14]

---

14 "'Seid Ihr wahnsinnig?' rief der Jüngling, und schlug den Arm um Josephen: 'ich bin Don Fernando Ormez, Sohn des Kommandanten der Stadt, den ihr alle

"Stone them! stone them!" evokes "crucify him!", of course, and hence continues the line of deviant biblical allusions that are prominent throughout the text: the image of original sin arose "in the convent garden" (*Klostergarten*, 131) but as Jeronimo's "full happiness" (*seines vollen Glückes*, 131). The valley outside the city had appeared as "the garden of Eden"—but only under the sign of the Kleistian "as if" (*als ob es das Tal von Eden gewesen wäre*, 136), and anachronistically following rather than preceding original sin (so much for returns to paradise through the back door). Josephe, Jeronimo, and Philipp evoke the holy family, but it is the woman who carries the biblical father's name, and they only get together under the polyvalently symbolic pomegranate tree—symbol of hope and community in the Christian context, but Persephone's tree in Greek mythology. Kleist's text—as an ever more rapid chase through a sometimes subtly and sometimes violently reconfigured and always destabilized Christian theo-teleology—culminates in a scene that reconceives of the crucifixion as filicidal barbarism organized not by God (the ultimate father) but by the "Prince of the satanic horde" (*Fürst der satanischen Rotte*, 144) himself, Pedrillo the shoe cobbler.

The following passages are excerpts from the scene of catastrophic culmination: "so Josephe placed (*setzte*) little Philipp, whom Jeronimo had carried up until then, together with the little Juan, into Don Fernando's arm, and said: go, Don Fernando, save your two children, and leave us to our fate."[15] Anybody who has dealt with babies and toddlers knows that it is entirely impossible to carry two of them in one arm, especially in the middle of violent commotion; Josephe's gesture and Fernando's acceptance thereof, beyond the register of verisimilitude to which Kleist is alternately highly attuned and entirely

---

kennt.' Don Fernando Ormez? rief, dicht vor ihn hingestellt, ein Schuhflicker, der für Josephen gearbeitet hatte. . . . Wer ist der Vater zu diesem Kinde? wandte er sich mit frechem Trotz zur Tochter Asterons. Don Fernando erblaßte bei dieser Frage. . . . Josephe rief, von entsetzlichen Verhältnissen gedrängt: dies ist nicht mein Kind, Meister Pedrillo, wie Er glaubt; indem sie, in unendlicher Angst der Seele, auf Don Fernando blickte: dieser junge Herr ist Don Fernando Ormez, Sohn des Kommandanten der Stadt, den ihr alle kennt. . . . Nun traf es sich, daß in demselben Augenblicke der kleine Juan, durch den Tumult erschreckt, von Josephens Brust weg Don Fernando in die Arme strebte. Hierauf: Er *ist* der Vater! schrie eine Stimmme; und: er *ist* Jeronimo Rugera! eine andere; und: sie *sind* die gotteslästerlichen Menschen! eine dritte; und: steinigt sie! steinigt sie! die ganze im Tempel Jesu versammelte Christenheit!" Kleist, 142–3.

15 "so setzte Josephe den kleinen Philipp, den Jeronimo bisher getragen hatte, samt dem kleinen Juan, auf Don Fernandos Arm, und sprach: gehen Sie, Don Fernando, retten Sie Ihre beiden Kinder, und überlassen Sie uns unserem Schicksale!" Ibid., 143.

indifferent, are purely symbolic of the dual fatherhood that is now at stake in this text. Josephe's act is *setzen*, once again evoking the name of the law, *Gesetz*. They succeed in leaving the church and "believed themselves saved. But hardly had they entered the equally crowded square in front of the church when a voice cried out of the raging horde (*dem rasenden Haufen*) that had pursued them: this is Jeronimo Rugera, you citizens, for I am his own father!"—note that he doesn't say I know who he is because I am his father but he *is* who he is because I am his father (*denn ich bin sein eigner Vater*), inverting the biblical for this is my own son—"and, next to Donna Constanze, stretched him to the ground with a monstrous strike of a club."[16]

Jeronimo's father had never before appeared or been mentioned in the text—his only function, at this point, is to introduce the topos of filicide that will dominate the remainder of events. Donna Constanze, taken for Josephe, is killed as well (a death that might be motivated as much by her name, constancy/faith, as by the logic of substitution); Don Fernando pulls his sword and attempts but fails to kill Pedrillo:

> But since he could not overpower the crowd which pressed upon him: farewell, Don Fernando with the children! cried Josephe—and: here, murder me, you bloodthirsty tigers! and threw herself amongst them voluntarily in order to put an end to the fight. Master Pedrillo struck her down with the club. . . . Thereupon, entirely splattered with her blood: send the bastard after her to hell! he cried and advanced again, with yet unsatisfied lust to murder.[17]

Josephe miscalculates in her assumption that *she* can serve as the ultimate sacrificial object—a mistake René Girard reproduces in his reading of the text that also understands her to be "the ideal sacrifice."[18]

---

16 "glauben sich gerettet. Doch kaum waren sie auf den von Menschen gleichfalls erfüllten Vorplatz derselben getreten, als eine Stimme aus dem rasenden Haufen, der sie verfolgt hatte, rief: dies ist Jeronimo Rugera, ihr Bürger, denn ich bin sein eigner Vater! und ihn an Donna Constanzens Seite mit einem ungeheuren Keulenschlage zu Boden streckte" (ibid.).

17 "Doch da er die Menge, die auf ihn eindrang, nicht überwältigen konnte: leben Sie wohl, Don Fernando mit den Kindern! rief Josephe—und: hier mordet mich, ihr blutdürstenden Tiger! und stürzte sich freiwillig unter sie, um dem Kampf ein Ende zu machen. Meister Pedrillo schlug sie mit der Keule nieder. Darauf ganz mit ihrem Blute besprützt: schickt ihr den Bastard zur Hölle nach! rief er, und drang, mit noch ungesättigter Mordlust, von neuem vor" (ibid., 144).

18 René Girard, "Mythos und Gegenmythos: Zu Kleists *Das Erdbeben in Chili*," *Positionen der Literaturwissenschaft*, 145.

Violence and reconciliation (or rather its bitter parody), here depend not on the sacrifice of the woman, but that of the son—it is only Juan's death that silences the crowd, the last in a line of J's invoking the death of Jesus:

> Don Fernando, the divine hero, now stood, his back leaned against the church; in the left he held the children, in the right the sword. . . . Seven bloodhounds lay dead before him, the prince of the satanic horde himself was wounded. But Master Pedrillo did not rest before he had one of the children pulled from his breast by the legs and, swung high in a circle, smashed it against the edge of a church pillar. Hereupon it became quiet and everybody left.[19]

The pillar of the church doubles the pillar of the jail from which Jeronimo had planned to hang himself in the opening scene, but it is Juan who, as it were, comes full circle and terminates the line of substitutions enacted at the end—substitutions that are anything but arbitrary. Here is the famous last sentence:

> Don Fernando and Donna Elvire accepted the little stranger as their foster son (*nahmen den kleinen Fremdling zum Pflegesohn an*); and when Don Fernando compared Philipp to Juan, and how he had acquired both, he almost felt as if he ought to rejoice.[20]

These may well be the most unsettling lines in a text full of disturbing implications. Don Fernando, comparing his adopted son to his natural son, seems to think that the former is superior to the latter, a superiority that also or perhaps especially manifests itself in terms of the manner of their respective acquisition—sexual reproduction emerges as inferior to the work of heroic rescue and legal adoption. In a text of obsessive doublings, it is the second son, the one whose filiality is designated by law not by sperm or marriage, whose existence effects reconciliation, the German term for which is *Versöhnung*—and German texts, despite the different etymology, have heard the *Söhne*, the sons, in *Versöhnung*

---

19 "Don Fernando, dieser göttliche Held, stand jetzt, den Rücken an die Kirche gelehnt; in der Linken hielt er die Kinder, in der Rechten das Schwert. . . . Sieben Bluthunde lagen tot vor ihm, der Fürst der satanischen Rotte selbst war verwundet. Doch Meister Pedrillo ruhte nicht eher, als bis er der Kinder eines bei den Beinen von seiner Brust gerissen, und, hochher im Kreise geschwungen, an eines Kirchpfeilers Ecke zerschmettert hatte. Hierauf ward es still, und alles entfernte sich." Kleist, 144.
20 "Don Fernando and Donna Elvire nahmen den kleinen Fremdling zum Pflegesohn an; und wenn Don Fernando Philippen mit Juan verglich, und wie er beide erworben hatte, so war es ihm fast, als müßt er sich freuen." Ibid., 145.

at least since the Baroque. Only, of course, there is no reconciliation—Don Fernando does not rejoice, he *almost* feels *as if* he *ought to* (irrealis, *müßte*) rejoice. While the two sons—the dead one and the live one, the natural one and the legal one—split between them Golgotha and the resurrection, this split can precisely not lead to Christian joy—Juan's crucifixion, after all, is a smashing of the brain, a destruction of the mind, unredeemable even by the strongest desire to retrospectively impose upon it rational meaning. The two sons may explicitly be linked to two competing and overlapping modes of fathering, but the Laiusian mode—fatherhood as filicide—overshadows both.

The Foundling

If we were yet tempted to read *Earthquake* as a however cautious celebration of a heroic fatherhood, *The Foundling* undermines that option. Again, we have two sons, the natural one and the adopted one, and the *Findling* of the title may well echo the *Fremdling* of *Earthquake's* ending. In the beginning, the merchant Piachi, accompanied by Paolo, his son from his first marriage, travels into a region affected by the plague (or rather a "plague-like illness," *pest-artige Krankheit*, 182); turning back too late, he out of pity picks up an afflicted boy, Nicolo. Since in Kleist no good deed goes unpunished, Piachi is arrested and the three are quarantined by force. Piachi stays healthy, Nicolo recovers, but Paolo, the natural son, is infected and dies after the symbolic "three days" (183)—another Christian inversion predicated on an oedipal plague. While the natural catastrophe, the earthquake, figures prominently in the earlier story, *The Foundling* quickly bypasses the plague and moves into the story of Piachi and Nicolo, whom the merchant adopts in his son's stead. Again, the substitution seems advantageous—in a mercantile echo of the ending of *Earthquake*, Piachi, "in an easily understandable manner, had grown to love the boy to the extent to which he had acquired him at great expense."[21] While Piachi is troubled by the boy's religious affiliation to the Carmelites, and Piachi's wife Elvire (in a typically Kleistian ironic juxtaposition) disapproves of his precocious sexual activities, Nicolo pleases his new parents so much that Piachi, "with the exception of a small capital which he kept to himself transferred to him all the property that was the basis of his trade in goods" (184), a transaction whose legal nature is stressed: *auf gerichtlichem Wege*, "by way of the courts."[22] This gesture—incidentally recommended by Montaigne, whom Kleist read, to curb patricidal

---

21 "in dem Maße lieb gewonnen, als er ihm teuer zu stehen kam" (ibid., 184).
22 "auf gerichtliche Weise, mit Ausnahme eines kleinen Kapitals, das er sich vorbehielt, das ganze Vermögen, das seinem Güterhandel zum Grunde lag" (ibid).

tendencies in sons—backfires badly. Nicolo develops lecherous designs on Elvire; when he comes home from a costume ball dressed as a Genoese knight, she faints at his sight. Later, he surprises Elvire on her knees in front of a (usually veiled) portrait that depicts a young man—an actual Genoese knight, as it happens—who had once saved young Elvire from certain death and had died three years later of the wounds he sustained in the rescue. When Nicolo inspects the painting later, in the presence of his and the bishop's lover and her illegitimate daughter, the little girl claims that it is a portrait of himself. Nicolo, playing down the resemblance, replies, "truly, dearest Klara, the painting resembles me as much as you resemble the one who believes himself to be your father,"[23] a sentence that directly evokes the ambiguities of paternity and its unstable manifestation in resemblance. However, once he discovers that the name of Elvire's lover, Colino, is an anagram of his own, Nicolo develops a plan to rape Elvire in the disguise of Colino but is interrupted in the attempt by Piachi who "just at this hour" enters the room. Nicolo, already trying to revive the once again unconscious Elvire with "hot kisses on breast and lips," begs forgiveness; when Piachi, "bent towards resolving the thing quietly, . . . speechless, . . . merely took the whip from the wall, opened the door for him and showed him the way he immediately was to take."[24] Nicolo instead expels his adoptive father on the basis of the transfer documents Piachi had signed. Piachi's appeals to the law prove fruitless; since Nicolo promises to marry the bishop's mistress, of whom the bishop wants to rid himself, "evil triumphed" (*das Böse siegte*, 186), and a new document is composed: "due to negotiations of this cleric [*dieses geistlichen Herrn*], the government passed a decree in which Nicolo was confirmed in his property and Piachi was ordered to not inconvenience him therein."[25]

Meanwhile, Elvire dies, presumably in consequence of the shock she has sustained in the attempted rape, and Piachi, furious, returns to his house, "threw Nicolo, who was weaker by nature, down and pushed in his brain against the wall. The people who were in the house did not notice him until the deed was done; they found him when he held Nicolo between his knees and forced the decree into

---

23 . . . "das Bild gleicht mir, wie du demjenigen, der sich deinen Vater glaubt!" Ibid., 190.
24 "Und in der Tat war der Alte auch geneigt, die Sache still abzumachen; sprachlos . . . nahm er bloß, indem er die Vorhänge des Bettes, auf welchem sie ruhte, zuzog, die Peitsche von der Wand, öffnete ihm die Tuer und zeigte ihm den Weg, den er unmittelbar wandern sollte" (ibid., 195).
25 "die Regierung erließ, auf Vermittlung dieses geistlichen Herrn, ein Dekret, in welchem Nicolo in den Besitz bestätigt und dem Piachi aufgegeben ward, ihn nicht darin zu belästigen" (ibid.).

his mouth."[26] Piachi, tried and sentenced to death, does not yet feel filicidally satisfied; he refuses to let himself be absolved by the priests, an act required by law (!) from all executees. Refusing confession and the rites of last unction, Piachi asserts: "I do not want to be saved. I want to ride down to the lowest bottom of hell. I want to find Nicolo again, who will not be in heaven, and I want to resume my revenge which I here could only satisfy incompletely."[27] The scene is repeated three times until Piachi, "cursing the inhuman law which would not let him go to hell," threatens to strangle one of the priests. "When this was reported to the Pope, he ordered to execute him without absolution; no priest accompanied him, one strung him up, in all quiet, on the square del popolo."[28] The last execution of the piece is ordered by yet another father figure, the pope, *il papa*, whose title oddly resonates with the place (*Platz*) of the people.

The Foundling takes up and rearranges numerous motifs from both *Marquise* and *Earthquake*: unconscious women, rape, uncertain paternity (several Kleist readers have mused on the question whether Colino could be Nicolo's father), the house of the father, documents, deviant doublings, anticlerical themes, adoption, oozing brain matter, filicide, and a couple of names (Elvire, Constanza). Reading the three novellas as companion pieces allows us to conclude that Kleist is involved in a systematic project to undermine all forms of fatherhood—a process that moves from the irony and uncertainty surrounding sexual or spermal fatherhood in the *Marquise* over the still ambivalent filicidal violence of *Earthquake* to the unambivalent one of *The Foundling*. The *Foundling*'s filicide is not merely unredeemed by any act of forgiveness or the kind of "closure" that *Earthquake* appears to offer, it is portrayed as nothing less than transcendent—an infinite act of murder that cannot end even in death.

While *Earthquake* presented a last vision (or rather fantasy) of a fatherhood both heroic and tender, if displaced from the natural to the "acquired" son, *The Foundling*, not by coincidence the narrative that most loudly seems to cry out for a Freudian reading, negates all

---

26 "warf . . . den von Natur schwächeren Nicolo nieder und drückte ihm das Gehirn an der Wand ein. Die Leute, die im Haus waren, bemerkten ihn nicht eher, als bis die Tat geschehen war; sie fanden ihn noch, da er den Nicolo zwischen den Knien hielt, und ihm das Dekret in den Mund stopfte" (ibid., 196).
27 "Ich will den Nicolo, der nicht im Himmel sein wird, wiederfinden, und meine Rache, die ich hier nur unvollständig befriedigen konnte, wieder aufnehmen" (ibid.).
28 "Als man dem Papst dies meldete, befahl er, ihn ohne Absolution hinzurichten; kein Priester begleitete ihn, man knüpfte ihn, ganz in der Stille, auf dem Platz del popolo auf" (ibid.).

possibility of reconciliation, *Versöhnung*, both in the secular and the sacred realm. Imagery of castration abounds—while Nicolo is sexually overactive, Elvire "no longer has any hope of receiving children from the old man."[29] Piachi, after being banned from his own house, "lays down the whip as if disarmed,"[30] and his attempts to gain justice are likened to "powerless levers" (*machtlose Hebel*, 195). Like so often in Kleist, however, the imagery proves misleading—Piachi might be sexually impotent, but he is stronger than Nicolo, and the scene where Piachi stuffs Nicolo's mouth with the very decree Nicolo took to contain all his power can be read, without too much stretch, as the final rape scene of the story, rerelating power to fatherhood in a mode of murder where strength "by nature" trumps the document, that is to say, culture.

In general, it seems as if Kleist's fathers win all the battles. Many scholars have noted that the various orders of paternity—biological, cultural, symbolic—, while either subtly undermined or violently threatened, are consistently reestablished at the end. Power always returns to the fathers, to the Marquise's father and the Count of F...; to Rugera the Elder, the Canon, and Don Fernando; to Piachi, the Pope, and the Law. This hardly means that Kleist endorses such victories; as Anthony Stephens suggests, Kleist exposes the "seeming self-evidence" of paternal authority and entangles it in the "the discourse of the unnatural (*Diskurs der Unnatur*)." One should also not forget that in Kleist's work, patriachal authority, far from being a homogenous system of shared power, emerges as highly fractious: as Gail Newman notes, "[t]he realm of the father [is] a realm framed by generally acknowledged institutions and discourses. . . . But . . . the patriarchal authority [is] irrevocably split within itself—Piachi turns to the law, Nicolo to the church, which represents all that was opposed to the bourgeois Enlightenment associated with the 'wohlhabender Güterhändler' Piachi."[31]

I think that Newman may still somewhat overestimate the extent to which fatherhood is supported by "generally acknowledged institutions and discourses"—there is not a single one of these discourses that is not up for grabs or demolition in Kleist, and his work brings into sharp relief the contradictory and at times mutually exclusive logic of their constructions. His stories and plays are documents of *Ungleichzeitigkeit*, nonsynchronism, a phenomenon Ernst Bloch describes as follows:

---

29 "welche sich von dem Alten keine Kinder mehr zu erhalten hoffen konnte" (ibid., 184).
30 "wie entwaffnet, legte er die Peitsche weg" (ibid., 195).
31 Newman, "Family Violence," 297.

Not all people exist in the same Now. They do so only externally, by virtue of the fact that they may all be seen today. But that does not mean that they are living at the same time with others. Rather, they carry earlier things with them, things which are intricately involved. . . . Times older than the present continue to affect older strata; here it is easy to return or dream one's way back to older times. . . . In general, different years resound in the one that has just been recorded and prevails.[32]

The concept of fatherhood is both a repository and a powerful agent of nonsynchronicity in this sense. By Kleist's time, so many ideological, cultural, and political contradictions have accrued around the image, idea, and practice of fatherhood that a radical questioning of the concept was inevitable. And yet, any attempts to seriously dismantle paternal power are either reversed or do not go very far, and the father will remain unquestionably the head of the bourgeois family for a long time to come. A number of scholars have argued that the politics and the rhetoric of the French Revolution either initiate or complete a paradigm shift in the legitimization of power, from the paternal to the fraternal, the vertical to the horizontal, the sacred to the secular,[33] but what Bloch calls "older strata" defined much of the practices and desires which their intellectual present had declared obsolete.

Kleist, a keen but ambivalent witness of the Revolution and its aftermaths, is a master at exposing the nonsynchronicity of paternity, but certainly not as an exercise in historical dialectics; the conflicting strata—fed by mythology, literature, biology, political philosophy, successful and failed revolutions, cultural change and the desire for permanence—resist all reconciliation in his work. In what only seems to be a paradox, it is precisely the survival of his fathers that marks this resistance; while it is striking that his texts do not include a single instance of patricide, this does not mean that Kleist endorses traditional paternity.[34] Rather,

---

32 Bloch, "Nonsynchronism and the Obligation to Its Dialectics," 22.
33 In *The Sexual Contract*, Carol Pateman locates the fraternalization of power in the political thought of seventeenth and early-eighteenth-century England, especially in the writings of Hobbes and Locke. The political history of the Greek city-states, especially the transition from the Tyrants to Athenian democracy, points to a comparable process in antiquity, and Freud, of course, argued in *Totem and Taboo* that a similar shift had to occur in prehistoric times. To me, this discrepancy suggests that the tension between the fraternal and the paternal is part of the patriarchal order, and that fraternal assaults succeed only intermittently, if at all.
34 Gelus reads Kleist as "split within himself between the steadfast upholder of patriarchal values and the androgynously subversive dismantler of stable meaning" ("Patriarchal Boundaries," 60), but I am not convinced that the patriarchal victories Kleist stages correspond to his own ideological desires.

he provides powerful testimony to its enduring power at an age where the rhetoric of fraternity threatens not so much to dislodge or replace but rather to conceal it. I wonder whether feminist accounts that see in patriarchy "the only concept that refers specifically to the subjection of women"[35] do not ultimately participate in this concealment—patriarchy names first of all the rule of the father *over the child*, and no progress in gender equality will set the real and the symbolic children free.

Kleist's work demonstrates that, ultimately, the ideology of fatherhood needs no fathers, and that it can so reliably reproduce them precisely *because* it does not need them to take any specific form. They can be installed through the language of blood or the language of the law, visible or invisible, disembodied or spectacularly physical, heroic or decrepit, human or divine, filicidal or sacrificial; they will resist and survive natural catastrophes as well as all social, legal, or ideological reforms as long as we are governed by those desires we imagine fathers can grant—the desire for protection that is inscribed into us during childhood; the desire for reconciliation that is part of our historical heritage of history itself; and, most importantly, the desire for conflict that renders oedipal even the most radical critique of the patriarchy, and hence in the very moment of its success can only reproduce the most powerful father of them all, the dead one. That he knew this is, I think, the ultimate irony in Kleist's filiarchal demand.

---

35 Pateman, *The Sexual Contract*, 20.

Section V
Freud's Fatherhood II

Ten The *Gschnas*, or the Path to the Fatherless Society

Children are both self and other, Freud told us. They are revenants, separate human beings who embody a number of yet different others—the father's actual and symbolic fathers, along with submerged fantasies of what he could have been. As if the ensuing multitude of simultaneous but irreconcilable relations were not enough, the most difficult tension fatherhood has to bear, the discrepancy between symbolic and familial fatherhood—that is, the Laius Complex in all its variations—makes the experience of modern fatherhood one of incurable inadequacy. It is here that Freud's historical position as one who is thinking in the age of the death of God bears most decisively upon his unwriting of fatherhood.

In a footnote in the *Interpretation of Dreams*, Freud claims that "the father is the oldest, the first, and for the child the only authority out of whose omnipotence all other social authorities have developed over the course of human cultural history."[1] Freud does not see or does not say that those "other authorities," however, have long served to produce that very paternal authority in which they purportedly ground themselves. Fatherhood is said to be the primal institution, but precisely as the first effect of pure signification, it is also inherently dependent on the feedback of power along the metaphorical and metonymic chains it is said to anchor. In monotheistic cultures, more specifically, who can say whether it is the father who lends his authority to God or God who lends his authority to the father, as the very principle of the disembodied paternity to which actual fathers have no recourse? Since paternity, Joyce's "legal fiction," is in its traditional semiotic distinction from material maternity always disembodied in principle, incorporating it is unavoidably a process of destabilization. Certainly, as Andrew Parker has recently reminded us with some force, motherhood has always been multiple as well, has always hovered between the material, the metaphoric, and the symbolic, and recent developments in reproductive technology may

---

1 "[D]er Vater ist die älteste, erste, für das Kind einzige Autorität, aus deren Machtvollkomenheit im Laufe der menschlichen Kulturgeschichte die anderen sozialen Obrigkeiten hervorgegangen sind." *Die Traumdeutung,* 226fn. My translation.

have done nothing more than sharpen our understanding of a multiplicity that has always been operative.[2] But the point is not that motherhood cannot be reduced to the material aspects of pregnancy and birth—how could it be otherwise?—, but that fatherhood, before the advent of DNA testing, *had* no somatic dimension that could be empirically verified or observed in immediacy.

The father may be the figure of omnipotence to his young children, but never to himself, and least of all, perhaps, in gazing at his child.[3] The subjectivity of embodied fatherhood—as an experience of uncertainty, mortality, and an unrequitable love—is in stark contrast to the concept of (symbolic) fatherhood in which psychoanalysis has so heavily invested itself.[4] If and when it surfaces, however, it comes with a strong flavor of lack and insufficiency. In the Rome Discourse, Lacan writes that "even when in fact it is represented by a single person, the paternal function concentrates in itself both imaginary and real relations, always more or less *inadequate* to the symbolic relation that essentially constitutes it" (emphasis added).[5] Jean-Michel Rabaté echoes: "Who can be sure to be the father, who can be so self-confident as to utter without faltering, 'I am a fa . . .' and not crash down into the frozen lakes of doubt and incest that have nonetheless been safely crossed?"[6]

While the doubt is old, the faltering of the father's voice has a historical dimension as well. Around 1900, the stammering of the father is everywhere. We can hear it in a passage from Hofmannsthal's

---

2   See Andrew Parker, "Philosophy's Mother Trouble," in *The Theorist's Mother*, 1–27.
3   The theme of paternal uncertainty (or its inversion, in Oedipus's filial uncertainty) is the one red thread in the history of fatherhood; precisely because the bodily link between father and child is always dubious, paternity relies on and emerges as the archetype of signification.
4   Freud's blindness to the position of the father is, I think, intimately linked to his decade-long blindness to the phenomenon of countertransference. While he recognizes early on that the analyst's main task is to initiate, sustain, and bear the analysand's transference, within this transference, he will always figure as the father, even though in a fatherhood he can construct as fantasized, displaced, not his own. In response, analysis develops the analyst as a counter-father, benevolent, nurturing, sexually abstinent, and—ideally, or in theory—silent, without features, present but invisible. Invisible to the analysand, but invisible also to himself, and that is, perhaps, the greater problem.
5   "The Function and Field of Speech and Language in Psychoanalysis," in *Ecrits*, 67.
6   "A Clown's Inquest into Paternity: Fathers, Dead or Alive," in *Ulysses* and *Finnegan's Wake*," in *The Fictional Father: Lacanian Readings of the Text*, ed. Robert Con Davis (Amherst: University of Massachusetts Press, 1981), 73.

"Letter of Lord Chandos" (1902), which has been read as emblematic of the age:

> the abstract words of which the tongue must by nature make use in order to bring any judgment to light fell apart in my mouth like mouldy mushrooms. It happened to me that I wanted to rebuke my four-year-old daughter Catarina Pompilia for a childish lie of which she had become guilty and to lead her to the necessity to always be true, and in this act the concepts that flowed to me in my mouth suddenly acquired such a glittering coloration and flowed into each other to such a degree that, stammeringly finishing the sentence as well as I could, as if I had become unwell, and indeed pale in the face and with a heavy pressure on my forehead, I left the child alone."[7]

Hofmannsthal acknowledges both the father's function to speak for the law, to render it visible—"to bring . . . judgment to light"—and the impossibility of embodying this function at a time when fatherhood is no longer securely grounded by a paternal god who can serve as the ultimate moral instance guarding the distinction between truth and lie. Incapable of meeting the task of abstraction—that is, the task of masculinity in the semiotic gender system that still organizes Hofmannsthal's writing—, the father abdicates a discourse that has become purely external to him: the words "flow to him" as if of their own accord and disintegrate in his mouth, losing color, shape, and texture, becoming pure matter. Having to embody the function of the symbolic father, the real father's experience is one of mute surrender, making the voice falter in a mouth full of mush. True, this loss is recollected in some of the most exquisite German prose in existence, but the eloquence belongs to the gesture of abdication, and it cannot blind us to the fact that no voice can answer Kafka's "Letter to the Father," a text that like

---

7 "die abstrakten Worte, deren sich doch die Zunge naturgemäß bedienen muß, um irgendwelches Urtheil an den Tag zu geben, zerfielen mir im Munde wie modrige Pilze. Es begegnete mir, daß ich meiner vierjährigen Tochter Catarina Pompilia eine kindische Lüge, deren sie sich schuldig gemacht hatte, verweisen und sie auf die Notwendigkeit, immer wahr zu sein, hinführen wollte, und dabei die mir im Munde zuströmenden Begriffe plötzlich eine solche schillernde Färbung annahmen und so ineinander überflossen, daß ich, den Satz, so gut es ging, zu Ende haspelnd, so wie wenn mir unwohl geworden wäre und auch tatsächlich bleich im Gesicht und mit einem heftigen Druck auf der Stirn, das Kind allein ließ." Hugo von Hofmannsthal, *"Ein Brief"* in *Werke in zehn Bänden: Erfundene Gespräche und Briefe*, ed. Lorenz Jäger (Frankfurt am Main: Fischer, 1999), 25.

no other demonstrates how the very gesture of acknowledging (or alleging) the father's superior power condemns him to silence.

Let us return, in this light, to Freud's dictum that "the father is the oldest, first and only authority for the child, from the absolutism of which the other social authorities have developed in the course of the history of human civilisation." The thought itself, much quoted, is fairly unremarkable—this book is devoted to the long history of paternity as the master trope of legitimate power, though the stress is on the equally long history of its contestation. What matters more is that Freud identifies this father's traditional function to model social and political authority in a long footnote that, in a typical Freudian meander, ends up far more invested in the possibilities of revolution than in the social and political stability the paternal trope is evoked to support. It is long, but well worth repeating almost in its entirety. Here is the setup, Freud's dream:

I am back in front of the railroad station, but I am with an elderly man, invent a plan to remain unrecognized, but see this plan already carried out. Thinking and experiencing are, as it were, the same thing. He pretends to be blind, at least on one eye, and I hold a male glass urinal in front of him (which we had to buy or did buy in town). I am, then, a caretaker of the sick and need to give him the glass container because he is blind.[8]

Here is the footnote accompanying this dream:

I here add some material for interpretation. Holding the urinal recalls the story of a peasant who tries one glass after another at the opticians, but still cannot read (peasant-catcher, like girl-catcher in a portion of the dream). The treatment among the peasants of the father who has become weak-minded in Zola's *La Terre*. The pathetic atonement that in his last days the father soils his bed like a child; hence, also, I am his sick-attendant in the dream. Thinking and experiencing are here, as it were; the same thing recalls a highly revolutionary closet drama by

---

8 "Ich bin wieder vor dem Bahnhofe, aber zu zweit mit einem älteren Herrn, erfinde einen Plan, um unerkannt zu bleiben, sehe diesen Plan aber auch schon ausgeführt. Denken und Erleben ist gleichsam eins. Er stellt sich blind, wenigstens auf einem Auge, und ich halte ihm ein männliches Uringlas vor (das wir in der Stadt kaufen mußten oder gekauft haben). Ich bin also ein Krankenpfleger und muß ihm das Glas geben, weil er blind ist. Wenn der Konducteur uns so sieht, muß er uns als unauffällig entkommen lassen. Dabei ist die Stellung des Betreffenden und sein urinierendes Glied plastisch gesehen. Darauf das Erwachen mit Harndrang." Freud, *Die Traumdeutung*, 220.

Oscar Panizza, in which the Godhead is treated quite contemptuously, as though he were a paralytic old man. There occurs a passage: "Will and deed are the same thing with him, and he must be prevented by his archangel, a kind of Ganymede, from scolding and swearing, because these curses would immediately be fulfilled." Making plans is a reproach against my father, dating from a later period in the development of my critical faculty; just as the whole rebellious, sovereign-offending dream, with its scoff at high authority, originates in a revolt against my father. The sovereign is called father of the land (*Landesvater*), and the father is the oldest, first and only authority for the child, from the absolutism of which the other social authorities have developed in the course of the history of human civilisation (in so far as the "mother's right" does not force a qualification of this thesis). The idea in the dream, "thinking and experiencing are the same thing," refers to the explanation of hysterical symptoms, to which the male urinal (glass) also bears a relation. I need not explain the principle of the "Gschnas" to a Viennese; it consists in constructing objects of rare and valuable reputation (*Ansehen*) out of trifles, and preferably out of comical and worthless material—for example, making suits of armor out of cooking utensils, sticks and "salzstangeln" [elongated rolls], as our artists like to do at their jolly parties. (Ibid., 225–6fn)

This extraordinary passage might well be worth its own chapter, but let's cut to the chase: this is a passage dedicated to the paternal triad, the equivalence of father, king, and god. Sovereignty both political and divine is paternal and paternity is sovereign, indispensable to the patriarchy in the narrow and the broader sense. But what is its figure? Freud's answer is nothing less than stunning: it is the *Gschnas*, a comical hodgepodge, an imitation object of great repute that on closer inspection consists of worthless trifles. As the image of power, fatherhood is not just a simulacrum, but a hysterical (!) joke. In turn, omnipotence—the convergence of will and deed, wishful thought and actual experience—, the hallmark of paternal divinity, is exposed as a dangerous affliction in need of quasi-medical intervention, a hysterical symptom.

Freud's line of the father as "the oldest, first and only authority" has been cited in the literature over and over again—but in isolation, as if that old, primal, sole authority were not here urinating into a glass, half or fully blind, soiling the bed, good for a laugh at the kind of parties artists arrange.[9] But isn't it Freud himself who is either half

---

9   Just a few examples here: Timothy Beal and D. M. Gunn, eds., *Reading Bibles, Writing Bodies: Identity and the Book* (London and New York: Routledge, 1997),

or fully blind here, "or pretends to be," as the easily missed and quite intriguing qualification suggests? As a great admirer of Freud's work, I want to believe the latter, I want to believe that he is fully aware of the scandalous import of this dreamwork. I want to believe that he knows that the triad of king and god and father has become a *Gschnas*. But it is a footnote, and what else is the footnote but the space below, the editorial equivalent realm of the act of negation where we can say what we are not quite ready to say, what we can only say in a footnote?

Freud, after all, is still writing and posing as the son, and at the threshold of our modernity, it is the sons who need the image of the powerful father the most, reassembling him from culture's leftovers all the better to ritually tear him down. Kafka is simply the most audible and the most eloquent of these filiarchs manqué; when Freud writes the *Traumdeutung*, the voice of the son has long begun to colonize literature, and the crisis of fatherhood manifests itself in a variety of (overdetermined) phenomena: the discovery of bachelorhood to which Eve Sedgewick has drawn attention,[10] the cult of male youth, the anti-organic themes of Huysman's *Against Nature*,[11] whose protagonist celebrates his impotence; the disquieting fascination with dead children in the same author's *Là-bas*; the pervasive anxiety concerning heredity (which always spells degeneration) in the wake of Darwin, to name just a few. In this light, the much-discussed "fear of the feminine" that pervades much of the literature of the time is a fear of procreation, a fear of engendering the child.[12] The great anxiety besetting the fin-de-siècle man, it is revealed, is not fear *of* the castrating father, but the fear of *becoming* the father; paternity, in turn, emerges as nothing but a different form of castration.

79; Matt Ffytche, *The Foundation of the Unconscious: Schelling, Freud and the Birth of the Modern Psyche* (Cambridge: Cambridge University Press, 2012), 266; Carl Schorske, *Fin-de-Siècle Vienna: Politics and Culture* (New York: Vintage Books, 1981), 197; Judith Van Herik, *Freud on Femininity and Faith* (Berkeley: University of California Press, 1982), 48.

10 Eve Sedgewick, *Epistemology of the Closet* (Berkeley: University of California Press, 1990), 188–212.

11 Joris Karl Huysmans, *Against Nature*, trans. Margaret Maulden (Oxford: Oxford University Press, 1998).

12 Here is a (fairly representative) passage from Zola's *The Sin of Father Mouret*: "A human smell rose from this heap of quivering houses. And the priest thought he was back in Désirée's barnyard, face to face with that endless swarm of multiplying animals. He felt the same heat of generation, the same continuous labor whose smell had made him sick. All day he had lived with this pregnancy of Rosalie's, and he finally thought of it as part of life's filth, of the flesh's drives, of the preordained reproduction of the species which sowed men like grains of wheat. The Artauds were a flock penned in by the four hills on the horizon, begetting, spreading out with each new litter from the females." Emile Zola, *The Sin of Father Mouret*, trans. Sandy Petrey (Lincoln/London: University of Nebraska Press, 1969), 57.

Decadence's most celebrated heroes—des Esseintes, Dorian in *The Picture of Dorian Gray*—are most decidedly unfatherly figures, and the most dire need of the "Jünglinge der Moderne," as Birgit Dahlke calls them,[13] may be the need for reliable contraception (although few will go as far as Weininger in his call for universal chastity). Over the long history of paternity, its greatest and most persistent problem had been paternal uncertainty—all of a sudden, paternal certainty may well prove more threatening. Aesthetic innovation had been securely tied to patricide for a while, but the anxiety of influence may well by now be outweighed by the anxiety of *being* one: "There is no such thing as a good influence, Mr. Gray. All influence is immoral," pronounces Wilde's Lord Henry.[14]

On the stylistic level, the most pertinent feature may be the famous catalogues of decadence, endless enumerations and descriptions of the inanimate that undermine organic aesthetics as well as narrative contracts built on the expectation of an integrating plot. These stalling narratives, too, point to a crisis of fathering: father-son succession is the master plot of myth and every patriarchal culture's founding narrative, a succession that often enough is staged as the failure of filicide (while their stories are very different, Zeus, Isaac, Oedipus, and Jesus are all sons who survive filicidal assaults).

In centering his enterprise on the name of the son, Freud formalizes and finalizes this crisis and makes it productive. While the dilemma of fatherhood is both ancient and overdetermined, I think there is little doubt that Freud's voice—so paternal, so patriarchal, so Laiusian in his lifelong struggle with the psychoanalytic progeny—has more than any other one generated the cultural space in which the sons will talk (and talk and talk and talk . . .) about their fathers, in tones of derision and regret, fear and love—but hardly ever about their sons, for they would, in that moment, risk becoming a *Gschnas* to themselves.[15] And since so many of these sons are fathers as well, both in biological, familial, and symbolic terms, the son's son becomes the twentieth century's most repressed figure. Quite appropriately, he makes a barely veiled appearance in Freud's essay "The Uncanny":

> The most prominent among the motifs that have an uncanny effect . . . the *doppelgängerdom* in all its gradations and forms . . . that one is led astray in contemplating one's I (*daß man an seinem*

---

13 Birgit Dahlke, *Jünglinge der Moderne: Jugendkult und Männlichkeit in der Literatur um 1900* (Cologne/Weimar: Böhlau, 2006).
14 *Collected Works of Oscar Wilde* (Hertfordshire: Wordsworth Editions, 2007), 15.
15 There are some notable exceptions here, of course; the most interesting one may be Yeats's work, especially his poems to his children and the Cuchulain plays, which culminate in filicide.

Ich irre wird) or puts (*versetzt*) the alien I in the place of the own, ergo I-doubling, I-splitting, I-substitution—and finally the eternal return of the same, the repetition of the same (*nämlichen*) facial features, characters, fates, criminal deeds, yes, of the same names through several successive generations.[16]

This doppelgänger is the son, is Oedipus as seen by Laius—familiar and alien, springing from the domestic uncanny of the lover's womb (*heimlich/unheimlich*), repressed but always returning, doubling the father, repeating his features, his crimes, his name, splitting his I, usurping his place, and at the same time, demanding to be loved without reserve.

Do fathers love their children? Of course they do, as a rule. Or so I believe. For the longest time, though, the love of the father, has most prominently articulated itself upon the child's loss or death.[17] If only the death of the child makes fatherhood speakable, then perhaps that is not only because losing a child is such a wrenching experience, but because that death resolves a profound ambivalence, cataclysmically releases the tension especially of fathering sons. When sons signify, simultaneously, a father's mortality and his immortality, the father-son relationship also balances—or fails to balance—identity and difference. The logic that governs it is supplemental, echoing the logic of the doppelgänger, and might in fact be its model.

The son is both promise and threat, beloved and feared, continuity and disruption, a gift and a monstrous imposition, another self and the worst possible rival, identity's futurity and its termination—and he is the one only because he is also the other. Precisely to the extent that paternity belongs to the public realm of order, law, and tradition, the son is *unheimlich*, the figure of the repressed other/self that comes from the home, and his death—real or fantasized—is the condition of love, or at least its articulation. Only the written child—written and hence both dead and alive—is the perfect child, or, as Ben Jonson has it, "his best piece of poetrie."[18]

---

16 "die hervorstechendsten unter jenen unheimlich wirkenden Motiven . . . das Doppelgängertum in all seinen Abstufungen und Ausbildungen . . . so daß man an seinem Ich irre wird oder das fremde Ich an die Stelle des eigenen versetzt, also Ich-Verdopplung, Ich-Teilung, Ich-Vertauschung—und endlich die beständige Wiederkehr des Gleichen, die Wiederholung der nämlichen Gesichtszüge, Charaktere, Schicksale, verbrecherischen Taten, ja der Namen durch mehrere aufeinanderfolgende Generationen." Freud, "Das Unheimliche," in *Studienausgabe*, 4:257.
17 See Conclusion: Dead Children.
18 See Silke-Maria Weineck, "Dead Childen: Ben Jonson Epitaph on my first sonne," in *Dead Lovers: Erotic Bonds and the Study of Premodern Europe*, ed. Basil Dufallo and Peggy McCracken (Ann Arbor: University of Michigan Press, 2007), 128–42.

And of course, fathering has been intimately linked to writing itself, from the moment Plato suggests, in the *Symposium*, that leaving behind logoi is far superior to leaving behind children—it's the only way to get rid of mothers, I suspect. That writing erases the writer, that the author dies in every work he produces, however, are insights we owe to the late nineteenth and early twentieth centuries; we also owe them, I think, to the unacknowledged experience of fatherhood that has so long functioned as creativity's ambivalent master metaphor.[19] Like writing, fatherhood is a form of suicide in the service of immortality, and every son an executioner. Of course, that is never the whole story, but in order to begin telling more of it, and to tell it differently, we had to imagine Laius again, and to finally imagine him from within: as a desiring subject, as the one who is called upon to say yes rather than no, yes to the child, and yes to his own death, releasing the son to the full potential of his otherness.

In imagining—or reimagining—Laius, he becomes visible as something other than a boy's fantasy, or a grown man's fantasy of what a boy's fantasy should look like. After all, Freud's account, though named for a tragedy, is strikingly untragic—the trade will work, he assures us, at least most of the time. Obedience will be rewarded with power, desire transferred, castration forestalled. The trouble will come only in dreams of murder and in footnotes, and when we wake up or return to the body of the book, the fathers and the sons alike will be safe, and as long as they are safe, those "other social authorities" whose appeal and legitimacy is grounded on a father's recollection of a son's fantasy of an omnipotent father will be safe as well.

Freud's theoretical gambit—to claim that the paternal triad as grounded by a hitherto unthought fourth figure, the psychic father, the father as inner object—exhibits the same ambiguity we have encountered before. Psychoanalysis stands in a long line of thought that seeks to recuperate fatherhood while abolishing its constitutive dimensions.

---

19 Plato, *Symposium*, 209a, trans. Michael Joyce: "But those whose procreancy is of the spirit rather than of the flesh . . . conceive and bear the things of the spirit And what are they? you ask. Wisdom and all her sister virtues; it is the office of every poet to beget them, and of every artist whom we may call creative." Aristotle, *Nicomachean Ethics*, 1168a, trans. J. E. C. Welldon: "Every artisan feels greater affection for his own work, than the work, if it were endowed with life, would feel for him. But nowhere I think is it so true as in the case of poets; they have an extraordinary affection for their own poems, and are as fond of them as if they were their children." Freud, writing to Edoardo Weiss about his anonymous publication of *Moses and Monotheism:* "My relationship to this work resembles that to a love child. . . . Only much later did I make this non-analytic child legitimate." Freud, *Briefe 1873–1939*, ed. Ernst and Lucie Freud (Frankfurt am Main: S. Fischer, 1968), 431.

Freud's affinity with Hobbes, in particular, is well established—the oedipal trade and the Hobbesian contract of submission are very close indeed, and both Hobbes and Freud end up as the great destabilizers of their time. But there is something new here: where previous reformulations of paternity were shot through with ambivalence, psychoanalysis is *itself* the theory of this ambivalence—as well as the theory of its concealment.

When paternal power emerges as a predominantly psychic effect that exerts its force in the mind of the child—and in psychoanalysis, all psyche is forever the psyche *of* the child—paternal subjectivity disappears from view. This is its peculiar strength in Freud's writing: fantasmatic fatherhood is far harder to dethrone than any given father could ever be. This is, after all, the central thesis of *Totem and Taboo*: the dead father, murdered by the band of brothers, returns first in the totem animal, then in the anthropomorphic immortal god, where he arises as more powerful than the primal patriarch—always vulnerable to the next usurper—could ever have hoped to be. Paternal power, in that model, depends on the empty space the actual father left behind, creating what Freud calls *Vatersehnsucht,* the guilty longing for the father that can cathect to any powerful male figure, actual or imagined. Unmoored from the triumphs or failures of any particular father, the force of the paternal becomes more mobile than it has ever been.

The chain of substitutions, however, is only as strong as its anchor in monotheism, which Freud reads as "the victory of the son's tender emotions over his hostile ones."[20] When psychoanalysis is born, Nietzsche had already proclaimed the death of God, and Freud himself is in the process of establishing himself as one of the most formidable atheists of all times. To be sure, in Nietzsche's words, "this monstrous event is still on its way and wandering,"[21] but the erasure of the supreme paternal signifier is on the wall. In consequence, the weight of patriarchal human history is lifting, and the paternal trope's enhanced mobility will eventually become a liability. Like the *Gschnas*, the figure of the father is cobbled together of bits and pieces, some useful, some obsolete, a bricolage of fear and desire, a repetition of memories and symptoms, of ancient mythologemes and fading ideologemes. The paternal system that had proven so resilient under millennia of

---

20 "Die ambivalente Einstellung gegen den Vater hat hier plastischen Ausdruck gefunden und ebenso der Sieg der zärtlichen Gefühlsregungen des Sohnes über seine feindseligen." Freud, *Totem und Tabu: Einige Übereinstimmungen im Seelenleben der Wilden und der Neurotiker*, (Leipzig/Vienna/Zürich: Internationaler Psychoanalytischer Verlag, 1922), 201.

21 Friedrich Nietzsche, *Sämtliche Werke: Kritische Studienausgabe*, 15 vols., ed., Giorgio Colli and Mazzino Montinari (Berlin: de Gruyter, 1967–77), 3:480.

repeated onslaughts enters a rapid oscillation: deeply entrenched in the collective psyche, and an object of derision and ridicule; part Darth Vader, part Homer Simpson.

The political implications—at the very least, the implications for the political imaginary—are vast, even though Freud himself will not be the one to spell them out. Despite the ubiquity of political or quasi-political allusions in Freud's writing, the fact remains that, as Mladen Dolar puts it,

> Freud . . . never engaged in political life, not in any significant way, not of his own accord, not until it was thrust upon him in the most insidious form of the rampant anti-Semitism, finally the occupation of his country which forced him into exile. Apart from this staggering ending, his relationship to politics was anecdotal. . . . Freud never proposed a political line that would follow from his discovery, a political stance to be taken. He avoided any reflection of the political impact that his discovery might have, in a way which cannot be unintentional, although never explicitly stated.[22]

As Dolar hastens to add, this absence of concrete political articulation does not mean that "the political" is absent from psychoanalysis, particularly if we think of politics as "constructing a collectivity" (ibid.)—be it via *Mass Psychology and the Analysis of the I* (1921), as Dolar does, or via reflections such as the late *Civilization and Its Discontents* (1929) or Freud's letter to Einstein, "Why War?" (1932). Ultimately, *Totem and Taboo* (1913) remains Freud's most enduring theory of political fatherhood, and it is nothing if not a theory of the very conditions of possibility of political organization. Like all of Freud's reflections on authority, it is organized around a theory of fantasmatic fatherhood, but it is crucial to remember that Freud's history—and he insists that it *is* a history—does not end with the conversion of the primal father's physical power into the dead father's psychic force. Many of *Totem and Taboo*'s most ingenious readers, such as Dolar, Jacques Lacan, Carole Pateman, or Eric Santner, restrict their accounts to this conversion, as if the father's power had forever been symbolic after his death by the sons' hands. This allows Dolar to claim that "with the advent of modernity—French revolution marking a symbolic cut and presenting a shorthand for many different processes—*it was the dead father himself who died*. He lost his symbolic impact, his name stopped being the foundation of authority, it was revealed as an imposture" (ibid.).

---

22 Mladen Dolar, "Freud and the Political," *Theory & Event* 12, no. 3 (2009) http://muse.jhu.edu/ (accessed March 30, 2014).

Freud, however, is exquisitely clear: after an interregnum about which he has very little to say, the dead father who exerted his power through representations in totem and divinity, is resuscitated and reinstated:

> With the institution of paternal deities the fatherless society gradually changed into a patriarchal one. The family was a reconstruction of the former primal horde and also restored a great part of their former rights to the fathers. Now there were fathers again but the social achievements of the brother clan had not been given up, and the factual distance between the new family fathers and the unrestricted primal father of the horde was great enough to ensure the continuation of the religious need, the preservation of the unsatisfied longing for the father.[23]

The father returns, Freud stresses, and "the revenge of the dethroned and reinstated father has become a hard one, *the rule of authority is at its height*" (ibid., emphasis added). Despite the lingering "achievements of the band of brothers," then, the new live fathers are actually *more* powerful than the old ones. Freud's account is not a linear one in which power, in a cataclysmic scene of primal patricide, becomes reinvested in symbolic placeholders, where it remains forever active as the power of the dead father. Rather, the surplus of the symbolic is channeled back into actual patriarchal power that has now acquired an *affective* hold to which the hypothetical primal father had no claim and no access until his murder. At least on Freud's terms, then, the execution of Louis XVI did not change much at all: notwithstanding Lacanian attempts to obfuscate Freud's somewhat embarrassing dependence on nineteenth-century social organization, the political psyche is not, for Freud, shaped by political systems. It is shaped by the experience of early childhood—that is to say, by the experience of the family as Freud both found and invented it.

The absence of paternal or patriarchal power was a fleeting state of affairs, then, no less lost in the fog of prehistory as the murder of the primal father itself. While Freud gestures, with uncharacteristic speculative humility, to the possibility of matriarchal interludes—"I do not

---

23 "Mit der Einsetzung der Vatergottheiten wandelte sich die vaterlose Gesellschaft allmählich in die patriarchalisch geordnete um. Die Familie war eine Wiederherstellung der einstigen Urhorde und gab den Vätern auch ein großes Stück ihrer früheren Rechte wieder. Es gab jetzt wieder Väter, aber die sozialen Errungenschaften des Brüderclan waren nicht aufgegeben worden, und der faktische Abstand der neuen Familienväter vom unumschränkten Urvater der Horde war groß genug, um die Fortdauer des religiösen Bedürfnisses, die Erhaltung der ungestillten Vatersehnsucht, zu versichern." *Totem und Tabu*, 201.

know to determine at what point in this development there finds itself a place for the great maternal deities"[24]—, Freud throughout his work declines to imagine in any detail "the fatherless society" he so briefly evokes, be it as historical past *or* possible future.

It is Paul Federn who, in 1919, resurrects that suggestive formula and fills the gap. *On the Psychology of the Revolution: The Fatherless Society* remains untranslated, even though no less than Ernest Jones suggested to Freud that he assign the task to James Strachey.[25] Federn's short essay—29 pages in print—makes explicit what Freud only implied, and implied ambivalently at best: if fatherhood is the key to political authority, then any lasting political change depends on changing the face of paternity.

A few words about Federn, who is barely known these days, might be called for. Paul Federn, born in 1871 and dead by his own hand in 1950, was an early and quite important associate of Freud's, having joined his inner circle in the early 1900s.[26] A founding member of the Vienna Psychoanalytic Society, which he led as acting chairman for years, as well as a leading training analyst of his time—his analysands included Wilhelm Reich—,[27] Federn frequently served as Freud's deputy at official functions and gave the radio address in honor of Freud's seventieth birthday. In Makari's account, Federn appears as a "bearded patriarch," a member of "the old guard," fanatically loyal to Freud, an opponent of all analytic innovation or revision, and a noticeably unpleasant character (an account strongly at variance with Edoardo Weiss's recollections).[28] It is certainly true that Federn was loyal to Freud and defended him vigorously from Freud's dissenting disciples, but it is equally true that his own work frequently and significantly departed from Freudian dogma, even if Federn himself was in a habit of downplaying the divergences. *The Fatherless Society*, both an explicit hommage to Freud and a subtle but deeply significant revision to Freud's theory of fatherhood, is deeply symptomatic of this tension.

The essay's first sentences are programmatic: "We can analyze societal order and its change as a technical program of organization

---

24 "Wo sich in dieser Entwicklung die Stelle für die großen Muttergottheiten findet, die vielleicht allgemein den Vatergöttern vorhergegangen sind, weiß ich nicht anzugeben." *Totem und Tabu*, 201.
25 Letter from Ernest Jones to Freud, October 17, 1920. *The Complete Correspondence of Sigmund Freud and Ernest Jones, 1908–1939* (Cambridge, MA: Harvard University Press, 1993), 289.
26 For further details, see Edoardo Weiss, "Paul Federn," in *Psychoanalytic Pioneers*, ed. Franz Alexander, Samuel Eisenstein, and Martin Grotjahn (New Brunswick, NJ: Transaction Publishers, 1995), 142–59.
27 Georg Makari, *Revolution in Mind: The Creation of Psychoanalysis* (Melbourne University Press, 2008), 397.
28 See Makari 397, 476ff.

or as a political problem, i.e. we can ask which interests and power factions battle each other and which means will serve each specific interest and faction of power. In the latter case, one will have to take the psychic processes into account in order to arrive at an etiological explanation."[29]

At stake, then, are the origins of political structures in or even *as* psychic phenomena, and it is not the least surprising that Federn, the analyst, will turn to the Freudian father, and in particular to the father of *Totem and Taboo*. Federn, the active and committed social democrat, however, veers into territory Freud himself never ventured to enter: he envisions, however tentatively, a change so radical that psychoanalysis—forever privileging continuity over change—would lose its tenuous hold on cultural theory altogether.

Federn is writing in the aftermath of World War I and the collapse of the Hapsburg monarchy, and like so many of his contemporaries, he senses the possibility of a truly new order: "For a long time—an unbearably long time where the socialist is concerned—our social order has retained the forms and laws of previous centuries" (4), he writes. It soon emerges that the form and laws of the previous centuries are nothing but the forms and laws of the paternal triad: the loss of traditional authority goes hand in hand with a loss of psychic equilibrium and social integration among his fellow citizens, whose previous submission to the general order he ascribes almost exclusively to the institutionalized force of the paternal.

> To date, the integration into the order of the state (*die staatliche Einordnung*) has been the consequence of the integration into the order of the family. But the family as a whole is not involved in the social aspect of ethical development to an equal degree. Rather, it is the position of the child with regard to the father which forms the foundation of all respect for authority.[30]

Federn himself calls this claim a *Binsenwahrheit*, a cliché, and to the extent that he is a good Freudian, he links it both to the current

---

29 "Man kann die Gesellschaftsordnung und ihre Umwandlung als ein technisches Problem der Organisation oder als politisches Problem behandeln, das heißt die Frage stellen, welche Interessen und Machtfaktoren miteinander kämpfen und welche Mittel jedem speziellen Interesse und Machtfaktor dienen. In diesem Falle wird man zu jeder ursächlichen Erklärung die seelischen Vorgänge mitberücksichtigen müssen." Federn, 4.

30 "Die staatliche Einordnung ist bisher die Folge der familiären gewesen. Aber nicht die gesamte Familie ist an dem sozialen Teil der sittlichen Entwicklung in gleichem Ausmass beteiligt. Vielmehr ist es die Stellung des Kindes zum Vater, die die Grundlage alles Autoritätsrespekts in ihm bildet." Ibid., 7.

organization of the family where the father is "indeed master of the child's fate" and to a long history where "the child only remained alive according to the will of the father." His account is exceedingly normative, but self-consciously so—while Federn refers to "the normal mother," who is said to idolize and serve her children, while "the typical father remains a stranger to the child," he acknowledges that such arrangements are "normal" or "typical" for the patriarchal family alone, itself one of those "unbearable" social forms of old. Still in step with Freud and his postulate of widespread *Vatersehnsucht*, Federn maintains that the relationship between father and child—distant, but reassuring—"remains undisturbed for only a short time, but long enough to continue unconsciously to exert an unextinguishable force in humans in the form of the need for such dependence (*Anlehnung*)" (8).

Where Freud defines filial ambivalence as the tension between affection and hostility, however, Federn's child does not need to come to terms with the father's possession of the mother but with the father's failure to live up to his image. The child soon learns, Federn maintains, "how limited the father's omnipotence really is," and it is this failure of the father which constitutes the "tragic moment" that "no boy is spared." Whereas Freud mourned his father's death as "the greatest loss" a man could endure, to Federn, the father has always already been lost. It is not the father's death but the father's life that constitutes the trauma, the series of "repeated disappointments" that constitutes the "fall from sheltered safety" (8). Like all trauma, the failure of the father "appears to be continuously forgotten" but constitutes "one of those experiences that are re-lived again and again—every time an authority in his life is felled" (8).

To be sure, Freud does reflect on this sort of disillusionment at times, not least with regard to his own father, but for Federn, the necessary fall of the father is nothing less than the condition of political life, for "usually, the child has no choice—to put it crudely—but to search for a new father, again and again. And since society and culture have developed on the basis of patriarchal authority for millennia, the child, who leaves the family behind to enter life, will find in teacher, priest, mayor, king, and emperor plenty of contenders for the paternal post that has become vacant within himself."[31]

For a while, this wide distribution of *Vatersehnsucht* works well enough—different aspects of the father image attach to different

---

31 "Gewöhnlich kann das Kind nicht anders, als sich – banal ausgedrückt – immer wieder einen neuen Vater suchen. Und da seit Jahrtausenden sich Gesellschaft und Kultur auf der Basis patriarchalischer Autorität entwickelt haben, findet das aus der Familie ins Leben tretende Kind im Lehrer, im Pfarrer, im Bürgermeister, in König und Kaiser genug Anwärter auf diesen in seinem Innern freigewordenen Vaterposten." Ibid., 9.

figures, some loved, some feared, and the relationships that develop tend to be more realistic while "the psychic tie that was torn away from the real father is attached to each new powerful authority." Since those "powerful authorities" tend to be powerful in general, the substitute fathers create a substitute community of siblings when "thus all the individual sons unite as subjects to the paternal authoritarian state" (*Autoritätsstaat*, 9). The flaws each secular authority exhibits, furthermore, are erased in "God-the-father whose perfection exceeds all worldly measure and reaches the glory of the original childish father version" (*Vaterfassung*). Thus, secular and divine fathers shore up the filial disposition" (*Sohneseinstellung*, 9), and the complicity of church and state secures the "patriarchal establishment state" (*patriarchaler Obrigkeitsstaat*)—paternal power emerges on the basis of paternal weakness.

Within the paternal series, emperor and god, two points of the paternal triad, are of special importance since unlike the familial father, neither one of them incites a sense of rivalry—the submissive political subject "is attached to them without wanting to compete or ascend to their height" (10). Thoroughly modern, Federn's account is entirely centered on the needs, desires, and psychic activity of the sons. There is no paternal subject: Federn's patriarchy knows only sons (and occasionally daughters), and the fathers themselves have no inner life of their own—they are, in fact, coterminous with the state itself, and equally faceless.

By now, Federn has constructed a model of filial submission so firmly rooted in the political psyche that revolution—the very theme of the essay—appears impossible. In order to conjure revolutionaries where none can exist, Federn turns to *vaterlandslose Gesellen*, "thugs without a fatherland," a term widely (and symptomatically) used at the time to denounce the communist and socialist left. In a brilliant move, he recasts the fatherlandless as the fatherless, a band of dissenters whose oppositional spirit can be bound and made fruitful by socialist consciousness. The aim of fraternal political organization, then, is to liberate its participants from their habits of filiality—a feat whose accomplishment, given Federn's insistence on the ubiquity and force of *Vatersehnsucht*, comes as a bit of a surprise until we learn that it was accomplished only because the "national heroes and leaders" of social democracy usurped the vacant paternal position (10).

Federn's argument has become unstable—the future of the revolution, it seems, no longer depends on the erasure of the filial disposition but threatens to emerge as just another battle between competing fathers. We might say that the essay repeats its argument as performance: Federn himself cannot conceive of authority as anything other than paternal authority. Fittingly, this is the point where Federn relates the anecdote of an "elderly comrade" who, at a national assembly, is able to articulate "the most radical demands loudly, fluently, and with full conviction," but "falters twenty times in the few sentences" that relate to the abdication of the emperor. The "child loyal to the emperor" (*das kaisertreue Kind*) left the "social democratic man" speechless, Federn concludes, but in Federn's own essay, the social democratic child takes over the language of the revolutionary (12).

How, then, are these unbearable forms and laws to be erased if even their most devoted critics cannot shed the habits that sustain them? Federn maintains that "unconscious bonds are uprooted when they no longer meet the old, unconscious desire that created them"—but as we recall, unmet desire for powerful fathers to replace the failing ones who cannot meet it is itself the very engine of the father series: "The child has the desire to depend on a beloved being whose greatness, power, and knowledge grant him absolute security and protection. The wish for such a father is precisely what makes the real father fall" (13).

Clearly, what would need to be uprooted is the desire itself rather than the political bondage it creates, but neither Freud nor Federn can account for any condition of that erasure's possibility. The next best hope, then, is the total and simultaneous collapse of all authority, a cataclysmic, breakdown of *all* patriarchal institutions that removes all contenders for the vacuum and leaves the filial subjects bewildered and abandoned. It is precisely this exceptional state Federn believes arrived at the end of the war: "Thus, in comprehensible inner confusion, there stood a crowd of fatherless folk whom the shared motherland and necessity forced to create a fatherless society."[32]

After this brief moment of imagined victory, however, Federn appears to lose faith in his own argument—his own filial disposition reasserts itself. The rise of the workers' and soldiers' councils, Federn's example for successful fatherless organization, makes for a slim foundation to erase what he had presented as a desire that was ubiquitous, ancient, and deeply rooted. As the structure of the family continued to shape the political psyche, previous attempts at fraternal organization, he admits, had failed, and while 1919 Austria may indeed have been characterized by a power vacuum, his fellow Austrians remain the product of the same families they had always been. And indeed, "[t]he congruence of the family with the fallen, patriarchally structured state and its incongruence with a fraternal organization is therefore the essential psychological problem in erecting a nonpatriarchal societal

---

32 "So standen plötzlich in begreiflicher innerer Verwirrtheit eine Menge vaterlose Gesellen da, welche das gemeinsame Mutterland und die Not zur Schaffung einer vaterlosen Gesellschaft zwingt." Ibid., 13.

order."³³ The battle to come, therefore, is to "make conscious" the filial condition and to thus render it opposable (*bekämpfbar*).

While Federn's tentative faith in the powers of social-democratic indoctrination, along with his conviction in the peaceableness of fraternal relations (26–7), must strike us as naïve, there is something quite touching in the sincerity of his fragile hope that Freud's story may finally find a different ending: "It would be a tremendous liberation if the current revolution, which is a repetition of very ancient revolts against the father, succeeded. The soul of mankind could perhaps become a more beautiful one, the patricidal feature could fade from its face."³⁴ And yet, here is the same conundrum again: Federn, advocating for the end of fathers, dreams of a humanity that is beautiful precisely because it no longer has to kill them. It is his horror of patricide, along with his own symptomatic longing for fathers and heroes, that prevents him from taking his argument to the only possible conclusion, that is, the abolition of *familial* fatherhood which Plato, in a different vision of a humanity more beautiful, had recommended thousands of years earlier. To be sure, Federn does know that nothing else will do, even if he only articulates that insight in passing, in the hope that "gradually, the structure of the family will adapt to the new order unless perhaps this new order will necessitate to substitute the family with child rearing according to matriarchal law or an unknown system."³⁵

This is the impasse, then, and we might call it Federn's paradox: the new order can only arise if there is a new family, and the new family can only arise if there is a new order. It is no wonder that he concludes with a coda noticeably lacking in revolutionary fervor: "The father-son motif has undergone the strongest defeat. It is, however, anchored deeply within humanity and will probably prevent this time as well that a fully 'fatherless society' will prevail."³⁶ It is difficult not to

---

33 "Die Kongruenz der Familie mit dem gestürzten, patriarchalisch gebauten Staate und ihre Inkongruenz mit einer Bruderschaftsorganisation ist ·deshalb das eigentliche psychologische Problem der Aufrichtung einer nicht patriarchalischen Gesellschaftsordnung." Ibid., 17.
34 "Es wäre eine ungeheure Befreiung wenn die jetzige Revolution die eine Wiederholung uralter Revolten gegen den Vater ist, Erfolg hätte. Die Seele der Menschheit könnte vielleicht eine schönere werden, der parrizide Zug aus ihrem Antlitz verschwinden." Ibid., 22.
35 "allmählich wird die Struktur der Familie sich der neuen Ordnung anpassen, wenn nicht vielleicht diese einen Ersatz der Familie durch eine Aufzucht der Kinder nach Mutterrecht oder nach einem unbekannten System nötig machen wird." Ibid., 17.
36 "Das Vater-Sohn-Motiv hat die schwerste Niederlage erlitten. Es ist aber durch die Familienerziehung und als ererbtes Gefühl tief in der Menschheit verankert und wird wahrscheinlich auch diesmal verhindern, daß eine restlos 'Vaterlose Gesellschaft' sich durchsetzt." Ibid., 29.

conclude that psychoanalytic universalism defeats the political dream of change precisely because Federn's vision is itself a patricidal one, a revolt against Freud, the most powerful man in his own personal father series.

And yet, Federn has proven right in many ways. Certainly, the fatherless society has not prevailed if such a society were to consist of autonomous men and women who had both understood and overcome their longing to be safe in the hands of power. And yet, it seems undeniable that the Western family *has* changed. Federn's "normal mother" and "typical father" exist, for the most part, in the nostalgic fantasies of conservative cultural discourse, and even there, they are steadily fading from view. Fathers' legal rights are either identical to mothers' rights or actually lesser in number and nature. DNA testing has brought to an end the ancient history of paternal uncertainty, steadily eroding a gender system that grounded motherhood in the body, fatherhood in speech and law. I sincerely believe that to the extent that our laws and our institutions reflect our collective convictions, we no longer have any viable theory that would allow us to privilege fatherhood over motherhood or motherhood over fatherhood—in fact, we no longer have a viable theory that would allow us to distinguish between the two. In my most optimistic moments, I believe we might be on the verge of that unimaginable "unknown system" Federn invokes and abandons.

And yet, these moments are few, for I remember a time one of our faucets had been dripping for days. I finally found the time and motivation to get out the tools and take care of it. My four-year-old son had been watching me closely, in what I was sure had to be admiration. But not more than two hours later, he proclaimed, with unshakable conviction, that "Daddy fixed it." His father, it should be noted, is a scholarly man who has been able to avoid exposure to all hand tools, and he has never fixed anything of this sort in his life. I have been wondering ever since who this Daddy might have been, this father who lived in my son's mind, doing the fatherly things his father never did, and I feel a strange kinship with Paul Federn and his mournful conclusion.

Conclusion: Dead Children

One more story. This one is about David and Absalom, David's third son, renowned for his beauty and charm, and particularly for his gorgeous head of hair. Again, it is a story of conflict, violence, and bloodshed, and impossibly convoluted, even in light of the Bible's pervasive penchant for complications. The trouble between father and son begins when David's oldest son, Amnon, rapes Absalom's sister Tamar, Amnon's half-sister. A full two years later, Absalom organizes a mob to kill Amnon in revenge. David is upset, Absalom flees, and father and son don't see each other for years, though David longs for his beautiful son. Absalom is finally allowed to return home and, after another delay, to see the king's face again.

The reconciliation accomplished, he promptly begins to plot against his father, gaining the people's favor, raising his own army. This time, David flees. Absalom moves into town and establishes his claim to power by raping his father's concubines—and these are just some highlights, never mind the curious rumor that Absalom killed all of David's sons, or the fact that Absalom sets fire to the field of David's general Joab, just to gain an audience with the king, or that we are told exactly how much the hair Absalom cuts off each year weighs.

David, in the meantime, amasses his own army. Before the final showdown, David instructs his men to deal kindly with the enemy, and in particular to be gentle with his son Absalom, though you would think that Absalom, by now, had forfeited any right to paternal concern. On the day of the battle, Absalom's beautiful hair gets caught in the branches of an oak, his mule bolts, and David's men find him hanging from the tree, still alive. They call for Joab and remind him of David's order to spare his son. Joab acknowledges the advice, stabs Absalom through the heart with three separate spears, then has him beaten to death by ten soldiers. It is an astonishing act of overkill, perhaps meant to remind us that the Bible takes paternal power seriously. When David hears that Absalom is dead, he cries out, "O my son Absalom—my son, my son Absalom—if only I had died in your place! O Absalom my son, my son!"[37]

All books start with an intuition. This one became possible the first time I heard Heinrich Schütz's "Fili mi Absalon," a motet from the

---

37 2 Samuel 18.33, NKJV.

Symphoniae Sacrae (1629).³⁸ It remains the most moving piece of music I know, and it irrevocably shifted my perception of fathers and of fatherhood. Until then, the voice of paternity had belonged to Freud's fathers, laying down the law; to Kafka's fathers, hovering between myth and mockery; to the fathers wreaking psychic havoc on their children all over postwar German literature. Fathers, at least the ones to be encountered in the post-Freudian world, were stern or abusive, distant or absent, and faintly ridiculous at that, like Adorno's "angry father who yells at the children when they do not tumble down the stairs in jubilation the moment he returns home from business in a bad mood."³⁹

The voice of King David—ancient, but mediated through the musical language of the late Renaissance—added an entirely different dimension, the sound of an intense sorrow none of those other accounts seemed to hear. The composition leaves unchanged the stark elements of the Vulgata's lament—"fili mi Absalom fili mi Absalom quis mihi tribuat ut ego moriar pro te Absalom fili mi fili mi"—and arranges them into spirals of loss, a relentless grief circling around the son, his name, and the father's longing to have died instead:

> Fili mi, fili mi, fili mi, fili mi, Absalon, fili mi, fili mi, fili mi, Absalon, Absalon, Absalon, fili mi, Absalon, Absalon, Absalon, fili, fili mi, Absalon, fili mi, fili mi. Quis mihi tribuat, ut ego moriar, moriar, moriar pro te, quis mihi tribuat, ut ego moriar, moriar, moriar pro te, moriar, moriar pro te! Absalon, Absalon, Absalon, fili mi, fili mi, fili mi, fili mi, Absalon, fili mi, fili mi, Absalon, Absalon, Absalon, Absalon!

If you have not heard it, find it now; there are many different versions on youtube.

* * *

The literary history of fathers and their children is written through the specter of death and loss, real or averted. Kronos eats his children;

---

38 *Symphoniae sacrae I*, Op.6, SWV 269. An excellent performance, by Cappella Augustana, conducted and with organ by Matteo Messori and sung by Harry van der Kamp, bass, is included in a box set, *Heinrich Schütz Edition*, Brilliant Classics, 2012. Available at http://youtu.be/bjRfof7WsHo

39 "Die Ermahnung zur Happiness, in der der wissenschaftlich lebemännische Sanatoriumsdirektor mit den nervösen Propagandachefs der Vergnügungsindustrie übereinstimmt, trägt die Züge des wütenden Vaters, der die Kinder anbrüllt, weil sie nicht jubelnd die Treppe hinunterstürzen, wenn er mißlaunisch aus dem Geschäft nach Hause kommt." Theodor W. Adorno. *Minima Moralia*. (Frankfurt am Main: Suhrkamp, 2003), 38.

Oedipus kills his father and curses his sons to fratricidal bloodshed; Theseus's father jumps into the sea when he sees the black sails that he believes announce his son's death; Agamemnon sacrifices Iphigeneia; Abraham is ready to slaughter Isaac; Jacob mourns Joseph; David mourns Absalom; God sacrifices Jesus. Ben Jonson composes two sonnets—"On my first sonne" and "On my first daughter"—but only after they are gone. Goethe's father rides faster while the Erlking whispers to the son dying in his arms. Lessing writes his most famous letter on the occasion of his infant son's death. Odoardo Galotti sinks the dagger into Emilia. Philotas kills himself, but in the name of the father (even if the father himself no longer wants to be called by that name). Jacques-Louis David paints Brutus watching the lictors bringing home the bodies of his sons who were executed at his command. Old Father Briest sorrowfully abandons Effi, who dies of consumption. Mallarmé obsessively writes and rewrites a *tombeau* for his dead son Anatole, which he will never publish. Yeats's Cuchulain slays his son on Baile's Strand. In 1901, recovering from a life-threatening illness, Mahler composes the *Kindertotenlieder*. And so it goes on, more recently in novels such as Ford's *Sportswriter* (1986), Ian McEwan's *The Child in Time* (1987), or Robert Hellenga's *The Fall of a Sparrow* (1998).

These stories are all different, to be sure—different times, different genres, different media, different aims. Some are explicitly political, some intensely personal. Some may leave us cold or make us angry, others may break our heart. Each and every one of them deserves its own reading. Other stories have been told. And yet, there is, undeniably, an enduring theme here, a *basso continuo* of death.

Absalom belongs to the same mythic landscape in which fathers and children encounter each other within the politics of sacrificial violence. Like Iphigeneia, Oedipus, Isaac, or Philotas, Absalom is sacrificed to the nation. He is a rebel, his death restores the political order, and when they come to tell David that he is gone, they think they are bringing good news.[40] And they are, of course: Absalom's death is good news for the king. But it is devastating news for the father.

The Tragedy of Fatherhood is devoted to that split that runs through the figure of the father who has carried the weight of the violence that constitutes his power and leaves him bereft. "Fili mi Absalon" does

---

40 "Tidings, my lord the king: for the Lord hath avenged thee this day of all them that rose up against thee. And the king said unto Cushi, Is the young man Absalom safe? And Cushi answered, The enemies of my lord the king, and all that rise against thee to do thee hurt, be as that young man is. And the king was much moved, and went up to the chamber over the gate, and wept: and as he went, thus he said, O my son Absalom, my son, my son Absalom! would God I had died for thee, O Absalom, my son, my son!" 2 Samuel 18.31–33, NKJV.

not pay attention to Absalom's revolt, to the rapes, the murders, the betrayals. Perhaps it is only in so starkly isolating the father's lament, by removing everything around it, that Schütz can lend the paternal subject such a powerful voice. But once you hear it there, you can hear it everywhere, as I have sought to show in the preceding chapters.

Much has been written about fathers and fatherhood, but very little about the father in mourning. And yet, he may be the emblematic figure of the long history of the paternal triad. Whenever children die for their fathers—or in the name of their fathers—, the power of the father, in reaching its zenith, abolishes itself. Freud may have gotten it wrong: the moment in which the *child* dies is the moment where fatherhood becomes symbolic fatherhood, disembodied. It is, to be sure, the moment where fatherhood articulates itself in writing—as lament, *nachträglich*.

We have no image for paternal grief: the parent who hovers over the body of the dead child is the mother; most of us recognize the image of the *Pietà* at a single glance. And there is no image for paternal tenderness, either—at least no canonical, collectively shared image, whereas mother and child, the Madonna, can be found everywhere a dead son can be found hanging on a cross. It is not as if fatherhood had not been painted or sculpted, of course, but none of those representations are seared into our shared visual vocabulary.

The body of parenthood, tactile and visible, has always been the body of the mother; the pervasive gender system that associates femininity with nature and soma and fatherhood with power and the law has all but barred the father's body from view—even if it is in full sight. The discussion of "Laocoön and his Sons" has shaped modern aesthetics like no other sculpture ever since, but with the exception of Goethe, the sculpture's admirers (Pliny, Winckelmann, Lessing, and Babbit, among others) don't pause to think about the fact that they are analyzing the representation of a father, failing. Sophocles wrote a tragedy about Laocoön as well, but just like his *Laius*, it is lost.

"Ugolino and His Sons," the Carpeaux statue you can visit at the gallery of the Metropolitan Museum in New York, is more sinister, though Ugolino's oddly muscular body ("oddly," because he is starving) clearly cites the Laocoön statue. Seen from the back—the title image of this book—, the sculpture hovers between violence, tenderness, and a disquieting erotic charge, appropriate for the depiction of a scene from Dante's *Inferno* where Ugolino's sons offer their starving bodies to feed their starving father:

"Father our pain," they said,
"Will lessen if you eat us you are the one

188   The Tragedy of Fatherhood

> Who clothed us with this wretched flesh: we plead
> For you to be the one who strips it away."[41]

Dante never quite tells us whether Ugolino partakes of his sons' flesh after they are dead:

> ... And I,
> Already going blind, groped over my brood
> Calling to them, though I had watched them die,
> For two long days. And then the hunger had more
> Power than even sorrow over me. (289)

Perhaps he ate them, perhaps he chewed on himself, perhaps he died of hunger before he could die of grief. It hardly matters—all of them have become meat. In Carpeaux's representation, the youngest son lies curled up at his feet, perhaps dead; two older ones cling to his body, beseeching him; the fourth one shelters his head under Ugolino's left arm, while their father looks into the distance, perhaps as not to be tempted by his children's offer to nurture him with their bodies, in a striking double reversal of a mother feeding her infant. Ugolino's posture seems oddly unaffected by his sons' distress; no part of his body accommodates them, as if he were barely aware of them. In Dante's text, Ugolino speaks eloquently of his own grief upon seeing the children die, one by one, but in a sculpture of five bodies, closely, even desperately intertwined, the father's body remains oddly untouched, or rather, perhaps, oddly untouching. Paternal tenderness, then, is a matter of words, of voice.[42]

* * *

Around 1900, paternal power suffers from multiple ailments: its symbolic ground, the narrative of God-the-father, has been shaking

---

41   Robert Pinsky, trans. *The Inferno of Dante: A New Verse Translation*. (New York: Noonday Press, 1996), 287.

42   I know of only one—rather obscure—story in which the death of the child does not lead toward the articulation of a heightened paternity, Damon Runyon's "Little Miss Marker." The main character, a thoroughly unappealing bookie named Sorrowful (!), takes in a little girl who deeply changes and humanizes him—a ubiquitous topos in modern literature, film, and television, but Runyon departs from the predictable storyline when upon the girl's death, Sorrowful simply reverts back to his former self, the child's presence leaving no trace: "And now as he is looking at the door a very strange thing seems to happen to his kisser, for all of a sudden it becomes the sad, mean-looking kisser that it is in the days before he ever sees Marky, and furthermore it is never again anything else" (101–2). In *Furthermore* (London: Constable and Company Ltd., 1938), 81–102.

ever since Spinoza began to rewrite the Old Testament's God in the spirit of a depersonalization that is always also a depaternalization. Its political analogue, kingship, is on its last breath. And in the absence of these traditional support systems, fatherhood's continuing fantasmatic support, far from shoring up the crumbling foundations, produces an overload far more crushing than any direct attack could be. If we accept that the unconscious is a repository not just of personal, but of cultural history as well—and how could it be otherwise?—, it releases images of powerful and terrifying fathers only to have them encounter *Peter Pan*'s hapless Mr. Darling who has taken up residency in the doghouse. This is no longer the father whose power can be removed or restricted only by a superior paternity, such as Abraham's God or Amphitryon's Zeus. "'Surely,' said John, like one who had lost faith in his memory, 'he used not to sleep in the kennel?' 'John,' Wendy said falteringly, 'perhaps we don't remember the old life as well as we thought we did.'"[43]

This is the comic register, but it's not so different elsewhere. Allow me to draw attention to two very different texts from the same period that have, in different ways, served as exemplary expressions of the age: the "Letter of Lord Chandos" (see Chapter 10), and *Sex and Character*, by Otto Weininger.

While Hofmannsthal, throughout his writings, seeks to recuperate the possibility of fatherhood, Weininger, with the psychotic clarity that pervades his work, pronounces that "fatherhood is a pathetic delusion." A delusion not because of the old lament of paternal uncertainty, or because insemination is too haphazard an event to ground fatherhood as an ethically significant relation, though that is certainly true for him, as well. More importantly, however, he argues that men's part in reproduction is limited: "the mother is being impregnated by all things, continuously, and all over her body. Hence fatherhood is a pathetic delusion as it must always be shared with an infinite number of things and people." Women—in their incarnations as either prostitute or mother—don't have intercourse with men; they are in a permanent state of coitus with the object world surrounding and penetrating them. Insemination is quantitatively, but not qualitatively, different from this ceaseless orgy of world and woman, "only a special case of highest intensity."[44] Weininger, by the way, is not talking metaphorically here, and he considers science to be squarely on his side (though science does not return the favor). On the contrary, he

---

43 Barrie. *Peter Pan in Kensington Gardens*, 213.
44 "nur ein Spezialfall von höchster Intensität" Otto Weininger. *Geschlecht und Charakter*, (Vienna and Leipzig: Wilhelm Braumüller, 1909), 307.

insists on the all-encompassing quality of this coition with staggering intensity:

> *Without difference* . . . , because woman is *only* and *throughout* sexual, and because this sexuality extends over her *whole* body and, in physical terms, is merely denser at some points than at others, *every* woman, feels herself sexually coited, perpetually and throughout her whole body, everywhere and always, without exception, by whatever it may be.⁴⁵ (Emphasis added)

This state of affairs will lead Weininger to the obvious conclusion: he advocates the end of reproduction: "Every form of fecundity is loathsome, and no one who is honest with himself feels bound to provide for the continuity of the human race. . . . On the contrary, it is immoral to procreate a human being for any secondary reason."⁴⁶

Needless to say, the end of fatherhood rarely takes such radical form; Weininger is merely the most symptomatic of a group of very different writers who are attuned to a version of what Eric Santner has called "the crisis of investiture." "Symbolic investiture," Santner notes, entails the orders, rites, and procedures by which:

> [A]n individual is endowed with a new social status, is filled with a symbolic mandate that henceforth informs his or her identity in the community. The social and political stability of a society as well as the psychological "health" of its members would appear to be correlated to the efficacy of these symbolic operations—to what we might call their *performative magic*—whereby individuals "become who they are," assume the social essence assigned to them by way of names, titles, degrees, posts, honors, and the like.⁴⁷

Santner, here following Lacan's analysis, defines this crisis as "a 'foreclosure' of the paternal metaphor, the Name-of-the-Father" (61),

---

45 "Unterschiedslos . . . fühlt sich jede Frau, da das Weib nur und durchaus sexuell ist, da diese Sexualität ueber den ganzen Körper sich erstreckt und an einigen Punkten, physikalisch gesprochen, bloss *dichter* ist als an anderen, fortwährend und am ganzen Leibe, überall und immer, von was es auch sei, ausnahmslos *koitiert*" (emphasis added). Ibid.

46 "Alle Fécondité ist nur ekelhaft; und kein Mensch fühlt, wenn er sich aufrichtig befragt, es als seine Pflicht, für die dauernde Existenz der menschlichen Gattung zu sorgen. . . . Im Gegenteil: es ist unmoralisch, ein menschliches Wesen zur Wirkung einer Ursache zu machen, es als Bedingtes hervorzubringen" *Geschlecht und Charakter*, 469.

47 Eric L. Santner. *My Own Private Germany: Daniel Paul Schreber's Secret History of Modernity*. (Princeton, NJ: Princeton University Press, 1996), xii.

but I am arguing that it is the father himself, not his metaphoric or symbolic substitutes, who can no longer assume his position, who can no longer "become what he is" and yet is still meant to be.

The father, I think, can no longer speak because, as Kafka's letter, which I quoted in the introduction, demonstrates, filiality has usurped the language and writing of modernity. I am not talking in terms of biography, of course. Many of the fin-de-siècle's seminal writers are indeed fathers in the literal sense. What I do mean to say is that they rarely write *as* fathers, in the way that, say, Lessing or Fontane did—they still write about fathers, no doubt, but, as a rule, from a distance that denies the possibility of identification. This is nowhere more striking than in Freud's *Interpretation of Dreams*, where, after stressing the role of his father's death in the conception of the work, Freud suggests that "to my readers the material from which they learn to evaluate and interpret dreams will be a matter of indifference."[48]

Quite the contrary: Freud's dead father and dead fathers in general have been anything but a "matter of indifference" in the reception of the Dream Book, and few if any have questioned the supreme oddity of Freud's self-analysis. Why would the death of one's father, however important or poignant it may be, be "the *most* important event" in a man's life, why "the *most* incisive (*einschneidendsten*) loss"? And why only in the life of a man (*eines Mannes*)? I suspect that the answer has little to do with the father himself, or with what has been lost *in him*, but with a loss within the life of the son: he has been cut off from sonhood itself. Like the birth of a child, the death of a parent changes our position in the generational scheme: both move us one step closer to death. But while the son who becomes a father can yet remain, in actuality, a son, the death of *his* father dooms him to an uninhabitable paternity. When being a son means being Oedipus, being a father means being Laius. It means to arrive at the crossroads where the son waits, politely asking the old man to step out of the way (or into the kennel). The son, needless to say, is carrying a stick.

As we have seen, when it comes to the stories of paternal violence, the most important ones—Kronos/Zeus, Laius/Oedipus, Abraham/Isaac, God/Jesus—have not told the story of the child who dies but of the boy who lived. Zeus does not die on Mount Olympus, Oedipus does not die on Mount Kithairon, Isaac does not die on Mount Moriah, and Jesus, while he does die on Mount Golgotha, revives. But even when the child does not make it, the topos of the dead child paradoxically

---

48 "Für den Leser mag es aber gleichgültig sein, an welchem Material er Träume würdigen und deuten lernt." Strachey's translation, in: Sigmund Freud, *The Interpretation of Dreams,* trans. James Strachey (New York: Basic Books, 2010), xxvi.

centers stories of *continuity* in which is inscribed a violence that affirms the paternal principle far more often than they call it into question. That is even or especially true when, as in *Emilia Galotti*, the child herself incites filicidal violence—she does so in the name of Roman fatherhood and of the law to which Odoardo appeals in the play's closing words.

Toward the end of the nineteenth century, this structure seems to lose its power, and children can no longer be sacrificed to that name of the father that had always spelled Moloch. What fails, to put it differently, is the transition from actual to symbolic fatherhood. One of the most vivid examples in this regard is Zola's *The Masterpiece*, first published as a novel in 1886. Long recognized as a roman à clef about Zola's relationship with Cézanne, the novel tells the story of Claude Lantier, a revolutionary painter denied recognition by the artistic marketplace of his day. Lantier's greatest ambition concerns the annual salon at the Académie des Beaux-Arts, the temple of the arts establishment, where year after year he fails to place one of his pieces. While he is working on a nude for which he holds the highest hopes, his son, a pale and sickly figure, dies. In a scene that begins in considerable poignancy but quickly shades into acute creepiness, Lantier abandons what was to be his masterpiece:

> He had so often been disobedient; this time he had obeyed only too well. She [Lantier's wife] had told him so often to "be quiet and let father get on with his work" that now he was going to be quiet for a long, long time.... Claude had begun to walk to and fro across the studio out of the sheer nervous desire to keep moving. His face was convulsed with grief, but his tears came slowly and he wiped them away mechanically with the back of his hand. Every time he passed the child's dead body he felt obliged to look at it, as if the glassy, staring eyes were exercising some kind of power over him. He tried to resist it at first, but the attraction grew stronger and stronger to the point of obsession, until at last he gave way, fetched out a small canvas and set to work on a study of the dead child. For the first few moments his vision was fogged by tears, but he kept on wiping them away and persisted in plying his wavering brush. Work soon dried his eyes and steadied his hand, and the dead body of his son became simply a model, a strange, absorbing subject for the artist. The exaggerated shape of the head, the waxlike texture of the skin, the eyes like holes wide open on the void, everything about it excited him, filled him with ardor and enthusiasm. He stood back to see the effect; he was pleased, and a vague smile appeared on his lips as he worked.[49]

---

49 Émile Zola, *The Masterpiece*, trans. Thomas Walton and Roger Pearson (New York: Oxford University Press, 2007), 262–3.

Conclusion: Dead Children 193

In the days of *Aufhebung*, the death of the child would have been recuperated in the birth of art; from Plato on, poiesis and paternity had gone hand in hand, with the production of art and logoi a superior path to immortality than mere reproduction. Zola, fully aware of this tradition, lets it collapse. Yes, *The Dead Child*, as the painting will be called, is accepted into the Salon, but only after prolonged politicking. When Lantier arrives at the Salon, he at first cannot find his painting, until he finally discovers it, upon his third pass through the Eastern Gallery. The small canvas is surrounded by an immense painting depicting the Deluge, and next to representations of an aging general, a moonlit nymph, a murdered woman, and assorted "pink effect, mauve effects, a variety of sorry visions. . . . And there, high up among all its sickly-looking neighbors, the little canvas, so much bolder in treatment than all the rest, stood out in violent contrast, like a monster in pain. . . . Hanging where it did it was just a confused mass, like the carcass of some shapeless creature cast up by the tide" (290). With the dead child just one more object of representation, the thoroughly denarrativized painting is ignored, and Lantier hangs himself in his studio not much later. If, as I have argued earlier, the living father has become the figure of impotence, his complementary figure, the dead child, no longer serves as a sacrifice to either history or art, and if fathers nonetheless dream of it at times, they will rarely make it known. Why did Freud remain largely silent on that particular fantasy? If we have learned anything from him, then surely that we are forever tied to the unspoken and the unspeakable. Nothing allows us to stipulate a sentimental exemption for the bond between father and child, least of all psychoanalysis, and yet, Freud either does not hear the voice of Laius or he deliberately silences it. But surely, *fort/da* is a game for all ages? If this book has any merit, the only way to become a father would be to come to terms with the seduction of filicide. Certainly, paternal abdication may be far more alluring. But we delude ourselves, I think, if we imagine that such abdications will set the children free: the gap between actual and symbolic fatherhood creates a vacuum quickly filled by the market forces of an industry Pamela Paul, in a recent book, has dubbed "Parenting Incorporated," more damaging, perhaps, than fathers ever were. Assuming responsibility for our most frightening fantasies, however, also means that we need to relinquish the image of the *other* murderous father who sustains our own filiality—and to shoulder the burden of embodying this image in turn. Of all the ethical demands that psychoanalysis exerts, then, the call to fatherhood might be the hardest one. The father can only relinquish his power if he first, knowing better, consents that it is real. In other words, modernity's call to fatherhood is the call to become what we are: a fantasy.

Bibliography

Abramovitch, Henry Hanoch. *The First Father Abraham: The Psychology and Culture of a Spiritual Revolutionary*. Lanham, MD: University Press of America, 1994.
Adorno, Theodor. *Minima Moralia*. Frankfurt am Main: Suhrkamp, 2003.
Aeschylus. *Seven against Thebes*. In *Aeschylus*, edited by Herbert Weir Smyth. Vol. 1. Cambridge, MA: Harvard University Press; London: William Heinemann Ltd., 1926.
Agamben, Giorgio. *Homo Sacer: Sovereign Power and Bare Life*. Translated by Daniel Heller-Roazen. Stanford, CA: Stanford University Press, 1998.
Airaksinen, Timo and Arto Siitonen. "Kant on Hobbes, Peace, and Obedience." *History of European Ideas* 30, no. 3 (2004): 315–28.
Anker-Mader, Eva-Maria. *Kleists Familienmodelle: Im Spannungsfeld zwischen Krise und Persistenz*. Munich: Wilhelm Fink, 1991.
Annas, Julia. *An Introduction to Plato's Republic*. New York: Oxford University Press, 1981.
Apollodurus. *The Library*. Translated by Sir James George Frazer. 2 vols. Cambridge, MA: Harvard University Press; London: William Heinemann Ltd., 1921.
Arendt, Hannah. *The Human Condition*. Chicago: University of Chicago Press, 1958.
Aristotle. *Generation of Animals*. Translated by A. L. Peck. Loeb Classical Library 366. Cambridge, MA: Harvard University Press, 1942.
—"History of Animals." In *Complete Works of Aristotle: The Revised Oxford Translation*, edited by Jonathan Barnes, translated by D'Arcy Wenworth Thompson. Vol. 1. Bollingen Series 71:2. Princeton, NJ: Princeton University Press, 1984.
—*Nichomachean Ethics*. Translated by J. E. C. Welldon. London: Macmillan and Co., 1892.
—*Nichomachean Ethics*. Translated by Horace Rackham. Cambridge, MA: Harvard University Press; London: William Heinemann, Ltd., 1934.
—*Rhetoric*. Translated by J. H. Freese. Vol. 22, *Aristotle in 23 Volumes*. Cambridge, MA: Harvard University Press, 1926.
Ashley-Cooper, Anthony, Third Earl of Shaftesbury. *Characteristics of Men, Manners, Opinions, Time*. Edited by Laurence E. Klein. Cambridge Texts in the History of Philosophy. Cambridge: Cambridge University Press, 1999.
Auerbach, Erich. *Mimesis: The Representation of Reality in Western Literature*. Translated by William R. Trask. New York: Doubleday/Anchor, 1957.
Bai, Tongdon. "Plato, Strauss, and Political Philosophy: An Interview with Stanley Rosen." *Diotima: A Philosophical Review* 2, no. 1 (2001). http://college.holycross.edu/diotima/n1v2/rosen.htm
Balmary, Marie. *Psychoanalyzing Psychoanalysis: Freud and the Hidden Fault of the Father*. Translated by Ned Lukacher. Baltimore: Johns Hopkins University Press, 1982.
Barrie, J. M. *Peter Pan in Kensington Gardens: Peter and Wendy*. Oxford: Oxford University Press, 2008.
Bartlett, Robert C. "Aristotle's Science of the Best Regime." *American Political Science Review* 88, no. 1 (1994): 143–55.

Bibliography

Beal, Timothy K. and D. M. Gunn, eds. *Reading Bibles, Writing Bodies: Identity and the Book*. Biblical Limits. London & New York: Routledge, 1997.

The Believer. Written and directed by Henry Bean. Performed by Ryan Gosling, Summer Phoenix, Peter Meadows, et al. Drama, 2001. Lions Gate, 2003, DVD.

Benardete, Seth. *The Argument of the Action: Essays on Greek Poetry and Philosophy*. Chicago: University of Chicago Press, 2000.

Bergmann, Martin S. *In the Shadow of Moloch: The Sacrifice of Children and Its Impact on Western Religions*. New York: Columbia University Press, 1992.

Bernhard, Wolfgang. *Das Ende des Ödipus bei Sophokles: Untersuchung zur Interpretation des 'Ödipus auf Kolonos.'* Munich: Beck, 2001.

Blackenhorn, David. *Fatherless America: Confronting Our Most Urgent Social Problem*. New York: Basic Books, 1995.

Blackstone, William. *Commentaries on the Laws of England: In Four Books*. Oxford: Clarendon Press, 1775.

Bloch, Ernst. "Nonsynchronism and the Obligation to Its Dialectics." Translated by Mark Ritter. *New German Critique* 11 (1997): 22–38.

—"Ungleichzeitigkeit und Pflicht zu ihrer Dialektik." In *Erbschaft Dieser Zeit*. Zürich: Oblecht & Helbling, 1935.

Blumenberg, Hans. *Paradigms for a Metaphorology*. Translated by Robert Savage. Signale: Modern German Letters, Cultures, and Thought. Ithaca, NY: Cornell University Press, 2010.

Bohnert, Joachim. "Kleists Fichte ('Amphitryon')." In *Resonanzen: Festschrift für Hans Joachim Kreutzer zum 65. Geburtstag*, edited by Sabine Doering, Waltraud Maierhofer, and Peter Philipp Riedl, 241–55. Würzburg: Königshausen & Neumann, 2000.

Boxer, Sarah. "How Oedipus Is Losing His Complex." *New York Times*, December 6, 1997. http://www.nytimes.com/1997/12/06/theater/how-oedipus-is-losing-his-complex.html

Brown, Wendy. *Manhood and Politics: A Feminist Reading in Political Theory*. Totowa, NJ: Rowman & Littlefield, 1988.

Cain, Albert S. "Who Should Fight America's Battles?" *New York Times*, February 24, 2003, sec. Section A, Editorial Desk.

Caruth, Cathy. *Unclaimed Experience: Trauma, Narrative and History*. Baltimore, MD: Johns Hopkins University Press, 1996.

Chapman, Richard Allen. "Leviathan Writ Small: Thomas Hobbes on the Family." *American Political Science Review* 69, no. 1 (1975): 76–90.

Cohen, Leonard. "The Story of Isaac." *The Lyrics of Leonard Cohen*. London: Omnibus Press, 2009.

Corngold, Stanley. "Nietzsche, Kafka, and Literary Paternity." *Lambent Traces: Franz Kafka*. Princeton, NJ: Princeton University Press, 2004.

Dahlke, Brigit. *Jünglinge der Moderne: Jugendkult und Männlichkeit in der Literatur um 1900*. Cologne/Weimar: Böhlau, 2006.

Davis, Michael. *The Politics of Philosophy: A Commentary on Aristotle's "Politics."* Lanham, MD: Rowman & Littlefield, 1996.

Delaney, Carol Lowery. *Abraham on Trial: The Social Legacy of Biblical Myth*. Princeton, NJ: Princeton University Press, 1998.

Deleuze, Gilles and Félix Guattari. *Anti-Oedipus: Capitalism and Schizophrenia*. Translated by Robert Hurley, Mark Seem, and Helen R. Lane. Minneapolis: University of Minnesota Press, 1983.

—*Kafka: Towards a Minor Literature*. Translated by Dana Polan. Minneapolis: University of Minnesota Press, 1986.

Derrida, Jacques. *The Gift of Death*. Translated by David Willis. Chicago: University of Chicago Press, 1996.
Devereux, Georges. "The Cannibalistic Impulses of Parents." *Psychoanalytic Forum* 1 (1966): 114–30.
—"Why Oedipus Killed Laius." *International Journal of Psychoanalysis* 34, no. 1 (1953): 131–41.
Dolar, Mladen. "Freud and the Political." *Theory & Event* 12, no. 3 (2009), http://muse.jhu.edu/ (accessed March 30, 2014).
Dutoit, Thomas. "Rape, Crypt and Fantasm: Kleist's *Marquise of O* ..." *Mosaic* 27, no. 3 (1994): 45–64.
Dylan, Bob. "Highway 61 Revisited." *Bob Dylan: Lyrics, 1962–2001*. New York: Simon & Schuster, 2004.
Eisenhower, John S. D. "Presidential Children Don't Belong in Battle." *New York Times*, September 28, 2008, sec. Op-Ed. http://www.nytimes.com/2008/09/28/opinion/28eisenhower.html
Elshtain, Jean Bethke. *Public Man, Private Woman: Women in Social and Political Thought*. Princeton, NJ: Princeton University Press, 1981.
Erikson, Erik. "Reflections on the Dissent of Contemporary Youth." *International Journal of Psychoanalysis* 51, no. 1 (1970): 11–22.
Euripides. *The Phoenissae*. Translated by E. P. Coleridge. Vol. 2 of *The Complete Greek Drama*. New York: Random House, 1938.
Euripides and T. A. Buckley. *The Bacchae*. In *The Tragedies of Euripides*. London: Henry G. Bohn, 1850.
Federn, Paul. *Zur Psychologie der Revolution. Die Vaterlose Gesellschaft*. Leipzig and Vienna: Anzengruber Verlag, 1919.
Fenucci, Valeria. "Introduction: Genealogical Pleasures, Genealogical Disruptions." In *Generation and Degeneration: Tropes of Reproduction in Literature and History from Antiquity to Early Modern Europe*. Edited by Valeria Fenucci and Kevin Brownlee, 1–16. Durham/London: Duke University Press, 2001.
Ffytche, Matt. *The Foundation of the Unconscious: Schelling, Freud, and the Birth of the Modern Psyche*. Cambridge: Cambridge University Press, 2012.
Filmer, Robert. *Filmer: Patriarcha and Other Writings*. Edited by Johann P. Sommerville. Cambridge Texts in the History of Thought. Cambridge: Cambridge University Press, 1991.
Flashar, Hellmuth. *Sophokles: Dichter im Demokratischen Athen*. Munich: Beck, 2000.
Foucault, Michel. *La volonté de savoir*. Paris: Gallimard, 1994.
Freud, Sigmund. *Briefe 1873–1939*. Edited by Ernst Freud and Lucie Freud. Frankfurt am Main: S. Fischer, 1968.
—*The Complete Correspondence of Sigmund Freud and Ernest Jones, 1908–1939*. Cambridge: Harvard University Press, 1999, 3.
—"Nachwort: Zur 'Frage der Laienanalyse.'" In *Ergänzungsband: Schriften Zur Behandlungstechnik*, edited by Alexander Mitscherlich, Angela Richards, James Strachey, and Ilsa Grubrich-Simitis, 342–9. *Studienausgabe*. Frankfurt am Main: S. Fischer, 1997.
—*Totem und Tabu: Einige Übereinstimmungen im Seelenleben der Wilden und der Neurotiker*. Leipzig/Vienna/Zürich: Internationaler Psychoanalytischer Verlag, 1922.
—*Die Traumdeutung*. Edited by Alexander Mitscherlich, Angela Richards, and James Strachey. Vol. 2. of *Studienausgabe*. Frankfurt am Main: S. Fischer, 1972.

—"Das Unheimliche." In *Psychologische Schriften*, edited by Alexander Mitscherlich, Angela Richards, James Strachey, and Ilsa Grubrich-Simitis, 241–74. Vol. 4 of *Studienausgabe*. Frankfurt am Main: Fischer, 1989.

Frömmer, Judith. *Vaterfiktionen: Empfindsamkeit und Patriarchat im Zeitalter der Aufklärung*. Munich: Fink, 2008.

Gelus, Marjorie. "Patriarchy's Fragile Boundaries under Siege: Three Stories of Heinrich von Kleist." *Women in German Yearbook* 10 (1995): 59–82.

Girard, René. "Mythos und Gegenmythos: Zu Kleists Das Erdbeben in Chili." In *Positionen der Literaturwissenschaft: Acht Modellanalysen am Beispiel von Kleists 'Das Erdbeben in Chili,'* edited by David E. Wellbery, 130–48. Munich: Beck, 1985.

Goux, Jean-Joseph. *Freud, Marx: Economie et symbolique*. Paris: Editions du Seuil, 1973.

—*Les iconoclastes*. Paris: Editions du Seuil, 1978.

—*Oedipus, Philosopher*. Translated by Catherine Porter. Meridian: Crossing Aesthetics. Stanford, CA: Stanford University Press, 1993.

—*Symbolic Economies after Marx and Freud*. Translated by Jennifer Curtiss Gage. Ithaca, NY: Cornell University Press, 1990.

Gray, Richard T. *Stations of the Divided Subject: Contestation and Ideological Legitimation in German Bourgeois Literature, 1770-1914*. Stanford, CA: Stanford University Press, 1995.

Griffith, Mark. "Brilliant Dynasts: Power and Politics in the 'Oresteia.'" *Classical Antiquity* 14, no. 1 (April 1995): 62–129.

Gunther-Canada, Wendy. "Catharine Macaulay on the Paradox of Paternal Authority in Hobbesian Politics." *Hypatia* 201, no. 2 (2006): 150–73.

Gustafson, Susan. "Abject Fathers and Suicidal Sons: Lessing's Philotas and Kristeva's Black Sun." *Lessing Yearbook* 24 (1997): 1–29.

—*Absent Mothers and Orphaned Fathers: Narcissism and Abjection in Lessing's Aesthetic and Dramatic Production*. Detroit, MI: Wayne State University Press, 1995.

Hall, Donald. "My Son, My Executioner." In *Fathers and Sons: An Anthology*, edited by David Seybold. Reprint. New York: Atlantic Monthly Press, 1995.

Hart, Gail K. "A Family Without Women: The Triumph of the Sentimental Father in Lessing's *Sara Sampson* and Klinger's *Sturm und Drang*." *Lessing Yearbook* 22 (1990): 113–32.

Hartsock, Nancy. *Money, Sex and Power*. New York: Longman, 1983.

Hegel, Georg Wilhelm Friedrich. *Aesthetics: Lectures on Fine Art*, 2 vols., translated by T. M. Knox. Oxford: Clarendon Press, 1975.

—*Frühe Schriften*. Vol. 1 of *Werke*. Frankfurt am Main: Suhrkamp, 1986.

—*Vorlesungen über die Philosophie der Geschichte*. Vol. 12 of *Werke*. Frankfurt am Main: Suhrkamp, 1970.

—*Vorlesungen über die Philosophie der Weltgeschichte, auf Grund der Handschriften*, edited by Georg Lasson. Vol. 3, book. 2. Hamburg: Felix Meiner, 1976.

Heine, Heinrich. *Die Romantische Schule. Zur Geschichte der Religion und Philosophie in Deutschland*. Edited by Hans Kaufmann. Vol. 9 of *Sämtliche Werke*. Munich: Kindler, 1964.

Herik, Judith Van. *Freud on Femininity and Faith*. Berkeley: University of California Press, 1982.

Hinton, R. W. K. "Husbands, Fathers, and Conquerors I." *Political Studies* 15 (1967): 291–300.

Hobbes, Thomas. *De Cive*. Edited by Howard Warrender. Oxford: Oxford University Press, 1987.
—*The Elements of Law, Natural and Politic: Human Nature and De Corpore Politico*. Edited by J. C. A. Raskin. Oxford: Oxford University Press, 1999.
—*Leviathan: Parts I and II*. Edited by A. P. Martinich and Brian Battiste. New York: Broadview Press, 2011.
Hofmannsthal, Hugo Von. "Ein Brief." In *Erfundene Gespräche und Briefe*. Vol. 2. *Werke in Zehn Bänden*. Frankfurt am Main: Suhrkamp, 1999.
—*Oedipus und Die Sphinx. Tragödie in Drei Aufzügen*. Berlin: S. Fischer, 1906.
Hölderlin, Friedrich. "Anmerkungen zum Oedipus." In *Werke, Briefe, Dokumente, nach der kleinen Stuttgarter Hölderlin-Ausgabe*. Edited by Friedrich Beißner, selected and with an afterword by Pierre Bertaux. Munich: Winkler, 1963.
Hunt, Lynn A. *The Family Romance of the French Revolution*. Berkeley, CA: University of California Press, 1992.
Huysmans, Joris Karl. *Against Nature*. Translated by Margaret Maulden. Oxford: Oxford University Press, 1998.
Irigaray, Luce. "Questions to Emmanuel Levinas." In *The Irigaray Reader*, edited by Margaret Whitford, 178–89. London: Blackwell, 1991.
Jonnes, Denis. "Solche Väter: The Sentimental Family Paradigm in Lessing's Drama." *Lessing Yearbook* 12 (1981): 157–74.
Kafka, Franz. "Brief an den Vater." In *Hochzeitsvorbereitungen auf dem Lande und andere Prosa aus dem Nachlaß, Gesammelte Werke, Taschenbuchausgabe in acht Bänden*, edited by Max Brod. Frankfurt am Main: Fischer, 1983.
Kant, Immanuel. "On the common saying: 'This may be true in theory, but it does not apply in practice.'" In *Political Writings*, 61–92. Cambridge: Cambridge University Press, 1991.
—*Der Streit der Fakultäten. Anthropologie in pragmatischer Hinsicht*. Akademie Ausgabe VII. Berlin: de Gruyter, 1968.
Kass, Leon R. "Educating Father Abraham: The Meaning of Fatherhood." *First Things* 48 (December 1994): 32–43.
Keuls, Eva C. *The Reign of the Phallus: Sexual Politics in Ancient Athens*. New York: Harper and Row, 1985.
Kierkegaard, Søren. *Fear and Trembling*. Translated by Walter Lowrie. Princeton, NJ: Princeton University Press, 1970.
—"The Lilies of the Field and the Birds of the Air." In *Christian Discourses*, translated by Walter Lowrie. New York: Oxford University Press, 1962.
Kittler, Friedrich A. "Erziehung ist Offenbarung: Zur Struktur der Familie in Lessings Dramen." *Jahrbuch der deutschen Schiller-Gesellschaft* 21 (1977): 111–37.
—*Discourse Networks 1800/1900*. Translated by Michael Metteer with Chris Cullens. Stanford, CA: Stanford University Press, 1990.
Kleist, Heinrich von. *Briefe*. Edited by Siegfried Steller. Vol. 4 of *Werke und Briefe in Vier Bänden*. Frankfurt am Main: Insel, 1986.
—*Erzählungen*. Vol. 4 of *Gesamtausgabe*. Munich: Deutscher Taschenbuch Verlag, 1964.
Knox, Bernard M. W. *Oedipus at Thebes*. New York: W. W. Norton, 1957.
Koschorke, Albrecht. *Die Heilige Familie und ihre Folgen*. Frankfurt am Main: S. Fischer, 2000.
Koselleck, Reinhart. *Preussen Zwischen Reform und Revolution; Allgemeines Landrecht, Verwaltung und Soziale Bewegung von 1791 Bis 1848*. Stuttgart: Klett, 1967.

Kremer, Manfred K. "Does Emilia Use Force against Her Father? Reflections on Lessing's *Emilia Galotti*." In *Lessing and the Enlightenment*. Edited by Ed Alexej Ugrinski, 113–19. New York: Greekwood, 1986.

Krüger-Fürhoff, Irmela Marei. "Epistemological Asymmetries and Erotic Stagings: Father-Daughter Incest in Heinrich von Kleist's The Marquise of O..." *Women in German Yearbook* 12, no. 1 (1996): 71–86.

Künzel, Christine. "Heinrich von Kleists 'Die Marquise von O ...': Anmerkungen zur Repräsentation von Vergewaltigung, Recht und Gerechtigkeit in Literatur und Literaturwissenschaft." *Figurationen* 1, no. 1 (2000): 165–81.

Lacan, Jacques. "The Function and Field of Speech and Language in Psychoanalysis." In *Ecrits: A Selection*. Translated by Alan Sheridan. New York: W. W. Norton, 1977.

—"On a Question Preliminary to Any Possible Treatment of Psychosis." In *Ecrits: A Selection*. Translated by Alan Sheridan. New York: W. W. Norton, 1977.

Laqueur, Thomas. *Making Sex: Body and Gender from the Greeks to Freud*. Cambridge, MA: Harvard University Press, 1990.

Laslett, Peter. *The World We Have Lost*. London: Methuen, 1965.

—and Richard Wall, eds. *Household and Family in Past Time*. Cambridge: Cambridge University Press, 1972.

Le Guen, Claude. "The Formation of the Transference: Or the Laius Complex in the Armchair." *International Journal of Psychoanalysis* 55, no. 4 (1974): 505–12.

Lessing, Goffhold Ephraim. *Gesammelte Werke in zwei Bänden*. Munich: Hanser, 1959.

—"Philotas." In *Trauerspeiele*. Berlin: Bossischen Buchhandlung, 1798.

Levenson, Jon Douglas. *Inheriting Abraham: The Legacy of the Patriarch in Judaism, Christianity, and Islam*. Princeton, NJ: Princeton University Press, 2012.

Levy, Iris. "The Laius Complex: From Myth to Psychoanalysis." *International Forum of Psychoanalysis* 20, no. 4 (August 2, 2011): 222–8.

Locke, John. *Two Treatises on Government*. Oxford: 1821.

Lorenz, Dagmar. "Väter und Mütter in der Sozialstruktur von Kleists 'Erdbeben in Chili.'" *Études Germaniques* 33 (1978): 270–81.

Macfarlane, Alan. *Marriage and Love in England: Modes of Reproduction 1300–1840*. Oxford: Blackwell, 1986.

MacLean, Marie. "The Heirs of Amphitryon: Social Fathers and Natural Fathers." *New Literary History* 26, no. 4 (1995): 787–807.

Makari, Georg. *Revolution in Mind: The Creation of Psychoanalysis*. Melbourne: Melbourne University Press, 2008.

Malinowski, Bronislaw. *The Father in Primitive Psychology*. New York: W. W. Norton, 1927.

Martinich, Aloysius. *Hobbes: A Biography*. Cambridge: Cambridge University Press, 1999.

Masson, Emile. *La puissance paternelle et la famille sous la Révolution*. Paris: 1910.

Meier, Christian. *Die Politische Kunst der Griechischen Tragödie*. München: Beck, 1988.

Melchinger, Siegfried. *Das Theater Der Tragödie: Aischylos, Sophokles, Euripides auf der Bühne ihrer Zeit*. Munich: C.H. Beck, 1974.

Mette, Hans Joachim. *Der Verlorene Aischylos*. Berlin: Akademie Verlag, 1963.

Miller, David Lee. *Dreams of the Burning Child: Sacrificial Sons and the Father's Witness*. Ithaca, NY: Cornell University Press, 2003.

Müller-Seidel, Walter. "Der rätselhafte Kleist und seine Dichtung." In *Die Gegenwärtigkeit Kleists: Reden zum Gedenkjahr 1977*, edited by Wieland Schmidt, 9–29. Berlin: Erich Schmidt Verlag, 1980.

Naffine, Ngaire. *Law and the Sexes*. Sydney: Allen and Unwin, 1990.
Nauck, August, ed. *Tragicorum Graecorum Fragmenta*. Hildesheim: G. Olms Verlagsbuchhandlung, 1964.
Naumann, Thomas. "Die Preisgabe Isaaks: Genesis 22 im Kontext der Biblischen Abraham-Sara-Erzählung." In *Opfere Deinen Sohn!: Das "Isaak-Opfer" in Judentum, Christentum und Islam*, edited by Bernhard Greiner, Bernd Janowski, and Hermann Lichtenberger, 19–50. Tübingen: Francke, 2007.
Neuhaus-Koch, Ariane. *G. E. Lessing: D. Sozialstrukturen in seinen Dramen*. Bonn: Bouvier, 1977.
Neumann, Peter Horst. *Der Preis der Mündigkeit: Über Lessings Dramen*. Stuttgart: Klett-Cotta, 1977.
Newey, Glen. "Not a Woman-Hater: Hobbes's Critique of Patriarchy." In *The Politics of Gender: A Survey*, edited by Yoke-Lian Lee, 10–24. London: Routledge, 2010.
Newman, Gail. "Family Violence in Heinrich von Kleist's Der Findling." *Colloquia Germanica: Internationale Zeitschrift Fur Germanistik* 29, no. 4 (1996): 287–302.
Nietzsche, Friedrich. *Sämtliche Werke: Kritische Studienausgabe*. 15 vols. Ed. Giorgio Colli and Mazzino Montinari. Berlin: de Gruyter, 1967–77.
Nitschke, Claudia. *Der öffentliche Vater: Konzeptionen paternaler Souveränität in der deutschen Literatur (1755–1921)*. Berlin: Walter de Gruyter, 2012.
O'Brien, Mary. *The Politics of Reproduction*. London: Routledge, 1981.
Oedipus Rex. Directed by Pier Paolo Pasolini. Performed by Franco Citti, Silvana Mangano, Alida Valli, Carmelo Bene, Julian Beck, and Pier Paolo Pasolini. Drama, 1967. New York: Water Bearer Films, 2003. DVD. Original screenplay: *Oedipus Rex: A Film by Pier Paolo Pasolini*. Translated by John Mathews. New York: Simon and Schuster, 1971.
Okin, Susan Miller. *Justice, Gender and the Family*. New York: Basic Books, 1989.
—*Women in Western Political Thought*. Princeton, NJ: Princeton University Press, 1979.
Owen, Wilfred. "Parable of the Young Man and the Old." *Complete Poems and Fragments*. Edited by Jon Stallworthy. New York: W. W. Norton, 1994.
Parker, Andrew. *The Theorists's Mother*. Durham, NC: Duke University Press, 2012.
Pateman, Carole. *The Sexual Contract*. Cambridge: Polity Press, 1988.
Patterson, Cynthia. "'Not Worth the Rearing': The Causes of Infant Exposure in Ancient Greece." *Transactions of the American Philological Association* 15 (1985): 103–23.
Paul, Robert A. *Moses and Civilization: The Meaning behind Freud's Myth*. New Haven, CT: Yale University Press, 1996.
Pinsky, Robert, trans. *The Inferno of Dante: A New Verse Translation*. New York: Noonday Press, 1996.
Plato. *Laws*. Vols. 10 and 11 of *Plato in Twelve Volumes*. Translated by R. G. Bury. Cambridge, MA: Harvard University Press; London, William Heinemann Ltd., 1967–68.
—"Republic." In *The Collected Dialogues of Plato: Including the Letters*, edited by Edith Hamilton and Huntington Cairns, translated by Paul Shorey, 575–844. Bollingen Series 71. New York: Pantheon, New York.
—"Symposium." In *The Collected Dialogues of Plato: Including the Letters*. Edited by Edith Hamilton and Huntington Cairns, translated by Michael Joyce, 526–74. Bollingen Series 71. New York: Pantheon, New York.

Plutarch. *Moralia*. Translated by Frank Cole Babbitt. Vol. 4. Loeb Classical Library 305. Cambridge, MA: Harvard University Press, 2005.
Pomeroy, Sarah B. *Goddesses, Whores, Wives, and Slaves*. New York: Schocken, 1975.
Prutti, Brigitte. *Bild und Körper: Weibliche Präsenz und Geschlechterbeziehungen in Lessings Dramen*. Würzburg: Königshausen und Neumann, 1996.
Rabaté, Jean Michel. "A Clown's Inquest into Paternity: Fathers, Dead or Alive, in Ulysses and Finnegan's Wake." In *The Fictional Father: Lacanian Readings of the Text*. Edited by Robert Con Davis. Amherst: University of Massachusetts Press, 1981.
Robert, Carl. *Oidipus: Geschichte eines poetischen Stoffs im Griechischen Altertum*. 2 vols. Berlin: Weidmann, 1915.
Ross, John Munder. "Oedipus Revisited: Laius and the Laius Complex." *Psychoanalytic Study of the Child* 37 (1982): 169–200.
—"The Darker Side of Fatherhood: Clinical and Developmental Ramifications of the 'Laius Motif.'" *International Journal of Psychoanalytic Psychotherapy* 11 (1985): 117–44.
—*What Men Want: Mothers, Fathers, and Manhood*. Cambridge, MA: Harvard University Press, 1994.
Rousseau, Jean-Jacques. *Social Contract and Discourses*. Translated and with an introduction by G. D. H. Cole. New York: E. P. Dutton & Co., 1913.
Runyon, Damon. "Little Miss Marker." *Furthermore*, 81–102. London: Constable and Company Ltd., 1938.
Santner, Eric L. *The Royal Remains: The People's Two Bodies and the Endgames of Sovereignty*. Chicago: University of Chicago Press, 2011.
Schlipphacke, Heidi. "The Dialectics of Female Desire in G. E. Lessing's Emilia Galotti." *Lessing Yearbook* 33 (2001): 55–78.
Schmitt, Carl. *Political Theology: Four Chapters on the Concept of Sovereignty*. Translated by George Schwab. Chicago: Chicago University Press, 2005.
Schneider, Helmut J. "Lebenstatsachen: Geburt und Adoption bei Lessing und Kleist." *Kleist-Jahrbuch* (2002): 21–41.
Schochet, Gordon. *The Authoritarian Family and Political Attitudes in Seventeenth-Century England: Patriarchalism in Political Thought*. New Brunswick, NJ: Transaction Publishers, 1988.
Schorske, Carl E. *Fin-de-Siècle Vienna: Politics and Culture*. New York: Vintage Books, 1981.
Schütz, Heinrich. *Symphoniae sacrae I*, Op.6, SWV 269. Performed by Cappella Augustana; Matteo Messori conductor and organ; Harry van der Kamp, bass. On disk one, Heinrich Schütz Edition (box set). Released May 29, 2012. Brilliant Classics B007762J4K. Available at http://youtu.be/bjRfof7WsHo
Schwab, Dieter. "Die Familie." In *Geschichtliche Grundbegriffe. Historisches Lexikon Zur Politisch-Sozialen Sprache in Deutschland*, edited by Otto Brunner, Werner Conze, and Reinhart Koselleck, 2:253–301. Stuttgart: Klett-Cotta, 1975.
Sedgewick, Eve. *Epistemology of the Closet*. Berkeley: University of California Press, 1990.
Simpson, Peter. *A Philosophical Commentary on the Politics of Aristotle*. Chapel: University of North Carolina Press, 1998.
Sinclair, T. A. *A History of Greek Political Thought*. Cleveland/New York: Meridian, 1968.
Sophocles. *Oedipus The King*. Translated by Stephen Berg and Diskin Clay. New York: Oxford University Press, 1978.

—*Oedipus Tyrannus*. Vol. 1 of *Plays and Fragments*. Edited and translated with notes by Richard C. Jebb. Cambridge: Cambridge University Press, 1914.

—*Sophocles: Works*. Edited and translated by Hugh Lloyd-Jones. Vol. 2. Loeb Classical Library 20–1. Cambridge, MA: Harvard University Press, 1994.

Stephan, Inge. "'So ist die Tugend ein Gespenst': Frauenbild und Tugendbegriff im bürgerlichen Trauerspiel bei Lessing und Schiller." *Lessing Yearbook* 17 (1985): 1–20.

Stephens, Anthony. "Kleists Familienmodelle." *Kleist-Jahrbuch* 1988–9 (n.d.): 222–41.

Stevens, Jacqueline. *Reproducing the State*. Princeton, NJ: Princeton University Press, 2012.

Strauss, Leo. *The City and Man*. Chicago: University of Chicago Press, 1978.

—*The Political Philosophy of Hobbes: Its Basis and Its Genesis*. Translated by E. Sinclair. Chicago: University of Chicago Press, 1952.

—"Progress or Return?" In *The Rebirth of Classical Political Rationalism: An Introduction to the Thought of Leo Strauss*, edited by Thomas L. Pangle, 227–70. Chicago: University of Chicago Press, 1989.

Szondi, Peter. "Analysen Des Tragischen." In *Schriften I*. Frankfurt: Suhrkamp, 1978.

Taylor, Mark C. "Journeys to Moriah: Hegel vs. Kierkegaard." *Harvard Theological Review* 70, no. 3/4 (October 1977): 305–26.

Tuana, Nancy, ed. *Feminist Interpretations of Plato*. University Park: Penn State University Press, 1994.

Van Herik, Judith. *Freud on Femininity and Faith*. Berkeley: University of California Press, 1982.

Vernant, Jean-Pierre. "Greek Tragedy: Problems of Interpretation." In *The Structuralist Controversy*, edited by Richard Macksey and Eugenio Donato, 273–89. Baltimore, MD: Johns Hopkins University Press, 1970.

Vernant, Jean-Pierre and Pierre Vidal-Naquet. "Oedipus without the Complex." In *Tragedy and Myth in Ancient Greece*, translated by Janet Lloyd, 85–113. Sussex: Harvester Press, 1981.

—*Tragedy and Myth in Ancient Greece*. Translated by Janet Lloyd. Sussex: Harvester Press, 1981.

Walsøe-Engel, Ingrid. *Fathers and Daughters: Patterns of Seduction in Tragedies by Gryphius, Lessing, Hebbel and Kroetz*. Columbia, SC: Camden House, 1993.

Weineck, Silke-Maria. "Dead Childen: Ben Jonson Epitaph on my first sonne." In *Dead Lovers: Erotic Bonds and the Study of Premodern Europe*, edited by Basil Dufallo and Peggy McCracken, 128–42. Ann Arbor: University of Michigan Press, 2007.

—"'Invisible Person': Carl Schmitt and the Master Trope of Power." *Germanic Review* 84, no. 3 (Summer 2009): 199–221.

Weininger, Otto. *Geschlecht und Charakter: Eine Prinzipielle Untersuchung*. Munich: Matthes & Seitz, 1980.

—*Sex & Character*. London: W. Heinemann, 1907.

Weiss, Edoardo. "Paul Federn." In *Psychoanalytic Pioneers*, edited by Franz Alexander, Samuel Eisenstein, and Martin Grotjahn, 142–59. New Brunswick, NJ: Transaction Publishers, 1995.

Weiss, Hermann F. "Precarious Idylls. The Relationship Between Father and Daughter in Heinrich von Kleist's *Die Marquise von O*." *MLN* 91, no. 3 (1976): 538–42.

Wellbery, David E. "Semiotische Anmerkungen Zu Kleists Das Erdbeben in Chili." In *Positionen Der Literaturwissenschaft: Acht Modellanalysen Am Beispiel von Kleists "Das Erdbeben in Chili,"* edited by David E. Wellbery, 69–87. Munich: Beck, 1985.

Wender, Dorothea. "Plato: Misogynist, Paedophile, and Feminist." *Arethusa* 6 (1973): 75–90.

Wilde, Oscar. "The Picture of Dorian Gray." In *Collected Works of Oscar Wilde*. Hertfordshire: Wordsworth Editions, 2007.

Wittkowski, Wolfgang. "Bürgerfreiheit oder—feigheit? Die Metapher des 'langes Weges' als Schlüssel zum Koordinatensystem in Lessings politischem Trauerspiel Emilia Galotti." *Lessing Yearbook* 27 (1985): 65–87.

Wright, Joanne H. "Going against the Grain: Hobbes's Case for Original Maternal Dominion." *Journal of Women's History* 14, no. 1 (2002): 123–55.

Wurst, Karin. *Familiale Liebe ist die 'Wahre Gewalt': Die Repräsentation der Familie in G.E. Lessings dramatischem Werke*. Amsterdam: Rodopi, 1988.

Yack, Bernard. *The Problems of a Political Animal: Community, Justice, and Conflict in Aristotelian Political Thought*. Berkeley: University of California Press, 1993.

Ziegler, Konrat and Walter Sontheimer, eds. *Der kleine Pauly: Lexikon der Antike in fünf Bänden*. Munich: dtv, 1979.

Žižek, Slavoj. *Did Somebody Say Totalitarianism?: Four Interventions in the (Mis)Use of a Notion*. London: Verso, 2002.

—*The Ticklish Subject*. London: Verso, 2000.

Zoja, Luigi. *The Father: Historical, Psychological and Cultural Perspectives*. Translated by Henry Martin. East Sussex: Brunner-Routledge, 2001.

Zola, Émile. *The Masterpiece*. Translated by Thomas Walton and Roger Pearson. New York: Oxford University Press, 2007.

— *The Sin of Father Mouret*. Translated by Sandy Petrey. Lincoln/London: University of Nebraska Press, 1969.

Index

Abraham 41–4, 58–73, 77, 107, 119, 186, 189, 191
Absalom 107, 184–7
Adorno, Theodor W. 7, 185, 195
Aeschylus 33, 40–3, 56
Agamben, Giorgio 77–8, 82, 112
Agamemnon 39–40, 186
akedah, the binding of Isaac 40, 59–60, 62–7, 69, 74
Aristotle 9–10, 42, 45–6, 56–7, 77–87, 89, 92–108, 117, 173
Athens 5, 40–1, 52, 62, 72, 77, 82, 88, 91, 94, 96, 145; *see also* Jerusalem
Auerbach, Erich 61–2

Bachya ben Asher 60
Balmary, Marie 7, 37–8, 71
Barrie, J. M. 4, 189, 195
biology 7, 82, 108, 144, 160
bios 8, 77–9, 82, 107–8, 112, 141, 144
Blackstone, William 108
Bloch, Ernst 95, 159–60
Blumenberg, Hans 10–11
body of the father 77, 79, 81, 83, 85, 87
Brod, Max 1
Brutus 60, 186

Cadmus 51–2, 72
cannibalism 40, 100, 197
Carpeaux, Jean-Baptiste 187–8
castration 23, 159, 170, 173
Chrysippus 33–4, 37–8
Cohen, Leonard 65, 73
Cronus 39–41, 51

Dante Alighieri 187–8; *see also* Ugolino and his sons
Darwin, Charles 170
dead father 17, 39, 71, 96, 174–6, 191
death of god 2, 4, 147, 165, 174
Deleuze, Gilles 2–3
democracy, democratization 5, 10, 56, 81, 94–5, 109, 160, 180–2
Derrida, Jacques 74, 107
Descartes, René 11
DNA testing 176, 193
Dylan, Bob 65–6

empathy and identification with the father 4, 19–20, 39–40, 46–7, 191
Enlightenment 24, 42, 48, 132, 134–5, 141, 147, 150–1, 159
Eteocles and Polyneices 44, 52–3, 137
Euripides 33–4, 37, 51–2, 56, 79

family 3–7, 15, 24, 26, 44–5, 47, 52, 58, 80–1, 90–3, 96, 98, 101, 104, 107, 117–18, 120, 123, 129–30, 135–6, 141–3, 145–7, 149–50, 153, 159–60, 176, 178–9, 181–3, 196, 198–202
Federn, Paul 4, 177–83
figure of the law, father as 4, 140
filiarchy, filiarchal 3, 50, 131, 137, 140, 143, 161
filicide, filicidal 23–4, 26, 36, 39–40, 44, 47, 52, 58–60, 65–6, 68, 70–1, 88, 129, 131–2, 134, 137–8, 145, 151, 153–4, 156, 158, 161, 171, 192–3

filisuicide 128, 137
Filmer, Sir Robert 108, 116–17, 122, 136
Fontane, Theodor 186, 191
Ford, Richard 186
Foucault, Michel 78, 99
fragility of fatherhood 10, 17, 73, 121, 139, 151
French Revolution 6–7, 160, 175
Freud, Jakob 19–21
Freud, Sigmund 2–5, 7, 13, 15–22, 24–9, 33, 35–9, 45–7, 50–1, 54–5, 59, 66–7, 70–1, 82, 94, 131, 135, 145, 158, 160, 163, 165–6, 168–79, 181–3, 185, 187, 191, 193

gender 6, 79–82, 89–92, 103, 115–22, 146–7, 161, 167, 183
Genesis 40, 59, 61, 64, 70–2, 114, 117, 120
Girard, René 154
Goethe, Johann Wolfgang von 136, 186–7
Gschnas 33, 165, 167, 169–71, 173–5, 177, 179, 181, 183
Guattari, Félix 2–3
guilt 1, 3, 38–9

Hall, Donald 24
Hamlet 33, 45–6
Hegel, Georg Wilhelm Friedrich 4, 45, 47–50, 56, 68–70, 136, 145
Heine, Heinrich 3–4
Hellenga, Robert 186
Hobbes, Thomas 4–5, 107–23, 130, 136, 160, 174
Hofmannsthal, Hugo von 7, 35–6, 38, 166–7, 189
Hölderlin, Friedrich 45, 49, 55
Homer 9, 37, 43, 100, 175
Huysmans, Joris-Karl 170

idealism 45, 48, 50

immortality (paternity as) 9, 18, 41–2, 68, 172–4, 193
Iphigeneia 186
Irigaray, Luce 23, 199
Isaac 39–40, 59–62, 64–5, 69–70, 72–4, 107, 171, 186, 191, 196

Jacob 107, 186
Jerusalem 40, 62, 72, 77, 108, 140–1; *see also* Athens
Jesus 39–40, 45, 152, 155, 171, 186, 191
Jonson, Ben 172, 186
Joyce, James 7, 165

Kafka, Franz 1–3, 167, 170, 185, 191
Kafka, Hermann 1–3
Kant, Immanuel 67–70, 73, 123–4, 147, 151
Kierkegaard, Søren 59, 62, 69–70
Kittler, Friedrich 135–6
Klein, Melanie 2
Kleist, Heinrich von 134, 144–61

Lacan, Jacques 4, 6, 17, 28, 33, 166, 175–6, 190
Laius, Laiusian 7, 10, 16–17, 24, 26, 28–9, 33–45, 47, 49, 52–3, 57–60, 62–4, 70–1, 88, 115, 128, 131, 151, 156, 165, 171–3, 187, 191, 193, 197, 200, 202
Lessing, Gotthold Ephraim 115, 127, 129–44, 186–7, 191–2
Lévi-Strauss, Claude 38
Locke, John 116, 118, 122, 136, 160

Macaulay, Catharine 120–1
Mahler, Gustav 186
Malinowski, Bronislaw 87
Marcuse, Herbert 7
marriage, martial 1, 42, 52, 90, 108, 135, 146, 150, 155–6
McEwan, Ian 186

Mendelssohn, Moses 141
metaphor 8–9, 11, 107, 111, 116, 136, 151, 173, 190
Mitscherlich, Alexander 15
monarchy 4, 41, 94–8, 109–10, 116–17, 120–2, 151, 178
monotheism 41, 58, 63, 71, 98, 100, 108, 115, 130, 141, 165, 173–4
motherhood, maternal 6, 8, 10, 16, 24, 34, 36–7, 40–1, 50, 54–5, 63, 73, 77, 82–3, 86–7, 92–3, 103, 107–8, 111–20, 122, 124, 129, 134–6, 142, 147–8, 150, 165–6, 169, 173, 177, 179, 183, 187–9
Mourning and Melancholia 2; see also Freud, Sigmund
myth, mythology 7, 16–17, 24, 29, 37–8, 40–1, 44–5, 48, 52, 59, 62–3, 67, 72, 88, 96, 131, 145, 153, 160, 171, 185

nachträglich 72, 187
Nietzsche, Friedrich 3–4, 45, 136, 147, 174
nomos 8, 96, 99, 107–8, 112, 141, 144; see also bios

Oedipus, oedipal 3, 7, 10, 15–17, 24, 28–9, 33–60, 63–4, 66, 70–1, 88, 115, 129, 131, 135, 137, 139–40, 145, 151, 156, 161, 166, 171–2, 174, 186, 191
overdetermination of fatherhood 9–10, 88, 170–1
Owen, Wilfred 64–5

Pasolini, Pier Paolo 7, 36, 38
paternal triad 5, 9, 15, 41, 58, 71–3, 99–100, 107, 109, 117–18, 120, 133, 140, 150, 169–70, 173, 178, 180, 187
paternal uncertainty 26, 77, 87, 111, 114, 144, 147, 166, 171, 183, 189

patriarchy, patriarchal 5–6, 9, 16, 24, 39, 41, 48–50, 58, 60, 100–1, 116, 120, 123, 131–2, 134, 139–41, 143–4, 151–2, 159–61, 169, 171, 174, 176–7, 179–81
patricide, patricidal 5, 24, 35, 39, 41, 47, 59, 71, 88, 106–7, 151, 156, 160, 171, 176, 182–3
Pelops 33–4, 37, 39–40
Plato 8, 33, 37–8, 89–96, 99–100, 102, 104, 107, 173, 182, 193
polis (Greek) 52–3, 55–8, 78–81, 88–9, 97–8, 101–2
political fatherhood 4, 64, 75–124, 140, 175, 177–83
Presence in absence 35
Pseudo-Apollodorus 34
psychoanalysis, psychoanalytic 2, 4–5, 7, 15–16, 28, 36–7, 40, 43, 45, 50, 54, 135, 166, 171, 173–5, 177–8, 183, 193

revenants, children as 20–3
Ross, John Munder 7, 36–7, 131
Rousseau, Jean-Jacques 116, 118, 123, 136
Runyon, Damon 188

sacrifice 7, 22, 37, 39, 41–4, 58–9, 63–7, 70, 73–4, 91, 93, 119, 132, 134, 154–5, 193
Sarah 67, 73, 77
Schelling, Friedrich Wilhelm Joseph 45, 170, 197
Schiller, Friedrich 45
Schmitt, Carl 8–9
Schnitzler, Arthur 15
Schütz, Heinrich 184–5, 187
secular, secularization 5, 8, 15, 47, 116, 122, 145, 147, 152, 159–60, 180
Shaftesbury, Earl of (Anthony Ashley Cooper) 122–3, 130
Sidney, Algernon 118

Socrates 63, 89–93, 102–4
Sophocles 29, 33–4, 37–8, 42, 45–6, 48–52, 54, 56–7, 88, 115, 139, 187
sovereignty 8, 17, 57, 109–12, 114, 116–17, 121–2, 169, 202
sperm, spermal paternity 9–10, 40, 71–2, 77, 85–7, 108, 115, 117, 155
Spinoza, Baruch 130, 136, 189
Strauss, Leo 62–4, 89, 91–3, 120
subject position 7, 16, 52
symbolic fatherhood 40, 49, 95, 187, 192–3
Szondi, Peter 42

Tantalus 40
temporalities 10, 28, 49
The Interpretation of Dreams, 15–16, 18, 25–6, 28, 165, 191; *see also* Freud, Sigmund
Totem and Taboo 17, 71, 160, 174–5, 178; *see also* Freud, Sigmund
tragedy, tragic 2, 4, 6–10, 16, 18, 20, 22, 24, 26, 28–9, 31, 33–4, 36–8, 40, 42–6, 48–50, 52, 54–64, 66, 68, 70, 72, 74, 78, 80, 82, 84, 86, 88, 90, 92, 94–6, 98–100, 102, 104, 106, 108, 110, 112, 114–16, 118, 120, 122, 124, 127–8, 130, 132–6, 138–40, 142, 145–6, 148, 150, 152, 154, 156, 158, 160, 166, 168, 170, 172–4, 176, 178–80, 182, 186–8, 190, 192

Ugolino and his sons 198–9; *see also* Carpeaux, Jean–Baptiste
Uranus 40, 72

vaterland 26, 68
Vernant, Jean–Pierre 45, 55–6, 88, 95, 99

Weininger, Otto 17, 171, 189–90
Wilde, Oscar 171
Winnicott, Donald 2

Yeats, William Butler 171, 186

Zeus 39–41, 57, 72, 99, 171, 189, 191
Žižek, Slavoj 16, 39
Zola, Émile 168, 170, 192–3